Politics in Contemporary Southeast Asia

The countries of Southeast Asia continue to change, evolve and chart courses that sometimes leave outside observers puzzled. *Politics in Contemporary Southeast Asia* thoroughly assesses the political challenges and changes faced by the countries of Southeast Asia in the twenty-first century. Focusing on political processes throughout, Kingsbury introduces readers to the challenges of representation and accountability of the regional governments, degrees of good governance and transparency, and the role of elites and militaries in shaping or determining political outcomes.

This book provides:

- A comprehensive, but accessible, introduction to political change and processes in Southeast Asia.
- Analytic criteria for assessment of case studies.
- Detailed country-specific surveys.
- Information based on extensive research on, and work in, the region.

Providing cutting-edge coverage of South Asian politics in all regions, this highly accessible and comprehensive book is suitable for undergraduate and postgraduate courses on Southeast Asian Studies, Asian Politics, and Democratisation.

Damien Kingsbury holds a Personal Chair in the Faculty of Arts and Education and is Professor of International Politics in the School of Humanities and Social Sciences at Deakin University, Australia.

Politics in Contemporary Southeast Asia

Authority, democracy and political change

Damien Kingsbury

Routledge
Taylor & Francis Group

LONDON AND NEW YORK

First published 2017
by Routledge
2 Park Square, Milton Park, Abingdon, Oxon OX14 4RN

and by Routledge
711 Third Avenue, New York, NY 10017

Routledge is an imprint of the Taylor & Francis Group, an informa business

© 2017 Damien Kingsbury

British Library Cataloguing in Publication Data
A catalogue record for this book is available from the British Library

Library of Congress Cataloging in Publication Data
Names: Kingsbury, Damien, author.
Title: Politics in contemporary Southeast Asia : authority, democracy and political change /
    Damien Kingsbury.
Description: Abingdon, Oxon ; New York, NY : Routledge, 2017. | "2017 | Includes
    bibliographical references and index.
Identifiers: LCCN 2016013424| ISBN 9781138889439 (hardback) |
    ISBN 9781138889446 (pbk.) | ISBN 9781315712888 (ebook)
Subjects: LCSH: Southeast Asia—Politics and government. | ASEAN—Relations.
Classification: LCC DS526.7 .K56 2017 | DDC 320.959—dc23
LC record available at http://lccn.loc.gov/2016013424

ISBN: 978-1-138-88943-9 (hbk)
ISBN: 978-1-138-88944-6 (pbk)
ISBN: 978-1-315-71288-8 (ebk)

Typeset in Bembo Std
by Swales & Willis Ltd, Exeter, Devon, UK

For Rae,
with whom I share an active commitment to free, fair,
transparent, representative and accountable politics
and
for sharing our many rewarding journeys in that pursuit.
Long may they continue.

Contents

Acknowledgments

There are a number of people I would like to thank who have made the writing of this book possible. First and foremost, my wife, Rae, has been a constant source of positive support and encouragement, having faith in me when my own faith was sometimes lacking. Our shared values and her encouragement to put them into action remains a source of inspiration.

I also wish to thank my colleagues at Deakin University, who have similarly been supportive and engaging, and who have continued to provide encouragement and opportunities for research and writing. In particular, I would like to acknowledge Professor Matthew Clarke for his continued support. If a university is a place of scholarly reflection and the exploring and sharing of ideas, then I have been fortunate to make an intellectual home in such a place.

All work of this type is a reflection of accumulated experience; in this case, some of that experience has been made possible by previous grants from the Australia Research Council, as well as research support from Deakin University. At least as importantly, however, have been the many and diverse range of friends, colleagues and acquaintances from across Southeast Asia or who regularly work in the region who have generously shared their experiences, information and reflections. They have allowed opportunities and insights both rare and privileged.

Finally, the people of the region known as Southeast Asia that I have encountered in a wide array of circumstances have continued to demonstrate that, while we all look at the world in different ways, including within what is sometimes referred to as 'national' cultures, what we share is a common, often humbling and sometimes inspiring humanity. The wide variety of people across the region demonstrate, as elsewhere, all that is good with the world, some of which is mundane, a great amount of which is aspirational, and on the odd occasion that which is salutary if not always positively edifying. Each of these qualities can, perhaps, be found to a greater or lesser extent in us all. Learning, however, the circumstances and values that prompt or motivate such varying responses has been the most valuable part of this experience and, while it is not possible to offer specific thanks, I do extend a continuing sense of gratitude.

Foreword

Southeast Asia is quickly evolving as a political lynchpin region in a complex, challenging and increasingly uncertain world. Its countries represent the process of democratisation, failures of democratic experiments and the outright rejection of plural democratic processes. It has moved away from a self-defining (and ultimately limiting) claim to being the home of 'Asian values', towards a position of not apologising to the world for the political orientation of its constituent parts. Belying this seeming confidence, however, remain many internal challenges to the stability and orientation of its states: some of its constituent states have been, and continue to be, beset by separatism and Islamist subversion, while others struggle to organise themselves around what it means to be a nation and to represent and meaningfully include their citizens. This book is an attempt to capture these complex and often overlapping struggles as this dynamic region forges its place in the world of the twenty-first century.

The main themes of this book are the extent and type of, and challenges to representation and accountability of, the regional governments of Southeast Asia, degrees of good governance and transparency, and the role of elites and militaries in shaping or determining political outcomes.

This book specifically focuses on political processes, although it offers a broad socio-cultural overview of the region in the Introduction, and considers ways in which the regional states do or do not work to the advancement of their citizens' interests. The intention of focusing on events in the lead up to and following on from the turn of the century reflects some key changes that have affected both the world and the region, notably following the end of the Cold War, the effects of globalisation, the Asian financial crisis of 1997 and, to some extent, the so-called 'War on Terror'. Over that period, some states have seen momentous political change, while others have forestalled political change by liberalising their economies, and yet others have actively stifled calls for change.

The book is organised into the thematic groupings of Hard Single Party States (Vietnam, Laos, Cambodia), Soft Dominant Party States (Malaysia, Singapore, Brunei), Transitional States (Myanmar, Thailand) and Democratising and Democratic States (Indonesia, Philippines and Timor-Leste).

1 Introduction

The countries of the region known as Southeast Asia make, on face value, an odd combination. They comprise some very different countries, one being the world's fourth largest state by population – some 250 million predominantly Muslim people living on around a third of its almost 18,000 islands across a 5,000 kilometre-wide archipelago of almost two million square kilometres. This country, Indonesia, achieved independence in 1949, prior to which its constituent parts comprised the Dutch East Indies. At the other end of the scale is Timor-Leste, one of the world's smallest states by population, with around 1.2 million predominantly Catholic people living on little more than half of an island of a little over 15,000 square kilometres. It achieved independence in 2002, prior to which it was colonised by Indonesia for 24 years and, before that, by Portugal. All of the countries in between have been European colonies but for Thailand, which managed to avoid the formality of that arrangement by being allowed to remain as a buffer between British and French colonial interests.

The region that comprises Southeast Asia is bounded to the west by India, to the north by China, to the east by the Pacific Ocean and its island states and to the south by Australia. Like all such boundaries, these are somewhat arbitrary, marking roughly geographic, specifically colonial and sometimes ethnic distinctions. Manifested as states, Southeast Asia includes continental Myanmar, Thailand, Laos, Cambodia and Vietnam and the maritime Malaysia, Indonesia, Singapore, Brunei, the Philippines and Timor-Leste.

Like all such boundaries, the distinctions between these states and the people who live in them tend to blur and the lived reality is much less clear than the delineations on a map. If regions were identified by ethnicity rather than states' boundaries, there would be a considerable ambiguity around this region's edges. Yet Southeast Asia is an identified region and self-identifies, in regular discussion with itself through the Association of Southeast Asian Nations, on that basis.

The original inhabitants of the more southern parts of this broad region were Australoid peoples, limited remnants of whom occupy some of the mountainous areas (e.g. the Orang Asli of Malaysia). Subsequent populations arrived in the region in waves primarily from around 2000 BCE, having migrated south from the Tibetan plateau, overland from regions of what is now southern China and from south-eastern China and Taiwan out towards the Pacific Ocean.

Such waves of migration have, at least for the time being, effectively finished. However, one of the more recent waves of migration was the Hmong, from the highlands of southern China to the highlands of northern Vietnam, Laos and Thailand. Their migration began in the late eighteenth century and did not effectively conclude until the early 1970s.

While the waves of migration that have populated Southeast Asia can be characterised by relatively minor anatomical differences, more usefully they fall into phyla of languages: the Sino-Tibetan languages to the west, mostly Myanmar; T'ai-Kadai in Thailand, Laos and Myanmar's Shan state; and the Austro-Asiatic languages groups of Proto Mon-Khmer across the rest of mainland Southeast Asia. Austronesian languages of the Malayo-Polynesian group dominate throughout the archipelago, but for the Papuan phylum of the region's south-eastern edges, where Southeast Asia blurs with the south-west Pacific.

The region also has a significant Han Chinese (mostly Hoklo/Hakka) population of around 30 million, some of whom have been resident as traders for hundreds of years but many of whom migrated during the colonial era (or immediately after), taking advantage of increased economic opportunities. While many Chinese have intermarried with others or have assimilated in name and language (e.g. the Peranakan, or 'descendants' of Indonesia), there remain significant and often quite distinct ethnic Chinese communities throughout the region, notably in Singapore and Malaysia. There is also some European racial influence, with elements of Dutch in parts of Indonesia, more notably Portuguese in earlier trading centres of Malacca and Timor-Leste, and Spanish in the Philippines.

While there is much to distinguish the various ethnic groups of Southeast Asia, there are also a number of commonalities across the region. In particular, common to all but a few highland tribes is the cultivation of rice, particularly wet or paddy rice. While wet rice agriculture is not universal throughout the region – there is also some dry rice farming along with other staple crops – it has laid the foundation for the creation of the major civilisations and hence key cultural influences of the region. These large, settled civilisations that, at different times, held sway over significant empires, include the Angkorian Khmer empire, the dynasties of Central and East Java (the most extensive of which was Majapahit), the central Burman empires, the pre-Lao state of Lan Xang, the rise of Thai empires and the southward expansion of Vietnam.

Parallel to the establishment of this agricultural phenomenon, and the centralised political systems it helped engender, was the Hindu-inspired cult of the *deva-raja* (god-king) and the development of strongly hierarchical patron–client relations. This Hindu influence was noticeable across the region but for Vietnam, which was more strongly influenced by China, the eastern parts of Indonesia and the Philippines, whose first major external influence was Islam, and some of the south-eastern islands and the northern Philippines, where later forms of Christianity were most influential.

Prior to colonialism, with the exception of Vietnam, states in Southeast Asia did not have demarcated borders, but porous centres of power that waxed and waned. This dynamism of states based on an 'exemplary centre' has been likened by some scholars to a 'mandala' model of political organisation, where the god-king sits at the pinnacle of power, surrounded by successive circles of nobles, courtiers and others in descending order of political importance, often encompassing smaller sites of power within its larger framework and further sites of friendly and enemy states. By definition, in such a model, if an enemy state expands, one's own state contracts, and vice-versa, so that a shifting equilibrium becomes the only constant in inter-state affairs. Populations in this context were important much less in terms of their ethnicity than as a principal source of labour and hence power. Interrupted and in significant part shaped by colonialism, regional states have largely adapted to Westphalian state models, particularly around notions of fixed borders.

Within the traditional patron–client model, rulers usually had some degree of reciprocal relations with their subjects. This tended to decline in more centralised, mandala-type political systems where the monarch sat both at the centre and on top of the political system, protected by courtiers and other underlings in concentric circles of authority. More localised, village-level political systems relied on a much more direct relationship between the ruler and the ruled.

The notion of an all-powerful ruler has not entirely disappeared in Southeast Asia, and royalty and other strong leaders, and charismatic individuals, have frequently continued to reflect both the extraordinary status of royalty, such as Thailand's King Bhumibol Adulyadej or Cambodia's Norodom Sihanouk, or the personification of power. This personification of power can also be seen in Myanmar's Aung San, Ne Win, Aung San Suu Kyi; Cambodia's Hun Sen; Vietnam's Ho Chi Minh; Indonesia's Sukarno and Suharto; Malaysia's Mahatir Mohamad; Singapore's Lee Kwan Yew; the Philippines' Ramon Magsaysay and Ferdinand Marcos; Brunei's Sultan Bolkiah; and Timor-Leste's Xanana Gusmao.

Significant attributes of powerful rulers were reflected through the so-called 'Asian Values' debate of the 1980s and 1990s, in which there was claimed to be a specifically 'Asian' way of understanding and applying political power. This was said to reflect notions of the community over the individual and consequent reinterpretations of civil and political rights, respect for and obedience to elders and leaders, hard work, and the valuing of education. The difficulty with this assertion was that, although it contained elements of truth, there were perhaps more exceptions to the rule than there was agreement with it. Moreover, it neatly reflected the political interests of a specific status quo and disallowed, by definition, meaningful challenge to the assertion.

The 'people power' movement of the Philippines and the democratisation of Indonesia after 1998 did much to damage the 'Asian Values' claim. Singaporean leader Lee Kwan Yew later modified the term to mean 'Confucian Values', which, having a Chinese connotation, clearly did not apply to most Southeast Asians. In the end, what was purported to be a common characteristic of Southeast Asian people transpired to be a common characteristic of authoritarian leaders more widely dispersed. What it meant to be Southeast Asian was less such an overt political construction and more a matter of having to address common sets of challenges around development and, in some cases, democratisation and civil and political rights.

In common with many societies far removed from Southeast Asia, patron–client relations continue to form much of the basis of society and politics, and often of economies and commerce. At one level, this tends to construct a mutually supportive and reciprocal set of relations which help bond together particular societies or social orders. However, translated into the post-colonial era and in particular into a modern economy, such patron–client relations also lend themselves to corruption, particularly of political office where traditionally there was little or no distinction between power and reward. Once, without formal taxation, there was a requirement for rulers to run the state from their own funds and there was some notion of reciprocity. More recently, however, rulers have been able to rely on state revenue and the reciprocal link is largely broken, leading to corruption scandals such as the accumulation of more than US$5 billion by Ferdinand Marcos and approximately US$35 billion by Suharto and his family.

While it is relatively simple to identify social commonalities or the major racial or linguistic families across Southeast Asia, descending into ethnicity is vastly more complex. There are more than 90 language groups across the region, each often dividing into locally distinct languages and dialects. To illustrate, while there are two principle language groups in the tiny half-island of Timor-Leste, it has 28 distinct languages and a further 16 dialects among its 1.2 million people. Neighbouring West Papua (as part of Indonesia) has more than 300 distinct languages. Even relatively ethnically cohesive states, such as Vietnam, have more than 60 languages, which is a common experience throughout the region.

The region's linguistic diversity reflects its fractured geography, with steep mountains and seas dividing peoples into historically relatively isolated communities. It was through such relative isolation that not only did distinct languages arise, but so too did local customs, belief systems and specific forms of social organisation. Without Westphalian borders prior to colonialism, regional authority and influences waxed and waned. This left overlays of some cultures on others, for example the strong Javanese influence in Bali and Sumatran influences in peninsula Malaysia. In some cases, the overlay of some cultures all but eclipsed those they touched, for example the Khmer and Vietnamese diminution of the once strong Cham nation, linguistically related to the Acehnese of northern Sumatra, or the subjugation of the Mon to invading Burmans. There were also more constructive relations, such as ancient Khmer links to the Srivajaya empire, on Sumatra, and to Java, manifested in the joining of their respective royal dynasties.

More widespread influences came from India, beginning around 2000 years ago, with the consequent spread of Hinduism and then Buddhism. This left a deep imprint of not just religion but also the introduction of Sanskritic literature and the embedding of Hindu art, culture and aspects of social organisation. Similarly, the spread of Islam, particularly through the maritime areas, deeply influenced traditional belief systems, cultural practices and modes of social and political organisation. So too the later arrival of Christianity influenced some regional groups, if with lesser total reach. In many cases, these influences have led to a blending with pre-existing modes to form the syncretised cultures, for example, of animism and Buddhism in Myanmar; animism, Hinduism and Islam in Central and East Java; animism and Hinduism in Bali; and Catholicism and animism in the Philippines and, even more pronouncedly, in Timor-Leste.

The impact of competing colonialisms in particular has been profound, not least through the reaction to it informing nascent notions of nationalism. In many cases, this emergence of national identity was framed by the geography of colonialism; though each of Malay origin, Indonesia, Malaysia and the Philippines charted distinct national paths, but for a brief moment of pan-Malayism in 1963. Interestingly, too, despite rejecting colonialism, national identity has been framed not just around colonial borders (independent Thailand had its borders set in the west and south by the UK and in the east by France) but also by adopting internal colonial policies. Such policies include the relocation of majority populations and the displacement of original populations, regional exploitation to the benefit of the centre, and the domination of the state by ethnic majorities, often to the exclusion of minorities.

So, too, ethnic groupings of people that might have otherwise found cause for national unity were divided. The Lao were divided between Thailand and Laos, along the Mekong River as a boundary between two territories rather than an arterial route within one. The various Malay peoples were arbitrarily divided or incorporated into colonial entities according to deals done in Europe and the US. Arguably the Malays of the Malaysian Peninsula have more in common with the Malays of Sumatra, from whom many are descended, than the Malays of Sumatra have in common with their Javanese counterparts to the south. Similarly, the Malays of Brunei at once reflect a greater Malay identity as well as Brunei's loss of the north of the island, Borneo, the name of which is derived from that of the kingdom.

The single largest ethnic group in the Southeast Asian region is the Javanese, with some 135 million people, which tends to dominate the rest of Indonesia's population of some 245 million, scattered across 12 major ethnic groups and hundreds of smaller groups, in terms of politics and cultural influences. The Javanese were originally animist, but broadly adopted and adapted Hinduism from early in the first millennium CE, and then Buddhism towards the end of the first millennia CE, with Islam becoming more predominant from the fourteenth century onwards. There remains, however, a blending of beliefs among many Javanese, who overwhelmingly officially identify themselves as Muslim but whose religious practices and beliefs reflect elements of earlier traditions. To illustrate, the storylines and characters of the Hindu *Mahabharata* and *Ramayana* continue to resonate in traditional Javanese storytelling and plays, and the Sanskrit eagle, *garuda*, which occurs in Hindu mythology, provides the backdrop to Indonesia's coat of arms, as well as lending its name to the national airline.

While often characterised as largely homogenous, the Javanese are a useful case study about the unifying and also the dividing effects of ethnicity. Inhabitants of the island of Java, Javanese live in the centre and east of the island, the west being populated by ethnic Sundanese. Like all ethnic groups, the Javanese are not homogenous and manifest distinctions along a number of lines.

Perhaps the most notable distinction is between observant (*santri*) and nominal (*abangan*) Muslims, who are themselves broadly divided by an urban/rural split. This distinction is commonly identified as being along the lines of the modernist, urban-oriented organisation Muhammadiyah and the more traditionalist, rural-oriented Nahdlatul Ulama. However, there are also a range of other, smaller organisations, including Hizbut Tahrir Indonesia, segueing into activist groups such as Lembaga Dakwa Islam Indonesia (Indonesian Islamic Propagation Institute); militant Islamist organisations such as the Front Pembela Islam (Islamic Defenders Front); and Islamist terrorist groups such as the descendent organisations of the Darul Islam movements, for example Jema'ah Islamiyah and its successor organisations including Jamaah Anshorut Tauhid. At the other end of the religious scale are organisations such as the Jaringan Islam Liberal (Islam Liberal Network) and a plethora of less formally organised religious groups that are only tangentially or nominally Muslim.

The Javanese are traditionally also divided by status, reflected in distinct languages based on politeness for each status group, Ngoko (lower status), Krama Madyu (middling), Krama (high status) and Krama Inggil (highest status), as well as some 18 regional dialects. Beyond this, there are degrees of influence of colonialism and modernisation, which have impacted on much traditional culture and adherence to ideologies – for example the state ideology of Pancasila, or Five Principles – while communism was relatively popular in Java until its adherents were all but wiped out in the massacres and imprisonments of 1965–66. Then there is simply the fact that local villages and communities have developed in distinct ways relative to each other depending on prevailing influences and circumstances.

Vietnam's ethnic Vietnamese (formally: Khin) are the next largest ethnic group in Southeast Asia, numbering around 77 million of the country's population of 90 million. The Vietnamese originated in south-eastern China, occupying the Red River Valley from around 1,000 BCE. The expansion of the Han Chinese forced the Vietnamese largely out of lands in south-eastern China into the Red River Delta, and brought the people of the precursor state of Vietnam under largely continuous Chinese control until the tenth century.

Despite continuing tensions and occasional battles with the Chinese, and reflecting long periods of occupation by them, Vietnam bears the most distinct Confucian influence of any Southeast Asian state. Even its name is a juxtaposed approximation of the Chinese term for 'South Tribe'. Vietnam used the Chinese examination system and court culture until after the arrival of the colonial French, and employed Chinese characters until 1918. Despite formally rejecting Confucianism, its characteristic influences continue to pervade Vietnamese 'communist' society.

As Vietnam expanded southwards, between the fifteenth and eighteenth centuries, it conquered and largely absorbed the Indianised state of Champa and then the south-eastern portion of Cambodia around the Mekong Delta. This area is still referred to by Cambodians as 'Kampuchea Krom' (Lower Cambodia), while 'Khmer Krom' denotes the ethnic Cambodians who still live in the region.

With each of these influences the malleability of cultures and ethnicities has shifted, and it continues to shift. Arguably the greatest post-colonial impact upon notions of ethnicity has been the attempted standardisation of 'national' cultures, commonly built more around an idealised state norm than the common nineenth-century European notion of ethno-nationalism, in which there is a high degree of congruity between the ethnic or language group and the state.

Assuming that the idea of 'nation' is based upon a geographically specific bonded political group, there are two principal conceptions of 'nation' in Southeast Asia. The first is the more conventional ethno-nationalist model, which is demonstrated in the core populations of states such as Vietnam, Cambodia, Brunei, Singapore and Thailand. Even among these states, however, there are numerous ethnic groups which have at various times resisted central control or the imposition of dominant ethnic characteristics.

This resistance is more pronounced in less ethnically coherent states, including Indonesia, Myanmar and the Philippines. Each of these states has, at different times, experienced high levels of armed rebellion against national inclusion, and there have been and remain numerous assertions of distinct national identity and related claims to separate statehood within these states.

In Indonesia, while Aceh's most recent rebellion (1976–2005) against the state has ended, there remains among many within Aceh and among its diaspora a continuing claim for independence from the Indonesian state. West Papua, too, continues to experience claims for separate state status, based on the shared ethnic and racial identity of that territory's Melanesian population as distinct from the predominantly Malay racial background of most of the rest of Indonesia. Indonesia has experienced a number of rebellions over its relatively short history, with claims to separate national identity also in Ambon (Republic of the South Moluccas) and northern Sulawesi, based on competing understandings of culture, power and imposition.

Tensions have also arisen in Malaysia, Singapore and Timor-Leste over ethnic distinction, leading to inter-ethnic violence in both places. In neither case were there separatist movements, although in Malaysia in particular the distinction between the three main ethno-racial groups – Malay, Chinese and Indian (mostly Tamil) – remains pronounced and is institutionalised in political parties.

This brings us to the second and more common sense of nation in Southeast Asia, which is defined as a state that has had its borders defined not by a particular bonded ethnic group but by geo-colonial circumstances. In most cases, the borders of such states were defined by colonial powers, if in some cases approximating to pre-existing polities. To illustrate, Myanmar occupies a territory that approximates to an area ruled by the majority Bama peoples prior to colonialism, but which varied over time to include or leave out territories which were once under Bama imperial domination. The T'ai-speaking Shan state, in northeast Myanmar, has at times been a vassal state to the imperial powers located in what is now central Myanmar, but at others was independent.

Myanmar's north-west area, approximating to the western Sagaing Region (and now a Naga self-administered zone), was historically an area subject to no external rule, but was demarcated in 1826 under the Anglo-Burmese Treaty of Yandabo, which ended the first Anglo-Burmese War (and in which Burma lost the vassalage of Assam and Manipur), and the 1953 Indo-Burmese Boundary Demarcation. Assam, Manipur, Jaintia and Cachar, in what is now part of north-east India (and therefore technically part of South Asia), was under Bama domination until 1835; Asam itself was a T'ai-speaking kingdom from the fourteenth century and is therefore more closely related to Southeast than South Asia. Similarly, the Dao of Yunnan Province, China, are a T'ai-speaking people more closely related to Thais than to Han Chinese.

In terms of ethnic identity, the T'ai-speaking Dao, Shan, northern Thai (Lanna) and Laos also shared as much in common with each other as the northern and southern Thai, who have since become a nation within a unified state. (The Assamese were linguistically assimilated into the Indo-Aryan language family and now speak a version of Bengali).

While post-colonial states largely exist within exact or approximate colonial boundaries, the states themselves were mostly formed in opposition to colonialism. In one sense, there is an inherent contradiction in some of the more overtly constructed states having explicitly rejected colonialism, but having adopted colonial boundaries (and sometimes oppressive colonial-era laws) in the post-colonial setting.

In this state-centric approach, the sense of 'nation' is more highly constructed, including through the standardisation of a common language, requiring a common academic curriculum (which frequently valorises 'nationalist' heroes whose agendas were less encompassing), and often inclusion by force. This, then, divides the 'nations' of Southeast Asia between those that are largely voluntary and those that are based on a significant element of compulsion.

The people of the Indonesian province of Aceh, perhaps more than others, bring together some of the complementary and contradictory characteristics of ethnicity and nation. The people of Aceh are primarily of Malay stock but, occupying the north-western tip of the island of Sumatra at the entrance to the much-travelled Straits of Malacca, they have also been subject to numerous other influences. Commenting on the variation in physical features, many Acehnese say that it is not what one looks like that makes one Acehnese, but what is in one's heart. This then goes to the question of ethnicity.

Ethnically, being Acehnese is defined primarily by being able to speak Acehnese, an Austronesian language related to but not mutually intelligible with Indonesian (a dialect of Malay), and by being Muslim. Being at the first port of call in the region, Aceh was the first point in maritime Southeast Asia to receive Islam, and is colloquially known as *Serambi Mekkah* (Mecca's Veranda). As such, many traders intermingled with its earlier inhabitants, so that the racial characteristics of Acehnese are largely Malay but also reflect Arab and Tamil influences, among others. Interestingly, the ethnic group that the Acehnese are closest to is the remnant Chams of central Indochina, who speak a close dialect of the same Chamic language and who are also Muslim. There are indications that Aceh and the former state of Champa may have had close political and economic relations, or that Aceh was influenced by the rise of the Khmer empire and the southward movement of Vietnamese, forcing many Chams to flee to overseas locations.

Although based on predecessor states, Aceh developed most clearly as a state from the thirteenth century, rising to a position of being a regional power in the seventeenth century. A sense of distinct Acehnese national identity, based on a shared village order, religious belief and adherence to a central sultanate, can be clearly marked from this time. The practice of political power in Aceh has long rested on a complex of factors, with power-sharing traditionally expressed through what is referred to as the 'state code', translated as 'Power rests with the king, Law with the great imam of Syah Kuala [Bandar Aceh's great mosque], Tradition with the Princess of Pahang and Regulations with the Bentara [similar to a police chief].' Deleting the role of the Princess of Pahang, which refers to cultural matters, this traditional political system reflected a triumvirate in which no individual (or single group) dominated political relations. The Acehnese state, which manifested this sense of national identity, was internationally recognised until 1871, when the UK withdrew opposition to Dutch incorporation of Aceh into its East Indies colonial possessions, which started two years later. The Acehnese resisted the Dutch for 40 years, with limited guerrilla activity against the Dutch until Japanese occupation in 1942.

Some scholars have suggested that notions of Acehnese national identity were relatively recently constructed, as a means of providing an ideology for Aceh's separatist war (1976–2005). There is some truth in the assertion that Acehnese national identity has been valorised and reified, although a similar assertion can be made about many nationalist movements claiming a glorious past upon which to base contemporary nationalist claims. There has also been a claim that Aceh's participation in the war against the Dutch, and agreement to be part of a post-colonial Indonesia, limits nationalist assertions. However, the Acehnese had agreed to be an autonomous part of an Indonesian federation which, when undermined by incorporation into the wider province of North Sumatra and the abolition of Indonesian federalism in 1950, led to rebellion in 1953. That rebellion ended in 1963 with the promise of greater autonomy, which was not implemented and which, in turn, led to the renewal of armed separatist activity 13 years later.

Despite a 2005 peace agreement which saw the implementation of greater autonomy for Aceh, a local sense of a distinct 'national' identity in Aceh remains pronounced, and continues to be asserted by many Acehnese activists. This sense of nation, then, continues to sit at odds with Indonesia's assertion of an overarching 'national' identity, which is constructed around the state, a generic language and its own somewhat glorified 'national' history, much of which finds its foundations in the greatest (claimed) extent of the Majapahit Javanese empire of the fourteenth century.

While the example of Aceh stands out, it is indicative of the at times mutually engaging or overlapping but otherwise quite separate and competing histories of various peoples of the region, their assertions of particular identities and the extent to which they agree with or accept the confluence between ethnic identity and the state. The Islamic Malays of (the former kingdom of) Pattani in southern Thailand have long asserted an independent identity and a claim for separate status, as have the Islamic Moros (from the Spanish 'Moors', Moroccan Muslims) of the southern Philippines; the Karen, Mon, Kachin and others of Myanmar; the racially distinct Melanesians of West Papua from the rest of Indonesia; and, at various times, populations within Indonesia in Ambon, Sulawesi, West Sumatra, Riau and elsewhere.

The status of pre-colonial states, kingdoms and sultanates reflected a shifting ordering of the ethno-political geography of Southeast Asia, some of which was nominally locked in place under colonial administration but which rarely survived intact the experience of post-colonial state formation. In part due to this distinct prior status and in part due to the centralist qualities of most post-colonial states, Southeast Asia has, as a consequence, experienced widespread and often sustained separatist insurgencies.

Having noted this claim to non-state national identity, Thailand has been quite success-ful at building a sense of Thai national identity, if with a significant exception in the coun-try's Muslim Malay south. The Thais of Bangkok are, in many cases, ethnic Chinese, but have for over a century adopted 'Thai-ness' as their national marker, starting in 1913 with the compulsory use of Thai names in order to gain Thai citizenship. The northern Thais, who were of a separately administered region and, at different times, a separate country, are to outsiders effectively indistinguishable from southern Thais, while the Thais of the north-eastern Isan region, many of whom are ethnic Lao, have also increasingly assimilated their sense of 'Thai-ness'.

Similarly, the Indonesian state's intentional nation-building program has been increas-ingly successful, in that the Indonesian language is now dominant, if sometimes along-side local languages. There is also a greater sense of agreement with national identity, which is more firmly embedded than in the past. In particular, in the post-Suharto 'reform' era, there is more coherence around a sense of national identity based on a civic identity. Where once being 'Indonesian' implied agreement with a largely unresponsive authoritarian political system, it has increasingly come to mean a more nuanced and plural set of political values, including the opportunity for and right to disagreement, robust political debate and open participation in largely free and fair procedural democ-racy (there continue to be questions around more substantive aspects of Indonesia's democratic process).

Negotiations with the Moro Islamic Liberation Front (MILF) have also moved towards establishing greater regional autonomy within the framework of the pre-existing Philippines state. At one level, this also implies agreement, if a negotiated one, around the status of the state and supra-national identity. Elsewhere, what it means to be Filipino is broadly accepted, even where there remains an ideological contest over the orientation of the state. Philippine communists do not agree with the ideological orientation of the state of which they are, for technical purposes, citizens, but they do agree that they are Filipino.

So too in Myanmar, where there has been separatist rebellion predicated upon sepa-rate ethnic and national identities since just after independence, there has been move-ment towards agreement around a set of negotiated relations. This was intended to see previously opposed groups incorporated into the overarching state and thus, in a practi-cal sense, accepting at least some of what it means to be of Myanmar. Interestingly, on this point, there is debate within Myanmar about accepting the idea of being a constitu-ent member of the Myanmar nation but, if of Burman ethnic background, still being referred to as 'Burmese' rather than Myanmarese/Myanmese. This, then, distinguishes non-Burman citizens of Myanmar by their ethnicity and continues to reinforce the dichotomy that historically separated the central *Burma Pyima* (Burma Proper; *pyima*: ruling/administration/benefactor) and the peripheral ethnic groups as *Pyinay* (inferior/subordinate).

This goes to the question of geo-institutional arrangements, rather than to the sense of the shared identity upon which a coherent and politically bonded nation is predicated. In this respect, while many peoples of Southeast Asia accept, with varying degrees of will-ingness, their incorporation into particular states, their sense of bonded political identity may exist on quite a separate plane. Unlike in much of Europe and some other specific areas, states exist in Southeast Asia and nations also exist, but the confluence of both in the 'nation-state' exists, even in the strongest examples such as Vietnam or Cambodia, only in a qualified and distinctly multi-ethnic sense.

Contemporary Southeast Asia

Political events in Southeast Asia necessarily reflect the circumstances and historical trajectories of the specific countries of the region as well as having some, if often lesser, influence on each other. However, all of the states of Southeast Asia have, in their own ways and to a great or lesser extent, responded to external changes. The most profound of these changes was the end of the Cold War, and the further changes which that wrought on the global order. As with the ripples in a pond, the splash occurred elsewhere, but its effects were felt throughout this region, thus helping to set the contemporary stage.

One of the principal effects of the end of the Cold War was to lessen superpower support for client states, or the use of local combatants as proxies in wider ideological battles. There was also, in what was for a time a unipolar world, a shift towards a greater sense of humanitarian responsibility. How the states of Southeast Asia responded to this change in global politics set the stage for the political environment assessed here. There is no agreement about the precise date for the ending of the Cold War, it being a series of events rather than a single event. However, the dissolution of the former Soviet Union in December 1991 was perhaps its clearest single indicator.

The end of the Cold War and the collapse of numerous communist regimes that characterised one of its sides was argued by some as a triumph for, and of, democracy. Indeed, some scholars argued that 'democracy' had been proven to be the 'end' state for human politics (Fukuyama (1992) was the most prominent example of this assertion). Others, however, argued against the teleological assumptions implied not just in democracy's inevitability but also its longevity (O'Donnell 1996). There is no doubt that authoritarian and one party states, especially 'communist' states, came under increasing pressure to liberalise and even democratise. There is similarly no doubt that many such states went down this at least nominally democratic path. However, not all such democratic experiments were successful, especially if the term 'democracy' is understood in a more substantive rather than merely procedural sense. What had become clear, though, was that democracy (or something like it) had become the global benchmark for understanding and classifying political systems. Democracy may not have become universal, nor has it proven to be as robust as some might have suggested; it has, however, become a common, if normative, measurement against which other political forms are assessed.

The most immediate effect in Southeast Asia of the ending of the Cold War was the 1991 Paris Comprehensive Peace Settlement which ended Cambodia's civil war. That war was between its Vietnamese and hence Soviet-backed government and its former government and opposition comprised of the Khmer Rouge, supported by China, and the royalist Khmer People's National Liberation Front, supported by the US and Thailand. Cambodia's post-transition 'democracy' was, however, short-lived, with the royalist FUNCINPEC being forced into a coalition government by the electorally defeated Cambodian People's Party (CPP). The coalition was ended by a CPP coup in 2007, establishing Cambodia on its current path of free market one party domination.

So, too, in Vietnam and its close ally Laos; the collapse of the Soviet economy forced them both to recast their economies away from being state controlled to being largely free market, if still with significant state involvement. The end of the Cold War saw the end of Thailand's communist insurgency, despite continued instability and military intervention in its government. However, this instability and the wider democratic trend did produce the landmark 1997 Constitution, commonly hailed as Thailand's most democratic. That it arrived at around the same time as the Asian financial crisis, however, led to the fall of yet another government, setting up the deep division that continues to pervade Thai political society.

The Asian financial crisis also impacted heavily on Indonesia, where the previously Western-supported but deeply corrupt president was pushed from office, ushering in the country's increasing democratisation. This event also paved the way for the independence of Timor-Leste. The end of the Cold War had less impact on Malaysia, Singapore or Brunei, although in the first two instances there grew greater scope for reconsidering and even challenging the political status quo. As a small, oil-supported sultanate, Brunei remained largely impervious to external political events. In the Philippines, however, the decline of the Communist Party of the Philippines following the country's return to electoral politics in 1986 was further cemented, if only for a time, while the US withdrew from two key military bases and there was a peace agreement in principle with Islamic separatists.

Finally, while Myanmar had remained largely isolated from world affairs, the rise of a post-Cold War global 'responsibility to protect' in the late 1990s, formalised in 2005, left the country's military government increasingly exposed. Economic sanctions followed by a threat of intervention eventually pushed Myanmar into adopting both economic and political reform.

Some of these events were clearly linked to each other, some were a much more direct response to external events, and all were, to a greater or lesser degree, also a reflection of the internal dynamics of the respective states. But while the states of Southeast Asia that are with us in the early twenty-first century remain identifiable as a continuation of earlier iterations, they have also moved on and changed in ways that have not always been expected.

The states of Southeast Asia continue to change, evolve and chart courses that sometimes leave outside observers initially puzzled. They will continue to reflect their histories and cultural influences, colonial overlays, the exigencies of development and state maintenance, as well as the multiple influences of globalisation and, very often, the interests of their elites. There is a normative and rather hopeful value in suggesting that, one way or the other, the states of Southeast Asia are, or should be, progressing to more inclusive and equitable political outcomes. But such progress that has been made has often been shallow, unsustainable or susceptible to reverse. It is therefore more useful to focus on what is, how it came about and what might be in the contest of ideas, and on the extent to which and where such a contest is available.

2 Political processes in Southeast Asia

It is common for many developing countries to be beset by problems of corruption, lack of accountability, poor governance and limited political representation. Such countries seem to have only occasional and often poor engagement with notions of democracy, and a greater propensity to various degrees of failure of state institutions. To some extent, this perception is based on a history of failure of developing countries to consistently conform to a modernist western model of political processes, the value of which has been the subject of lively debate. To a considerable degree, too, many of these features are some of the defining characteristics of a developing country, particularly one that has not progressed in its overall political development.

The states of Southeast Asia cross the full range of development categories, from among the least developed countries in the world (in median income terms) such as Timor-Leste and Laos, to among the most developed (in per capita GDP terms) such as Brunei and Singapore. Yet each of them continues to display both attributes of development and many of the qualities and compromises of post-colonial states.

More specifically, the countries of Southeast Asia have each faced a range of economic, social and institutional challenges, some of which have been or are in the process of being successfully overcome and many of which have not. Those unresolved challenges can both be a product of and lead to the undermining of political representation, stability and what might be referred to as 'political development' (see Kingsbury 2007a). Within this framework, and recognising that individual countries are products of specific historical or more recently inherited sets of circumstances, there are elements of consistency between the issues they continue to face and which allows a general analysis of their politics which can be applied when understanding specific case studies.

This chapter sets out the main features of politics in Southeast Asia, indicating how the relationships between these elements forms a complex interweaving of factors that preclude providing simple answers to their multi-faceted problems.

This chapter is based on the idea that the processes by which people can improve their lives are in large part shaped by political and social freedoms and accountabilities. The idea of development has traditionally been focused on improvements in the material welfare of people. Some commentators and regional politicians have argued that economic or material development should take precedence over political development, and that political development should be put on hold to ensure that fragile or conflicted political environments do not hinder efficiencies of organisation necessary to lift poor countries out of poverty. In some cases, this position has also been allied with the view that political development (especially if that means democracy and civil and political rights) is a foreign imposition, does not necessarily accord with pre-existing cultural or political values, and may constitute a form of imperialism. The 'Bangkok Declaration' (1993) was perhaps the most pronounced regional statement on this issue (see also De Bary 1998).

Related to the view that economic development should take precedence over political development – that people will be unconcerned about politics if they do not have enough to eat – is the view that higher levels of material development are necessary to sustain higher levels of political development. That is, if people lack food security or are illiterate they will be not only less concerned about politics but less able to meaningfully participate in a given political process. This has been termed by some as 'rice before rights' or the 'full bellies thesis' (see Howard 1983).

A countervailing view is that if people have the opportunity to freely express themselves, and to hold their politicians accountable, they are more likely to be able to ensure there is adequate distribution of food and other available material goods, including education (see Sen 1999). This then raises the fundamental question of whether it is economics that drives politics, or politics that drives economics, or what has been referred to as the debate about the competition between structure and agency. These issues will be discussed within the context of wider interpretations of governance and evolving political practice.

The origins of Southeast Asia's contemporary states

While some can trace a pre-colonial history, with the exception of Thailand the states of Southeast Asia came into existence in the period following the Second World War, in which struggles for liberation that had begun to find their voice in the 1920s and 1930s became more compelling in the post-war era. Even Thailand was defined by aspects of the colonial experience, not least in terms of its borders and the status of its external relations.

There have been two defining qualities of Southeast Asia's states that derive from their post-colonial status. The first is that the successor states have almost all been based upon prior colonial boundaries, usually reflecting colonial convenience rather than prior ethno-linguistic unity. This is based on the principle of *uti possidetis*, or that which is possessed at the time of independence. This in turn is based on the maxim of Roman law, 'the doctrine of *uti possidetis ita possidetis* (as you possess, so you possess), which treats the acquisition of a state's territory as a given, with no territorial adjustments allowable without the consent of the currently occupying parties' (Mahmud 2011: 60). There have been exceptions to the application of this principle, in the case of French Indo-China (divided into three states) and the Malayan colonies (also three states). But the principle has otherwise been applied, and has thus created inherent problems of a disjuncture between the conception of 'nation' as a bonded political community and the heterogeneity of the state.

The second defining quality is that a number of Southeast Asian states came to independence through a military struggle (Myanmar, Vietnam, Laos, Cambodia, Timor-Leste), or other military involvement (Thailand, Philippines), with military forces and ideology subsequently coming to play a major and often self-defining role in the orientation of those states. This has resulted in the creation of hierarchical, unaccountable, power-oriented political structures.

Having achieved independence, there have been question marks over the extent to which states in Southeast Asia sustained the sense of unity of purpose that liberation helped engender. There have also been questions over whether these states have sustained their often claimed commitment to either a generalised sense of freedom or a representative, accountable and participatory political process. The aspirations often associated with independence – that independence will address the problems that beset the colonised territory – have commonly exceeded the capacity of the newly formed state to deliver. Indeed, such aspirations were often confronted by reduced state capacity as a result of war and the loss of colonial expertise, organisation and capital. Expectations of improvement in the lives of the people concerned not only went beyond that which the colonial power was able to provide, but were further out of touch with the reduced post-colonial environment (Chandler 2010: 170).

The gap between post-colonial expectations and the (lack of) capacity to fulfil them invariably produced political tensions (Jefferess 2008: 163). In multi-ethnic post-colonial societies, and in particular within the context of post-independence material scarcity, there has been a tendency for political leaders to reward their political supporters at the expense of other groups (Grawert 2009: 138). This form of patron–client relations has often been based along specific ethno-linguistic lines, although exceptions arose where patron–client groups formed around areas of geographic or, more commonly, economic interest. That is, while the bonds of a united struggle against colonialism may form an initial sense of unity, this unity was often not maintained in the post-colonial era.

In an open or plural political environment, such as post-colonial democracy, this lack of unity has in some cases manifested as political opposition and dissent. In cases where governments had little initial capacity, they have sometimes struggled to maintain organisational control and have consequently had a tendency to close political space and thus revert to forms of authoritarianism (Vietnam, Laos, Cambodia, Philippines, Myanmar, Thailand, Brunei, Indonesia), often employing repressive colonial-era legislation (Malaysia, Singapore) (see Collier 2009: 173–6, 186 on the relationship between state capacity and postcolonial democracies). In cases where such governments have derived from a military or revolutionary background that reflected a high degree of non-consultative hierarchical organisation, such organisation may be reflected in the political style and orientation of a subsequent government.

Political identity

Southeast Asia's independence movements were generally accompanied by a rise in the assertion of a nationalist identity, usually cohering around opposition to the colonial authority. But because most colonies were constructed according to geographic convenience rather than along ethnic or linguistic lines, they usually included distinct tribal or ethnic groups, many of which traditionally had ambivalent or even mutually hostile relations. Moreover, it was a common practice for colonial powers to employ one ethnic group in a position of advantage over others, as a mechanism for recruiting ethnic groups in support of the colonial enterprise (e.g. see Horowitz 1985: 527). In some cases, Southeast Asia's states succeeded in developing a sense of relatively coherent national identity (Thailand, Cambodia, Vietnam, Singapore) but in others, however, attempts to compel loyalty to the national project failed, especially where some ethnic groups felt discriminated against on the grounds of their ethnic identity and where the 'civic guarantee' of equal inclusion failed to apply (Myanmar, Indonesia, Philippines, Malaysia). This was particularly so where a specific ethnic group with a grievance within a reasonably geographically coherent area did not acknowledge the legitimacy of an administration from a separate location or over the claimed area, or where that sense of legitimacy was never adequately established or was lost, illustrated by separatist movements that affect or have affected many developing countries.

Southeast Asia's ethnically heterogeneous states in particular have tended to exhibit vertical or regionally based group tendencies, where they are constructed from multiple pre-existing and self-identifying communities and where the civic function of the state, in which all citizens are treated as equal, is weak. Given that most Southeast Asian states are 'ethnically diverse' (see Collier 1998 on the post-colonial experience more generally) and often have weak civic institutions, there is a tendency for such states to coalesce along ethnic rather than civic lines. In this, it is assumed that ethnically diverse states that have weak civic structures will necessarily employ a higher degree of compulsion in order to maintain state control. Conversely, ethnically diverse states that have stronger civic structures will have a greater proportion of voluntary inclusion within the state.

Given that many developing post-colonial states initially had and sometimes still have weak civic institutions – variable institutional capacity being a characteristic of the development process – few such multi-ethnic societies have made a fully successful transition to becoming voluntary states in which effectively all members freely choose to be citizens. Commonly, there has been an element of compulsion in accordance with an overt 'nation-building' project. Where this nation-building project has been predicated upon a higher degree of compulsion, it has tended to produce a reaction or to exacerbate existing tendencies, often by way of assertion of an alternative or separate identity. In the former case, where the distinction is between the ruling elite and the ruled, this can lead to 'horizontal' social divisions or class-based dissent, including 'classes' characterised by economic or political dispossession. In the latter case, the distinction is between ethnic groups, or vertical distinction (Eriksen 2002: ch. 3). This then raises two questions, the first being what it is that constitutes a nation, and how claims to nation can be assessed.

National identity as the basis for the assertion of nationalist claims can be characterised in two broad streams. The most common and primordial quality of national identity is based on ethnicity (Smith 1986: 22–46). As Anderson (1991) has noted, a common language is the principle mediator through which individuals who may not know each other can actually or potentially communicate across distance and hence perceive themselves as having a common interest.[1] This language can be commonly shared as the first quality of group formation, in that it was already spoken by the constituent members of the political group. In many developing countries, however, the state language is often not the first language of many of its citizens but may have been developed to help create a sense of common communication and hence identity. So too, it has been common for countries to emphasise elements of their history to help form a common political bond. However, basing the national project solely on an ascribed history or culture, i.e. what it means to be of a particular nationality, without extending that to include wider civic values, raises the prospect of reifying a mythical 'glorious past' (see Smith 1986: 174–208). In reifying itself, the state becomes inwardly focused, exclusivist and reactionary, which can lead to political division and conflict both with external nations (e.g. Khmers and Vietnamese in 1978) and within the state between constituent ethnic groups.

Historically, the territorial reach of nations has shifted, especially prior to the advent of modern state sovereignty (the Westphalian system of fixed borders), and populations were often fluid. These shifts were still underway when colonial powers cemented what were subsequently to become state borders.

The second defining quality for a more modernist, less ethnically prescriptive national identity is based on shared cultural or plural civic values (see Miller 1993, 1995; see also Smith 1998: 210–13). Shared plural, civic values correspond to a more voluntary, inclusive, participatory and open political society (for example, liberal democracy), usually based on an equally and consistently applied rule of law. An important element of this common civic identity is manifested as political participation.

Where national bonds are historically weak in relation to the state and civic bonds are not evident, states tend to compel membership of a 'national' community following, rather than preceding, the creation of the state. Compulsory membership of states by ethnic minorities is a feature of most Southeast Asian states. Such compulsion tends to preclude civic values, in which the state rules by (often relatively arbitrary and frequently oppressive) law, thus denying justice. This situation can be seen as applying in particular to Myanmar, Indonesia and the Philippines, and perhaps also Laos and to a lesser extent Malaysia, Cambodia and Vietnam. By contrast, voluntary nationalism, in which members freely embrace their agreed commonality, appears to provide a more stable basis for social equality of difference under rule of law (see Seymour 2000; Habermas 2001a, 2001b).

While Southeast Asia's states were historically divided and few could be said to have existed as coherent nations prior to independence, through the commonality of the struggle and, usually, the contiguity of the land, many did form strong national identities in direct response to the real or perceived depredations of the colonial experience and, in particular, wars of liberation. This further quality of defence, or security, in nation formation parallels and overlaps with Hobsbawm's (2004: ch. 4) and Gellner's (1983: ch 3) views on the role of industrialisation in nation formation. In this respect, the principles of defence (or a militant independence movement) require similar organisational structures to an industrial environment, with clear lines of management and control and the standardisation of communication (especially language) and worker/soldier practices. The importance of shared liberation struggles or mutual defence cannot be overstated. Where outsiders may argue that a 'nation' has not historically existed, given a common cause and organisation, as in the case of Timor-Leste for example, it can come into being relatively quickly and with a high degree of coherence and commitment in cases of mutual preservation.

The state

Several Southeast Asian states are based on colonies that did not necessarily reflect the unity or distinction of pre-existing ethnic identities, but they often had difficulty claiming the principle of *uti possidetis*, or full possession of prior claimed territory (ICJ 1986: 554), in establishing a non-ethnic (i.e. civic) form of national identity (Hasani 2003). As a result, there have been numerous claims to separate national identity which have led to competition between the self-identifying nation as a bonded political group and some Southeast Asian states.

The state, in a contemporary sense, refers to a specific and delineated area (Smith 1986: 235) in which a government exercises (or claims to exercise) political and judicial authority and claims a monopoly over the legitimate use of force up to the extent of its borders. Within a given territory, the state can be identified by the presence and activities of its institutions, which define its functional capacity (Krader 1976: 13). While a state claims authority within its borders, along with a monopoly on the use of force, it normatively does this on behalf of its citizens, as a manifestation of their political will. This implies a social contract between the state and its citizens, in which the state can expect, and compel, a duty to comply. In return, citizens can expect that the state will reflect and represent their interests. In reality, however, some states in Southeast Asia have only incomplete control of their territory, and their institutions do not always function, much less function well, up to the extent of their territorial borders. Moreover, such social contracts that exist between developing states and their citizens have been frequently undermined, compromised or arbitrarily changed to suit the needs and interests of ruling elites. In enforcing their will, particularly in relation to violent opposition, political elites in developing countries have resorted to using militaries for domestic purposes.

Militaries in politics

One of the most significant problems that has beset developing countries generally and those of Southeast Asia in particular has been the involvement of the military in civilian politics, in some cases disproportionately influencing government and in others taking control of the government. Militaries have been dominant in Southeast Asian countries but for Malaysia, Singapore and, arguably, Brunei. There have been many military coups or attempted coups, all reflecting, or contributing to, a high degree of political instability.

While almost all countries agree that they require the presence of a military, Desch (1999) has argued that civilian authority over militaries works best where a state faces high external threats and low internal threats. Civilian control of the military works worst, according to Desch, where a state faces high internal threats, such as separatism or revolutionary movements, and low external threats. Such could be said to be the situation in Myanmar, Thailand, Laos, Indonesia and the Philippines. In those conditions, the military is more likely to see – and has seen – itself as a political actor or as the protector of the state. This has often been justified by the role played by militaries (or their precursor guerrilla organisations) in independence movements. In conditions of high internal and external threats or low internal and external threats, Desch suggests, civilian control over the military sits in between the two extremes. In developed countries, however, the tendency has been for low internal and external threats to equate to greater civilian control over the military (see Lasswell 1941; Dains 2004). Militaries in Southeast Asia, notably in Myanmar, Indonesia, Thailand and the Philippines, have also interpreted as an internal 'threat' a perceived or actual lack of competence by civilian leaders.

Huntington (1957) argued that the most effective method of asserting civilian control over the military is to professionalise them, but a capacity to professionalise the military has often not been present in Southeast Asian states. This has been particularly so where the state has been unable to meet the full costs of the military, and hence militaries engage in private businesses outside civilian control, meaning they are less accountable to civilian governments and have political and economic interests that compete with their defence function (e.g. in Myanmar, Indonesia, Thailand, Laos, Vietnam and Cambodia).

Notably, too, when military organisations do influence or exercise political authority, they are by definition hierarchical, closed and relatively authoritarian (see Huntington 1957). This is especially the case where the military derives its ethos from revolutionary idealism, in which its role in the securing of independence is usually only the first step on the road to a wider social transformation, such as in Vietnam, Laos and Cambodia.

Where society is otherwise initially disorganised, where alternative legitimate sources of power have not yet become established or where the post-independence development project either heads towards failure or actually fails (e.g. Myanmar, Indonesia, Philippines), military control may be regarded by power holders as necessary to maintain state organisation or, in some cases, cohesion. This then has the capacity to devolve into a situation where the newly independent authority may lose legitimacy through its exclusive, non-participatory and non-representative system of organisation, or where it compels often geographically and ethnically specific reluctant citizens to remain within the state. Myanmar, Indonesia and the Philippines are again prime examples of this.

Again, too, a significant element of this tendency towards political closure in the face of state incapacity set against growing frustration and disappointment has come to characterise some Southeast Asian governments at different stages in their development, when tensions between increasing political closure on one hand and growing frustration on the other spilled over into violence. Governments moved to assert their authority, as was demonstrated in Myanmar immediately after independence, in Indonesia also from soon after independence, and in the Philippines in the 1950s and again from the late 1960s, but a breakdown of state institutions in a number of instances led instead to near state collapse, in some cases resulting in the even stronger assertion of the status quo, and in others in a generalised chaos and disfunction, and sometimes eventually in regime change, for example in Myanmar, Indonesia, Thailand, and the Philippines.

Democracy, democratisation and regime change

In the period since the end of the Cold War (*c.* 1991), there has been an upsurge in the number of states around the world that define themselves as 'democracies'. So too has this been the case in Southeast Asia, if incomplete in some areas and with reversals in others. This is in part due to the turn towards electoral processes in formerly authoritarian client states that have since lost the patronage of one or other of the two then superpowers. However, not all regime change has been democratic, democratic change is not inevitable and it has been shown to be possible for democracies to revert to other, less or non-democratic, forms of political organisation. Further, what is claimed to be 'democratic' may not be that, or it may be a procedural democracy, employing a relatively free electoral contest, but failing to provide a range of more substantive democratic qualities such as the separation of powers between government institutions, equitable and consistent rule of law, civil and political rights such as freedom of speech and assembly, or the opportunity to fully participate in the political process (see Schumpeter 1976; Dahl 1986; Burton *et al.* 1992: 1; Grugel 2002: 6).

In debates about democracy and democratisation, Fukuyama (among others) argued that there is only one final form of democracy – liberal democracy associated with free market economics (Fukuyama 1992). Such 'democratic absolutism' has frequently run contrary to the political experience or preferences in Southeast Asian countries, even where they accept a substantive democratic model, for example, with a higher degree of economic intervention. As a result, there has been considerable debate over the value and appropriateness of a 'one size fits all' democracy, not least in the Southeast Asian contexts.

There are, in theory, over 500 types of democracy (Collier and Levitsky 1996) – many more than there are national democratic governments. The principle distinction is between whether the democracy in question is a minimalist or proceduralist model, or maximalist and substantive, and how these qualities are manifested.

A procedural democracy is understood to hold reasonably regular elections which are more or less free and fair. A substantive democracy holds regular, free and fair elections, has state institutions capable of instituting government policies which are accountable and under government control, has a strong and active civil society, and is one in which law is equally and consistently applied and in which there are no meaningful challengers to the democratic process (Collier and Levitsky 1996: 10).

Despite Collier and Levitsky's argument for acknowledging 'diminished sub-types of democracy' (Collier and Levitsky 1996), it could also be suggested that there is a democratic 'cut-off point', less than which is not actually 'democracy' but a different political form that shares some democratic attributes. An 'expanded procedural minimum' model is equivalent to a democratic cut-off point in most Western democracies. This definition includes ('reasonably') competitive elections devoid of ('massive') fraud, with universal ('broad') suffrage, basic civil liberties such as freedom of speech, assembly and association, and an elected government with effective power to govern (institutional capacity). This may serve as a 'democratic benchmark'. See Table 1 for further comparison of the various terms used to designate alternative definitions and conceptions relating to democratisation.

There have also been objections to democracy, which have frequently been adopted by non-democratic governments to rationalise their political structure and orientation. Pre-democratic governments such as monarchies (e.g. Brunei) have generally been opposed to democracy on the grounds that it stands in opposition to hereditary right to rule. Authoritarian governments also argue that democracy promotes social division (Myanmar and Indonesia under military rule) and short-term interests (Singapore) over long-term planning (e.g. see Kaplan 2005; Hoppe 2001). In some cases, they also argue that democracy can imply a tyranny of the majority. Communist governments (Vietnam, Laos) have also argued that democracy is a subterfuge for capitalist control of society and that the only political choices are those between parties or individuals representing versions of exploitative capitalism (even though both are now functionally capitalist one party states).

In compiling a 'Democracy Index', the Economist Intelligence Unit Democracy in Southeast Asia noted that the quality of democracy in Southeast Asia differed widely (EIU 2014). No Southeast Asian country was, by this assessment, able to score at least eight of ten to be identified as a 'full democracy'. In assessing the level of democracy in each of Southeast Asia's countries, they were judged against five categories, which contained further questions. These included the extent of electoral processes and pluralism, functioning of government, political participation, political culture and civil liberties (EIU 2014).

Timor-Leste scored highest on the Democracy Index, with 7.16 following independence from Indonesia in 2002. It remains, however, a 'flawed democracy'. It was followed by Indonesia on 6.76, Thailand with 6.55 (but presumably prior to the 2014 coup), Malaysia on 6.41 and the Philippines with 6.30. Southeast Asia has two 'hybrid regimes', with a score below six, being Singapore on 5.88 and Cambodia on 4.96. There are also three 'authoritarian regimes' in the region, with scores below four, including Vietnam on 2.89, Myanmar on 2.35 (but with quasi-democratic elections in November 2015 which would have altered this assessment) and Lao PDR as the least democratic on 2.32. Brunei was not indexed by the EIU but it could have been expected to rank at or towards the bottom of the scale, given that it is an absolute monarchy. In terms of global rankings, Timor Leste ranked at number 43, Indonesia 53, Thailand 58, Malaysia 64, Philippines 69, Singapore 81, Cambodia 100, Vietnam 144, Myanmar 155 and Lao PDR 156.

Table 1 Definitional and conceptual benchmarks in research on recent democratisation terms used to designate alternative definitions and conceptions

	Electoralist definition	Procedural minimal definition	Expanded procedural minimal definition	Prototypical conception: established industrial democracy	Maximalist definition/conception
Associated Meanings	these are the principal definitions employed in the literature; often presented and applied with considerable care			not defined; plays important role in forming subtypes	often not explicitly defined
Reasonably competitive elections devoid of massive fraud, with broad suffrage	yes	yes	yes	yes	often not included
Basic civil liberties; freedom of speech, assembly and association	–	yes	yes	yes	often not included
Elected government has effective power to govern	–	–	yes	yes	often not included
Additional political, economic and social features associated with industrial democracy	–	–	–	yes	often not included
Socioeconomic equality and/or high levels of popular participation in economic, social and political institutions	–	–	–	–	yes
Examples	Kirkpatrick 1981: 326–7; Vanhanen 1990: 17–18; Fukuyama 1992: 43, 49–50; Chee 1993: 1; see also Schumpeter 1947	O'Donnell and Schmitter 1986: 8; Diamond, Linz and Lipset 1989: 6–7; Di Palma 1991: 16; Mainwaring 1992: 297–8; see also Linz 1978: 5	Karl 1991: 165; Schmitter and Karl 1991: 81; Huntington 1991: 9–10; Valenzuela 1990: 70; Rueschemeyer, Stephens and Stephens 1992: 43–4; Loveman 1994: 108	not explicitly discussed	Fagen 1986: 258; Harding and Petras 1988: 3–4; Jonas 1989: 129–30; Miliband 1992: 122–3; Rocamora and Wilson 1994; Harnecker 1994: 64

There has been a long-expressed view that notions of democracy are culturally specific and are not transferrable to non-western societies (e.g. see Zakaria 1994 re Singapore). 'With few exceptions, democracy has not brought good government to new developing countries . . . What Asians value may not necessarily be what Americans or Europeans value', Singapore's Lee Kuan Yew said by way of defending what were claimed to be 'Confucian values' (Han *et al.* 1998).

In cases where democracy is established, there can also be a democratic tension around the acceptance of a plurality of views, some of which might be antithetical to further such openness (e.g. majority imposition, or voting to end voting) and which may set up points of conflict within a society still struggling to come to grips with low levels of institutional and organisational capacity. Some Southeast Asian states have had difficulty in overcoming these tensions and have sometimes slipped into chaos, often ended when the military or another authoritarian party imposes its own undemocratic will (e.g. Myanmar, Indonesia, Thailand, Philippines). This then raises the issue of regime change, which in developing-country contexts may be towards or, possibly, away from open, plural political models.

Regime change

The issue of regime change is critical in the process of political development and is often the point at which options for democratic openings occur (e.g. the resignation of Indonesia's Suharto, the fall of the Philippines' Ferdinand Marcos). By regime change, what is meant is a fundamental shift of political values, which sometimes takes place not via an orderly handing over of government within an established and agreed political framework. Regime change usually follows a period of rising political tension, and its common feature is political instability in the period leading up to, surrounding and following such change. As a consequence, regime change can be accompanied by political violence, especially between groups representing the status quo and aspirants for change.

Regime change that is internally driven tends to reflect a failure of the existing system to fulfil the basic requirements of a key social sector or sectors, such as rural or urban workers, the middle class, business owners, traditional oligarchs, or the military. Regional examples of such a failure and consequent regime change were Thailand in 2006 and 2014, Indonesia in 1966 and 1998, Cambodia in 1992 and 1997, and the Philippines in 1986. This failure to satisfy such sectoral interests may reflect a basic ideological position that predisposes the government to ignore or oppose particular interests. Alternatively, it may also reflect a government's incapacity to function in favour of its preferred interest sector, such as where the government becomes excessively corrupt, factionalised or otherwise unable to exercise authority, or where its key institutions cease to meaningfully function. In this respect, regime change is most commonly a consequence of horizontal, interest-based political change (class- or social group-based revolutions).

Regime change tends to occur either when a government representing one horizontal group replaces another, or when a horizontal group or coalition of groups replaces its own, failed government. Regime change is rarely vertical, because vertical divisions that are so strong as to successfully challenge a government tend to want to establish a separate state, e.g. Timor-Leste's separation from Indonesia. Vertical regime change may, however, occur in tribal societies, where the government tends to reflect the assertion of specific ethnic or tribal interests within the state. To date, ethnic majorities have tended to ensure their continuity in Southeast Asia's multi-ethnic states.

The period of regime change is the point at which there is greatest political flux and hence both opportunity and threat. Where there is opportunity, it is usually associated with the end of a chaotic or dysfunctional regime. Sometimes, however, this change may be away from plural government towards a more closed or authoritarian political model (e.g. Brunei in 1962, Indonesia in 1966, Cambodia in 1997, Thailand in 2014). Even where new forms of government may have the external characteristics of democracy (such as in the Philippines in 1986, or Indonesia in 1998), there may be partially or completely hidden components that fundamentally compromise the capacity of the general population to meaningfully participate in political affairs or to be genuinely represented (see O'Donnell 1996 for discussion on this broader topic). That is, where regime change is towards democracy, it may be procedural, or less than procedural, rather than substantive.

Beyond this, although the tendency towards the end of the twentieth and in the early twenty-first centuries has been for regime change to move away from authoritarian models, it can also impose non-democratic or authoritarian rule. Regime change can be from or to any other particular regime type. O'Donnell and Schmitter (1986) identify eight basic political model types, each characterising degrees of democracy and liberalism. At the most authoritarian end of their scale, O'Donnell and Schmitter identify autocracy, or 'dictadura' (strong authoritarianism), as constituting low democratic capacity and low levels of liberalisation, moving to or from a plebiscitary autocracy usually via a coup or revolution. Graduating towards a medium level of liberalisation while retaining low levels of democratisation is characterised as liberalised autocracy, or 'dictablanda' (liberal authoritarianism), which might reflect a number of authoritarian but not dictatorial regimes (such as Singapore). Instituting limited political democracy with medium liberalisation, or 'democradura' (illiberal or hard democracy), opens the next political category, representing less authoritarian but still restrictive regimes, such as in Malaysia. O'Donnell and Schmitter's next category of political democracy, reflecting higher democratisation and greater liberalisation ('democrablanda'), does not generally appear to correspond to any Southeast Asian states.

Due to conflicting interests, much regime change will be opposed, and transitions especially from authoritarian to democratic models require a shift in allegiance of the military. The military itself will therefore often be politicised and divided between those who support regime change and those who oppose it. O'Donnell and Schmitter (1986: 15–17) characterise such military factions as 'hardliners' and 'softliners'. As these terms imply, hardliners oppose change, while softliners facilitate change, usually cautiously. Southeast Asian examples of successfully facilitated change by military softliners who have taken advantage of 'the military moment' (O'Donnell and Schmitter 1986: 39) include the Philippines in 1986, Indonesia in 1998 and Myanmar in 2015. Moreover, limited liberalisation away from direct military rule while retaining a capacity for existing elite control or liberalisation without introducing democracy may also be facilitated by such a softline military approach (for example, the removal of direct military rule in Indonesia 1986–88 and relative liberalisation without democratisation in 1991, and the military-led move from a 'dictadura' to a more liberal, and restricted electoral, process in Myanmar). Softliners, however, sometimes overestimate their popular support, and may engender a backlash that sets back movement towards liberalisation (O'Donnell and Schmitter 1986: 58). For example, in Indonesia, the resignation of President Suharto in 1998 following a shift by a majority in the military towards a softline position was in turn followed by a conservative or hardline backlash, in which Suharto's immediate successor, President Habibie, quickly failed in his bid to be elected to that position and his liberal successor,

Abdurrahman Wahid, was ousted halfway through his own presidential term. In the Philippines, between 1986 and 1990 there were six attempted military coups against the post-authoritarian government of President Corazon Aquino. In Myanmar, Aung San Suu Kyi, while enormously popular, was unable to convince prior power holders to allow her to assume the presidency.

As Dahl noted, a state is unlikely to quickly develop a democratic political system if it has had little or no experience of public contestation and competition, and lacks a tradition of tolerance towards political opposition (Dahl 1971: 208). That is, regime change in such a state is at least as likely to default to an alternative authoritarian government, or to partially do so. Similarly, although cautioning against political expectations arising out of such structural preconditions, Di Palma noted that economic instability, a hegemonic nationalist culture and the absence of a strong, independent middle class all impede transition from an authoritarian political model towards one that is more democratic (Di Palma 1991: 3).

Structure or agency?

There is debate in development politics over whether there is a structural or causal link between economic and political development. One view has it that societies need to reach a certain level of economic development before they can enjoy a similar level of political development (e.g. see Acemoglu and Robinson 2006: ch. 3). A competing view posits that a higher level of political development is possible without related economic development, as in e.g. Timor-Leste, Cambodia until the coup of 1997 and, arguably, Indonesia, or that economic development does not have a direct impact on democratisation, as in e.g. Thailand's democratic failure, Singapore's effective one party state status or Brunei's monarchy. This specific debate reflects a broader 'structure–agency' debate, in which there are competing views over whether material circumstances shape development outcomes or whether there is scope for human 'agency' or choice to determine how societies organise themselves.

In considering transitions from authoritarian to democratic models, there are a range of conditions that might be claimed to be essential for successful regime change. As noted by Dahl, these include control of the military and police by elected civilian officials, democratic beliefs and culture (Dahl 1989: 111) and no strong interference by foreign powers that are hostile to the change. Further, Dahl identified conditions that were not absolutely necessary, but which were favourable for the establishment of democracy, including a modern market economy and society, and weak sub-cultural pluralism (or lack of opportunity for inter-ethnic conflict) (Dahl 2000: 147; see also Dahl 1989: ch. 8).

In what Dahl has referred to as 'the democratic bargain' of trust, fairness and compromise (1970), this pact normatively corresponds to a type of social contract.

The evolution of political forms, from absolute autocratic rule towards civil government that encourages political participation, representation and accountability, requires a type of social contract between citizens and its government. Under absolute rule, a completely sovereign monarch or tyrant is not party to any contract but rules with unlimited authority. Under this form of government there is no neutral authority to decide disputes between the ruler and the citizen. Under the 'social contract' model, however, the government accedes authority to the population, mediated by an independent authority (for example, an independent judiciary) in return for the right to rule. This occurs on a sliding scale of a balance of authority until it is agreed that authority is ultimately vested in the citizens, is only held by the political leader or government on behalf of the citizens, and is able to be rescinded by the citizens in an agreed and orderly manner (that is, through regular elections).

In this, it is important that elites who intend to continue or expand their political rule are able to satisfy, or be seen to address, most outstanding demands while at the same time avoiding the strongest dissatisfactions manifesting into collective action. As O'Donnell and Schmitter noted, and which appears to be borne out by experience, regimes' transitions from authoritarianism tend to be smoother and more successful if they promote essentially conservative political outcomes (e.g. Indonesia, Timor-Leste, Philippines, Myanmar), as this is seen as less threatening to out-going authoritarian elites. Democratic 'idealists', usually on the left and centre-left, are only given the opportunity to engage in transitional processes if elite survivors from the previous regime are willing to negotiate a mutually satisfactory set of rules of the new game (O'Donnell and Schmitter 1986: 70). Where such negotiations fail, more active, usually leftist or strongly liberal-reformist, political actors may be rapidly marginalised, as occurred in post-1986 Philippines and in post-1998 Indonesia.

In the latter case, those demanding total reform of the political system were quickly marginalised, resulting in the fragmentation of the reform movement (comprised of particular students, civil society and humanitarian NGOs and coalitions). Of particular transitional note, however, was the role played by military softliner Susilo Bambang Yudhoyono, first as the leader of the reform faction of the Indonesian military in the early 1990s following dissent towards the then president, then as a political actor and finally as president himself.

Yet Yudhoyono was also victim of a conservative coalition, with his second and final term in office (2009–14) being noted for inaction. In the case of the Philippines, public protest against then President Marcos and the blatant falsification of election results, backed by sections of the military, led to his ousting and replacement by his electoral opponent, Corazon Aquino, the widow of Marcos' murdered former opponent, Senator Benigno Aquino. While Corazon Aquino came to power on the back of a popular protest movement, she in fact ushered in elite rule mirroring that of the oligarchic pre-dictatorship era. Under Aquino, the Philippines' elite structurally excluded genuine open participation in politics, despite it formally being an open electoral contest.

One interesting and sometimes important aspect of regime transitions is the role played by external events. Although there are numerous exceptions, it appears that critical political shifts most often occur at times of pronounced social, economic and/ or political dislocation. A range of pre-existing tensions or pressures must already exist in order to capitalise on the subsequent rupture, but the rupture itself appears to act as a catalyst for regime change (see O'Donnell and Schmitter 1986: 72), e.g. Indonesia in 1998, and arguably the impact of Cyclone Nargis on Myanmar's post-2008 political environment. Indeed, virtually the whole post-Second World War period of Southeast Asian decolonisation could be attributed, to a greater or lesser extent, to the direct and indirect economic, military and political effects of the war.

Transitions born of crisis are, of course, not consistent in their outcomes, as illustrated by the shifting contest between democracy and authoritarianism in countries such as Thailand and Cambodia. There are even cases of voluntary political redundancy, such as Indonesia's President Suharto's resignation, although this too might be seen as a political 'shock'. In some cases, the 'shock' itself, though, is little more than an excuse to exercise an overdue necessity, where an ossified regime is aware of its redundancy, yet still requires an excuse to dignify and hence ease its own departure.

As noted, not all regime changes are towards democracy. Some changes may be partial (for example, the Philippines post-1986, Cambodia in 1992 and 1998, Indonesia post-1998) or lead to conflict (such as Cambodia 1975–92). Others are simply a reversion from one type of authoritarianism to another, as has been the case in Myanmar until 2015. These different experiences of regime change invariably reflect competing views of what constitutes political progress; what is to some fairness is to others interference; what is to some freedom is to others disorder – depending, as discussed earlier, on how one views the basic concepts of freedom and equality.

The state, society and democratisation

Reflecting on the relationship between the state and society in the context of degrees of freedom, Stepan noted the putative if changing focus of the state from economic to political development:

> The assumptions of modernization theory that liberal democratic regimes would be inexorably produced by the process of industrialization was replaced by a new preoccupation with the ways in which the state apparatus might become a central instrument for both the repression of subordinate classes and the reorientation of the process of industrial development.
>
> (Stepan 1986: 317)

The development of 'Bureaucratic Authoritarian regimes' that are associated with, if not necessarily responsible for, economic development (seen as industrialisation) in a number of Southeast Asian states ('developmental states') has also fragmented and inhibited potential political opposition (Singapore is the prime example, followed by Malaysia). The rise in the relative authority of formal or recognised state institutions, and the non-negotiable imposition of their development programs, has diminished other political institutions, including both the formal pluralist institution of 'Opposition' and the capacity of civil society (Stepan 1986: 317). This in turn comes back to attempts to delegitimise political alternatives, in particular those that are necessary for a successful plural polity but which have an imposed reduced capacity that in turn delegitimises them, as for example in Indonesia until 1998.

If there is a differentiation between early and more recent approaches to institutions, it is in understanding institutions as not being just organisations of people with particular roles, but sets of rules or codes of behaviour that can include, for example, respect for the rule of law, notions of equality, and tolerance of or respect for alternative views. The key distinctions here are between formal and informal rules or codes of behaviour, with greater emphasis being placed on important informal rules that nonetheless effectively play a formal role in political society. An example of an informal rule that might be considered critical is the opportunity for the creation and maintenance of civil society organisations, which have a central role in the open political functioning of developing states. The 'rules' by which such groups organise themselves are one way in which they constitute institutions, but the fact of their existence and their shifting social and political roles have also become institutionalised. That is, there is an expectation that such organisations will exist in a developing country, will be acknowledged as existing and will from time to time contribute to public debate and decision-making.

In circumstances where legitimacy implies consent to rule it is normative, in that it reflects a social value-judgement about whether or not a ruler or government has the 'right' to occupy that political position. This in turn opens up questions of moral authority and the extent of correspondence between such matters and between ruler and ruled. Positive legitimacy implies explicit agreement about the circumstances that confer legitimacy, such as compliance with equal and consistent rule of law, and the correspondence between the action of the ruler and such compliance. That is to say, legitimacy of rule derives from a sense of justice in social and political relations; where a sense of justice prevails, the social and political circumstances may be regarded as legitimate.

The relationship between civil society and government has been proposed as an indicator of the democratic health of the state, with the varying capacities of each institution being a key determinant. Stepan posits four sets of relationships between the state and civil society, which are characterised as the following:

1   Growth of state power and diminution of civil society power, which often occurs during the closure of political space by governments.
2   Decline of state power and growth of civil society power, which has risen but tended to again decline in Southeast Asian states.
3   Growth of both state and civil society, which is unusual in Southeast Asian states but has occurred, if in passing, during democratic transitions.
4   Decline of both state and civil society (but with option of civil society growth outside the state), which tends to reflect failed-state status, e.g. Myanmar under the State Law and Order Restoration Council, Cambodia under the Khmer Rouge, pre-communist Laos.

(Stepan 1986: 318)

Stepan was primarily concerned with the growth of state power in developing countries at the expense of civil society, or the imposition of bureaucratic authoritarianism with a parallel reduction in the capacity of non-state actors to compete with state power. This situation could be said to be characteristic of 'strong states' such as Vietnam or Singapore in which an independent civil society is relatively weak. In the transitional phase away from bureaucratic authoritarianism, state power declines and civil society strengthens as a consequence of the opening of greater political space (for example, as military domination declined in Thailand).

Civil society may also increase in its own right and therefore act as a contributor to declining state power (for example, Indonesia prior to and just after the fall of President Suharto). Growth of both state and civil society power can be seen either in competition or as providing a balance for each other. With the former, the instability that derives from competition is unable to be sustained, and either the situation tends to degenerate into internal conflict or the state or civil society fails to sustain its position and hence declines in power relative to the other. More positively, however, state power can be defined not only as bureaucratic authoritarianism (negative state power) but also as benign state capacity or an ability to resist the influence of vested interests (positive power). In such cases, where there is strong civil society and strong positive state power, the two are likely to interact together to increase their respective capacities. There is little of this, however, apparent in Southeast Asia.

In cases where both state and civil society power decline, however, there is the possibility of state failure or reversion to pre-modern methods of state organisation (ASC *et al.* 2003: 4), as neither institutional segment is available to compensate for the weakness of the other. Such a power vacuum often draws external actors into the collapsed political space. This could be seen in the case of Timor-Leste from late April 2006.

State institutions

The role of institutions has been identified by the World Bank, among others, as being central to the success or failure of development projects, particularly in their larger and more bureaucratic sense. That is, the capacity of states to make use of aid, to deliver its benefits and to sustain the process of development generally is seen by the World Bank, and many others, to be vested in the institutions of the state. This thesis was first developed by Huntington (1968) and later addressed by Fukuyama (2004).

After his earlier foray into determinist normative claims of the inevitability of democracy and free market capitalism in developing countries, Fukuyama appeared to recognise that liberal democratic capitalist outcomes in developing societies such as those of Southeast Asia was not necessarily a given. Responding to his own country's assertion of military power, Fukuyama recognised two sets of closely related problems. The first was that the United States (and its allies) had intervened in the affairs of other states (most notably in the region: militarily in Timor-Leste, financially in Myanmar and to a lesser extent Indonesia) with the explicit intention of ending non-democratic regimes. Such intervention was justified on the positive grounds that it was intended to bring democracy or at least greater freedoms to these countries (or in the case of Indonesia to pressure it to allow intervention in Timor-Leste). However, local populations do not necessarily automatically see the benefits of a 'democratic' system of government when it appears to be imposed and an alien ideology. More to the point, it has been difficult to establish a democratic framework in states that did not enjoy the range of institutions that allow democracy to exist, much less flourish. It was the lack of such institutions that was in most cases responsible for allowing particular states to degenerate to the point where they were unable to prevent state collapse, state chaos or military coups.

Second, it was a failure of state institutions more generally that provided fertile ground for the establishment of organisations that might be seen as antithetical to political development, e.g. Jihadi organisations such as the Philippines' Abu Sayyaf Group or the communist New People's Army. Beyond this, the lack of capacity or performance of state institutions was widely and increasingly seen as a key reason that such states remained mired in under-development.

Governance

Along with normative claims to democratic principles, the issue of 'governance' has become central to developing countries in the period since the end of the Cold War. No longer able to rely on the support of patron states under which there were few respected rules in exchange for strategic loyalty, developing countries, including in Southeast Asia, have had to begin to order themselves in ways that conform to international standards. Reflecting donor countries' ideological shift away from government-centred approaches to development while at the same time recognising the limitations of neo-liberalism, at the peak of the Clinton-Blair political dominance, the World Bank and UNDP opted for a 'third way', reflected in a 'semantic shift' (Mazower 2012: 369) towards 'good governance'. As Mazower has noted, the business school model of 'corporate governance' adapted to development needs included a sense of social and environmental responsibility, along with poor – and usually large – government being regarded as the chief impediment to development (Mazower 2012: 369–70).

Having first arisen in public development discourse in the early 1990s, a 'Commission on Global Governance' was established in 1992 and its first report, *Our Global Neighborhood*, published in 1995. According to Mazower, a governance approach reflected 'a creed justifying far-reaching interventions in the public administration, law, and political systems of countries around the world' (2012: 370) UNESCAP identified good governance, in a more benign way, as accountable, transparent, responsive, equitable and inclusive, effective and efficient, following the rule of law, participatory, and consensus oriented (UNESCAP 2011). Each of these criteria accords with other general definitions, apart from that of being 'consensus oriented'. While consensus can be an important tool for resolving conflict and ensuring that no parties' fundamental interests are neglected, in traditional or developing societies it can also be used to impose the will of more powerful (and often self-interested) figures and may disempower the legitimate claims of less powerful groups. Moreover, consensus and rule of law do not sit easily together, especially where disputes arise over issues of law and equity.

Ideas of governance are closely related to institutional development, in particular regarding the capacity and probity of state institutions to undertake the functions that are allocated to them (World Bank 2011). In particular, the World Bank sees good governance linked to its anti-corruption activities as being important to its focus on alleviating poverty. The World Bank's Worldwide Governance Indicators (WGIs) project identifies aggregate and individual governance indicators for 213 economies over the period 1996–2009. Within the WGIs, the World Bank identifies six dimensions of governance, including 'Voice and Accountability', 'Political Stability and Absence of Violence', 'Government Effectiveness', 'Regulatory Quality', 'Rule of Law' and 'Control of Corruption'. The extent to which Southeast Asian states meet such criteria varies considerably but, it is important to note that none of them meet all of these criteria.

The Asian Development Bank (ADB) identifies a similar set of criteria for governance, including accountability, predictability, participation and transparency. Similarly, states in Southeast Asia meet these criteria to varying but usually limited degrees. The ADB's work in the governance field has been primarily in strengthening accountability institutions, including audit agencies, anti-corruption commissions and the judiciary. It notes that 'strengthening the rule of law . . . is crucial to encourage private sector investment and combat corruption' (ADB 2011). The ADB's criteria for governance differs in detail from those of the World Bank, but its basic goal of ensuring a safe, legal and consistent political and economic environment is consistent with that of the World Bank.

Notably, while both the World Bank and the ADB recognise there need to be different approaches to ensuring good governance in specific societies, both are equally focused on combating corruption in government institutions and agencies, as a primary means of ensuring the best possible environment for regional economic development. Increasingly, however, equal and consistent application of rule of law and ensuring regional governments that are open and responsive to citizens' needs, along with the other key qualities of good governance, is seen not just in instrumentalist terms of helping to ensure economic development.

Conclusion

No two countries in Southeast Asia have identical political histories, systems or processes, but many do share some of a range of characteristics that help to explain why they often demonstrate particular outcomes that often appear to meet less than a normative standard.

The way in which Southeast Asia's countries have come into being has included being physically shaped by colonial powers, having their sense of national identity informed by their opposition to the colonial experience and, not least, their political processes influenced by the wars that were often fought to end such colonialism. Having started from a low level of development in terms of economic and organisational capacity, some Southeast Asian states have subsequently slipped further, engendering disappointment and disenchantment with the independence process and tensions over the allocation of scarce resources.

Very often, where different ethnic groups have been brought together in one state as a consequence of prior colonial incorporation, such tensions can take on a tribal or 'nationalist' hue and, in cases where the ethnic group has a specific territory, can lead to claims for separatism, such as those that have affected Myanmar, Indonesia and the Philippines. These types of situations can become particularly problematic where states have limited capacity or skills to deal with such problems and, often through a military acculturation, respond with repressive measures, leading to a diminution of the legitimacy of the state.

Such states, such as Indonesia, Myanmar and the Philippines, may liberalise over time, especially in light of a lack of support from other, more powerful states that might have had an interest in maintaining particular regimes. In some instances, popular revolts (e.g. Philippines, Thailand) or the internal collapse of a prior regime (Indonesia) may also lead to democratic change. Too often, however, regime change is not permanent or even long-standing, and collapses of government, coups and so on can lead to a cycle of authoritarian or military government, a process of liberalisation and then a return to authoritarianism, and so on. Thailand's history of having elected governments interspersed with military coups has been a prime illustration of this particular phenomenon.

One of the main problems that arises from such political instability, and the lack of representative government and accountability that usually accompanies it, is that the mechanisms of government intended to ensure good government are rarely in place. As a result, the overall development project tends to struggle under a burden of corruption, inefficiency and sectional self-interest. This then feeds into a sense of disillusionment with, and the illegitimacy of, the state, which leads to the predictable government response and the cycle referred to above. This is not the only reason why some Southeast Asian states have failed to break out of a cycle of poverty, mismanagement and poor government, for many of their citizens, in some cases for over 60 years. But it has been and remains a common and significant contributing factor in the failure of the development process for many of these countries.

Note

1 Anderson's principal reference was to the use of print technology in the dispersal and standardisation of language, but the principle of a common language applies regardless of the mechanism of its dispersal.

3   Vietnam

Brief introduction to category: hard one party states

The hard one party states of Southeast Asia can be classified as 'authoritarian' by way of contrast with 'dictatorial' and 'totalitarian' states. There have been attempts at totalitarianism in previous Southeast Asian states, in particular in Cambodia under the Khmer Rouge, in Myanmar under the Burma Socialist Programme Party and then the State Law and Order Restoration Council, and, to a somewhat lesser degree, under the governments of Vietnam and Laos in the immediate post-1975 period. However, each of these states was operated by small committees (politburos) rather than by the direct rule of one person and hence, while totalitarian, could not be classified as dictatorial.

Notably, several of the states of Southeast Asia have had or continue to have a high level of military involvement in their political processes. The continued involvement of militaries in politics is not uncommon in states that have achieved independence through military struggles in which there was no functional separation between political and military wings of the independence movement. Militaries tend to involve themselves in civil politics particularly during times of institutional weakness, post-conflict rebuilding, or actual or perceived internal challenges to the status quo. As Desch has noted, when militaries have an external focus, they are more likely to respect civilian authority, but when they have an internal focus they are more likely to involve themselves in domestic politics (Desch 1999: 8–21).

Indeed, because militaries are hierarchical, authority-driven structures, their method of operation can easily be transferred to post-conflict environments. This reflects what Huntington noted as military's exaltation of 'obedience as the highest virtue of military men. The military ethic is thus pessimistic, collectivist, historically inclined, power-oriented, nationalistic, militaristic, pacificist, and instrumentalist in its view of the military profession' (Huntington 1957: 79).

Both the Philippines and Indonesia came close to formal dictatorship, the Philippines under the declaration of martial law by President Ferdinand Marcos between 1972 and 1981, and Indonesia, increasingly, under President Suharto, who assumed practical if initially shared power in 1966, from the mid-1980s until his political demise in 1998.

From May 2014, Thailand was under military rule in which all executive and legislative powers were vested in the military leader, General Prayut Chan-ocha, functioning under the guise of the National Council for Peace and Order (NCPO). While Prayut consulted with his senior officers, he was supreme commander and, hence, exercised what could be described as dictatorial powers in the sense that he issued 'dictates' or decrees which had legislative authority. However, while military control extended well into normally civilian areas of Thai life, there was less than absolute control of the media and other civil society organisations, so the state could not be considered totalitarian in either practice or intent.

Southeast Asia's hard one party states can be classified as 'authoritarian', in that they constitute non-participatory social orders characterised by intolerance of opposition or dissent. However, there is no single definition of 'authoritarianism', which, moreover, as a term would probably include Cambodia and might also be used to describe the political system of Singapore and perhaps even Malaysia. These three are not one party states as such, and manifest some tolerance of opposition and dissent. 'Hard one party states' are, therefore, by definition states in which one political party or ideology holds a functional monopoly on political power which is exercised in a relatively non-participatory or absolutist manner, and in which opposition or dissent is not tolerated.

Introduction: Vietnam

Vietnam was at the leading edge of the impact of the Cold War in Southeast Asia, from 1946 until 1954 with its revolution for independence from colonial France, and then from 1954 until 1975 with the war which ended in reunification. It was, throughout this period, the example *par excellence* of the Cold War in practice. It was also a key actor in, and illustration of, some of the changes at the point at which the Cold War ended.

In Vietnam the 'Vietnam War' is referred to as the 'American War', with the United States playing a direct and major role on behalf of one party to the conflict, and the Soviet Union and, to a lesser extent, China (Elleman 2001: 285) playing supporting but less directly interventionist roles on behalf of the independent government established in the north of the country.[1] But the American War was also, and perhaps as much, a war between two political elites within Vietnam, with different geographic bases of power and with competing views of the country's future. Both were nationalist, but from mutually exclusive and therefore competing ideological perspectives.

There has been suggestion from time to time that the north and the south of Vietnam are different, so much so that the two-state situation that existed from 1954 until 1975 was warranted. Vietnam is relatively homogenous, but far from entirely so. Apart from more than 50 ethnic minorities, there have been historical differences between north, centre and south of the country. With its more laissez-faire spirit of being a new (or occupied) territory, and reflecting an influx of Chinese traders, the south of the country had a stronger entrepreneurial orientation. This was enhanced by France's direct colonial rule in 'Cochinchina'. Even prior to French colonial occupation, capitalism had been the default position of the south, but was a much later arrival in the more tradition-bound north where, in line with Chinese Confucian influences, manufacturing and trade were considered low-status occupations (see Gernet 1962: 67–69 on the classifications of employment status in medieval China).

Setting aside the extent to which the government in what was briefly the Republic of (South) Vietnam was a proxy for external interests, first France and then the US, French influence in the south had always been stronger, there was a more developed capitalist system in place and its elites had interests distinct from those in the north which tended to be manifested in more conservative, status quo-driven political outcomes (Goodman 1973: 65–70). The north, on the other hand, had developed a stronger sense of anti-French and anti-colonial sentiment. Moreover, at the time of the partition of Vietnam, in 1954, ahead of what were intended to be national elections in 1956, up to a million largely, although not exclusively, Catholic Vietnamese fled to the south, further altering the balance of interests between the two parts of the erstwhile nation (see Frankum 2007).

However, the Kinh (ethnic Vietnamese) are the same people north and south, speak the same language and share the same traditions, even if capitalism came later to northern Vietnam and was never as deeply entrenched. As the heartland of the original Nam Viet state, Hanoi has always seen itself to be the true representative of what it means to be Vietnamese, and of the fact that, mixing with (if largely displacing) the original Cham and Cambodian residents of the centre and south and the influx of Chinese, the southerners were rather more free and easy about their cultural identity.

Consequences of ideology and struggle

As a result of its long struggle for independence and unity, Vietnam is a country in which the army and the Communist Party of Vietnam are conjoined twins, with no effective separation between them and no effective division between the party and other institutions of state (the armed forces held 11 per cent of Central Committee seats as of the 2016 12th National Congress). Vietnam does formally operate on the basis of *trias politica*, or the separation of powers between the executive, the legislature and the judiciary. But with all institutions being dominated by the Communist Party of Vietnam (CPV) and it, in turn, being controlled by the Central Committee, the separation between state institutions does not exist in practice.

While the CPV's 175 regular- and 25 alternate-member Central Committee only nominally elects the Politburo (party executive committee), it can overturn, and has overturned, politburo decisions. Perhaps the most pointed example of this was in 1996 when although two-thirds of the politburo voted in favour of Le Kha Phieu as General Secretary of the CPV (one of the party's most influential positions), the Central Committee voted against his election and overturned the Politburo's decision. Indicating, though, the Politburo's ultimate authority, Le was eventually installed as General Secretary the following year.

In theory, the National Congress of the CPV is its highest organ and it is this organisation that elects the Central Committee. However, as its membership only meets every five years, its powers are delegated, with the Central Committee making the major policy decisions and electing the senior leadership. Beyond the Central Committee, the National Assembly elects the President, who in turn appoints the Prime Minister and the Council of Ministers (the cabinet), who in turn control the day-to-day functions of the government (Constitution of Vietnam 2013: ch. 5).

Consistent with other communist parties based on Leninist organising principles,[2] the CPV's authority is, in theory, derived from its membership in a bottom–up structure. At one level, party membership could be seen to be popular with Vietnamese citizens, with membership growing from less than two million in 1986 to more than three and a half million by the 11th Party Congress in 2011 (Thayer 2015e). In large part, party membership has grown less because of an ideological commitment and more because it allows access to employment and better chances of promotion. And rather than the party being a strong grassroots organisation as its membership and theoretical structure might imply, in practice it is led by the party elite, which directs and effectively controls all political processes, or the framework within which such processes can occur. The 'Fatherland Front' (Mặt Trận Tổ Quốc Việt Nam), which includes the Vietnam Trade Union, the Vietnam Peasant Society, the Ho Chi Minh Communist Youth Union, the Vietnam Women's

Society and the Vietnam Veterans Society, acts as a mass 'solidarity' base for the government (Constitution of Vietnam 2013: ch. 1, section 9, sub-section 2), and members of its constituent organisations are usually CPV members.

Economic change

Vietnam's shift from tightly controlled economic centralism to economic liberalisation has enhanced its economic development, particularly from the political and economic depths of the late 1980s. Much of Vietnam's infrastructure was in ruins following the end of the American War, and from 1976 until 1980 the country was in recession. The system of collectivisation had led to a slump in agricultural output, and maintaining a large army in Cambodia and another on the Chinese border further drained the failing economy. It was increasingly clear that Vietnam's political leaders could successfully prosecute a war but had little understanding of how to run an economy.

Facing its own economic difficulties, Vietnam's main supporter, the Soviet Union, indicated from the mid-1980s that it would be moving towards winding down its foreign aid program. Soviet aid was significantly reduced following the introduction of its then new policy of *perestroika* (restructuring), which in turn reflected a slowing down in Soviet economic development and inadequate living standards. As Ho Chi Minh's generation began to retire, pragmatists and technocrats became increasingly influential, setting up a political competition that continues at the time of writing. In response, Vietnam instituted its policy of 'economic renovation' (*doi moi*) in 1986, following China's own cautious program of economic reorganisation instituted from 1978 onwards by Chairman Deng Xiaoping. Vietnam's own experiment with economic change may have come after that of China, but it advanced more quickly over a shorter period of time, and in part served as a marker for the economic changes undertaken by the Soviet Union around the same time.[3] This change in economic policy was formalised in resolution 13 at the meeting of Vietnam's Politburo in May 1988, in which it endorsed a 'multidirectional foreign policy' for the country's economy.

There was also pressure for Vietnam to reduce its military budget, at around 10 per cent of GDP or more than 60 per cent of government expenditure (Thayer 1994: 34), necessary to maintain Vietnam's military presence in Cambodia and along its border with China. Withdrawal from Cambodia, agreed to in 1987 (finalised in 1991), normalisation of relations with China[4] and a loosening of internal economic controls can be understood as part of the package of reforms that presaged and were part of the end of the Cold War. Soviet military aid, which had been critical to Vietnam's campaigns in Cambodia and against China, 'virtually ceased after 1990' (Thayer 1994: 34), adding further pressure for reform.

This multidirectional policy included an openly expressed desire to join ASEAN (Thayer and Amer 1999: 2–3). The extent to which change was influencing Vietnam, and in particular its Politburo, and which highlighted differences between reformers and conservatives, was reflected in the events of the following year in China. The Chinese Communist Party's crushing of a developing pro-democracy movement in a bloody crackdown focused on Tiananmen Square, Beijing, highlighted the challenge of political changes that might accompany rising expectations brought about by economic changes. As Vietnam's economy has increasingly opened, it has been widely noted, with an element of irony, that if the North beat the Americans in the war for reunification of the country then the South had beaten the Soviet Union on the economic front.

The purpose, and most significant consequence, of the opening of the Vietnamese economy has been that not only has the country lifted itself out of economic ruin, its people have also improved their average standards of living, having joined the 'medium human development category'. While the UNDP notes that the Human Development Index has changed criteria and hence cannot be compared across years, it is important to note that, in simple per capita gross national income terms, in 2005 purchasing parity prices, the country has risen from $845 in 1990 to almost $3,000 by 2012 (UNDP 2013c). While the majority Kinh have improved their lot, Vietnam's minorities have been left behind, making up to almost two-fifths of Vietnam's poor, but only a fraction of its population. But even while the structure of Vietnam's economy was allowed to change, that of its political organisation was not.

Factions

Vietnam is a one party state, but that does not mean that there are not competing interests and factions within that single party structure. The appearance – and reality – of unity at one level is beset by power plays at another. As with other political parties that contain differences within then, the CVP very rarely discusses its internal differences in public, but the behind-the-scenes manoeuvring can be quite intense, and the rise and fall of political figures is closely linked to such intrigues at least as much as it might be to individual capacity or merit (see Boehler 2012 for a brief account). In the CVP there are broadly four main factions, reflecting the broad spectrum of the party's origins, starting from where its more idealistic members would like it to be but focusing mostly on competition for resources based on its more contemporary circumstances.

The oldest faction within the CVP comprises the ideological remnants of the party's commitment to the key principles of Marxism-Leninism. Given that Vietnam still claims to be a 'communist' state, formal acknowledgment continues to be paid to Marxist-Leninist principles through institutes and studies. However, as a political force it is all but dead and, in some respects, is viewed in its original form by other political leaders as an impediment to continued economic development. This faction is, therefore, small and relatively ineffective other than as a link to the past, the rhetorical principle that originally informed that part of the independence movement, and as a link to the internally contradictory notion of a 'socialist oriented market economy'. In theory, this means an economy in which state-owned enterprises (SOEs) are dominant, although in practice Vietnam has been moving away from SOEs – a move which has marked many of the factional battlelines.

One of the two major factions can be classified as 'rent-seekers', or those senior officials who are connected to and receive payments, often through bribery and corruption, from SOEs and other protected local industries. Although 'corruption' is, in some respects, a contested concept – it can imply everything from direct skimming of profits and bribery to more rather than less favourable business deals and appointments – there has been a significant increase in corruption since the process of economic reform began in Vietnam (Gainsborough 2010: 50–57). In large part, this increase in corruption has reflected greater opportunity, but it has also reflected the lack of formal regulations around procedures, and 'grey' regulatory areas that can develop from lighter to darker shades.

Rent-seeking is essentially where governments provide advantages to local industries in order to protect their profits at the expense of competition, efficiency and often economic growth. These powerful elites have transitioned from the former Marxist-Leninist ideological base (or, more recently, have never been true adherents of it) to the financial status quo, being primarily concerned with protecting their own interests, including at the expense of human rights, openness and accountability. In this, Gainsborough has identified the considerable resilience of Vietnam's political elites in the face of change, adapting to such change without weakening their grip on power (2010: 156–8).

The other major faction within the CVP is associated with the country's new breed of moneyed elite. This group has already made its wealth, often through associated rent-seeking from SOEs, but has been moving away towards new enterprises that are increasingly independent and not state-reliant. As with the rent-seeking group, the new elite rich have been intent on protecting their own position, often at the expense of SOEs with which they seek to compete, but also at the expense of human rights and democratisation by way of tightly controlling land access, services and labour conditions. It is this group that, broadly, appears to have been in the ascendency.

Despite the privatisation of significant portions of Vietnam's economy and the decline of SOEs by more than half between 2000 and 2016, remaining SOEs continued as a financial power base for senior party figures, particularly the conservative faction. Many senior power holders also had significant shares in privatised SOEs.

Finally, there is also a small group of reformists which, although at odds with the previous three groups, may have some overlap with them, for example agreeing with the old guard about the undesirability of corruption or the attempted closure of debate. As with reformers elsewhere, there are also degrees of the extent of the desired reform, with more moderate reformers retaining closer links to other parts of the party structure, which continues to benefit them. The reformist group is relatively weak, given that it does not represent a clear interest. However, with growing disenchantment about the process of development among many politically lower-ordered Vietnamese, there is scope for the reform group to develop from a grassroots base and to find a presence in the National Assembly and hence in the Central Committee and decision-making processes. One element in favour of the continuing presence of the reformists is a slow but steadily increasing media openness, primarily due not to any policy decision but to a lack of awareness of how to control flows of information, particularly through the Internet and social media sites.

The Ministry of Information and Communications is focused primarily on print and electronic broadcasts, but the Director-General of the Postal Bureau, responsible for the Internet, struggles to filter or monitor all online usage. It did closely control local Internet Service Providers (ISPs) but was unable to adequately filter international ISP sources. Blogging and Facebook (especially since the advent of a Vietnamese-language outlet) are popular alternatives for non-authorised sources of news and information, if with all the caveats about reliability and accuracy that such sources retain.

The Internet had, in effect, full social penetration by 2006 (Hayton 2011: 120) and has thus become an important source of information in the dissemination of dissidence. One outcome of this has been that online networking and petitions have become an important medium for intellectuals and other influential figures to share ideas and opinions. These have ranged from topical and more or less apolitical issues to critical political discussions including questioning the political system and promoting liberal and democratic ideas (Morris-Jung 2015). But, beyond propagating a generic manifesto, there was a notable lack of a plan to provide a practical alternative, much less to bring down the CPV (Hayton 2011: 122).

There remains close scrutiny, however, of the print media, still perceived as the most influential form of communication, while electronic communication such as radio and television is mostly state-owned and -controlled. International subscription television stations are allowed, including potentially critical documentary and history programming, although news channels such as the BBC remained banned, including intermittent blockage of the BBC website.

Where factionalism and closure tends to be less important is in areas beyond domestic interests:

> Old ideological links are a significant part of Vietnam's two most significant military alliances: with Russia and with India. All three have declared themselves 'strategic partners' of the others. Russia is Vietnam's biggest weapons provider and India is helping Vietnam to build up an indigenous arms manufacturing base. They both have investments in Vietnam's offshore oil industry and they share several attributes which Vietnam finds attractive: they're large, they're players in the new multi-polar world, they're far away and they've both had conflicts with China. In other words, they'll assist Vietnam, but they won't dominate it.
>
> (Hayton 2011: 200)

The European Union is also important to Vietnam, effectively as much so as the US in terms of exports (17 per cent and 18 per cent respectively) (Hayton 2011: 201).

One area where central party control is limited is at the local level. A lack of practical central-control effectiveness means there is a practical element of autonomy in decision making. According to Hayton: 'The party is prepared to allow greater participation in the management of the state, especially at village level'. But, he notes, the CPV is not willing to create a direct electoral process. 'All the evidence suggests the Party intends to remain in charge of policy-making' (Hayton 2011: 226).

While one might view factionalism within the CPV generally and the Central Committee in particular as problematic in terms of creating tensions, they do have a more positive side. While the factions are not necessarily coherent in a formal sense, as parties tend to be, and do not formally caucus on issues of the day, they do provide a venue for some contest of ideas around the development and implementation of policy. This contest of ideas is somewhat less than democratic, but it is closer to a democratic model than that of more dictatorial 'communist' countries (such as North Korea), in that there can be active debate and what is often a meaningful vote, for example at the National Congress and Central Committee meetings.

One relatively small but particularly interesting move which may have reflected deeper issues in Vietnam's politics occurred when, in January 2015, the Central Committee of the Communist Party held a 'confidence' vote on its 16-person Politburo and 4-person Secretariat. In the vote, the 20 senior members were ranked by 197 of the 200 full and alternate Central Committee members as to whether they inspired 'high confidence', 'confidence' or 'low confidence'. (Chan Dung Quyen Luc 2015). The (unofficial) results of the vote showed a dispersal between 'high confidence' of between 152 (Prime Minister Nguyen Tan Dung) and 100 (Hanoi Party Secretary Pham Quang Nghi) but with a total 'confidence' vote of 174 and 164 respectively, and 'low confidence' of 23 and 33 respectively. Interestingly, both men were born in 1949 and were due for compulsory retirement, having passed the age of 70 by 2019, the last year of the 11th Congress (Thayer 2015d: 8). One or, much less likely, both were also being considered for special exemption from the compulsory retirement age, giving either one or, again less likely, both an inside running for a senior position such as communist party Secretary-General.

The 'confidence' vote might have been understood, at one level, to be about making the party's senior leadership more accountable. More probably, however, the vote reflected both a factional division within the party and an overarching tendency to want to show that, while some were more confidence-inspiring than others, all were still largely confidence-inspiring. The vote was, however, seen as a further consolidation of the power of the CPV's Central Committee relative to that of the Politburo, and a diffusion of political power overall within Vietnam's once concentrated political structure.

> Prime Minister Dung has been exerting growing influence over the Central Committee, gaining more power at the expense of his peers, especially General Secretary Nguyen Phu Trong and President Truong Tan Sang. This explains why the Central Committee reversed the Politburo's decision to discipline him, and denied Politburo membership for Thanh and Hue, who are both political rivals of Dung. It also partly accounts for the fact that Dung outperformed his peers in the Central Committee's confidence vote in January 2015.
>
> (Le 2015)

Pham Quang Nghi, ranked ninth in the party, was from the conservative wing of the party and was said to have helped enrich many of his key supporters (Wikileaks 2011). Vietnam's Prime Minister and third-ranked party member, Nguyen Tan Dung, was the youngest member of the Politburo when he was admitted in 1996, having been the protégé of both conservative former President Le Duc Anh and reformer, architect of '*doi moi*' and former Prime Minister Vo Van Kiet. In this respect, '[j]ust as it did in the mandarinate of seventeenth century Vietnam, success in the Party depends upon having a combination of three factors; talent, connections and money. Of the three, connections are the most important' (Hayton 2011: 106). Dung had all three, yet despite this political pedigree he was a relatively divisive figure, having been (unusually) publically criticised and told to resign in front of television cameras by a member of the National Congress in 2012 in relation to the stagnation of the Vietnamese economy and a string of high-profile scandals (BBC 2012).

The public rebuke followed more widespread concern about the government having presided over a culture of corruption at state-owned enterprises, including Vietnam Shipbuilding Industry Group (Vinashin), for which nine senior officials were jailed, and Vietnam National Shipping Lines (Vinalines) in which its former chairman was arrested abroad and extradited for 'economic crimes'. In 2013, there were 278 trials on corruption charges, with 80 new cases of fraud also being uncovered. Four officials from Vietnam Railways were also arrested, including deputy general director Tran Quoc Dong, for alleged involvement in a US$758,000 bribery case. While Vietnam was actively pursuing corruption cases, CPV General Secretary Nguyen Phu Trong said that the campaign had not met the expectations of the country's citizens (Boudreau and Diem 2014).

Dung had been promoted to the prime ministership for being able to bridge two main factions or tendencies within the party, rent-seekers and the moneyed elite. The public attack on Dung, therefore, could have represented either the open contest for influence between the rent-seeker and moneyed elites, with the latter decrying Dung's failures around SOEs and their drain on the economy, or an element of reformist anger at mismanagement being allowed to go unchecked (Vuving 2012).

While differences exist, open political dissent as such remains effectively forbidden, and political control remains centralised, tightly held and unlikely to change in the foreseeable future. Indeed, it could be said that the primary task facing the Communist

Party of Vietnam is how to remain in power while at the same time accommodating significant economic, technological and, increasingly, social change. Confrontation with and lingering distrust of China, and the collapse of the Soviet Union, pushed Vietnam's political leaders to embrace, at least in part, closer relations with its former nemesis, the US. The symbolic value of both China and the US – between conservatives and integrationists – also represents the broad divisions over tactics and personal association rather than strategy and ideology within the Vietnamese leadership (Hayton 2011: 190–5).

The real political questions for Vietnam have concerned the power plays within the party's central committee, revolving around minor variations on (slightly) more or (restrictively) less liberal approaches to political control and degrees of external influence and competition, corruption, and respect or otherwise for basic human rights. There was also a growing division over the issue of relations with China and Vietnam's approach to China's expansion into the South China Sea. Importantly, Prime Minister Nguyen Tan Dung had been planning to become CVP Secretary-General at the 2016 party congress, meaning he sought an unprecedented exemption from rules requiring no more than two terms in office and retirement at 65. Dung had been deeply critical of China's expansion into the South China Sea and enjoyed strong support within the Central Committee, if less so in a divided Politburo (Thayer 2015c: 3). That he should even have considered being exempted from the CVP's rules on retirement indicated that he believed that his 'pragmatic' faction in the CVP had gained the upper hand.

The Communist Party of Vietnam's retirement age of 65 and limit of two terms in office ensures a relatively high degree of turnover and, in theory, limitations on potential official corruption. However, given that the top five leadership positions – party secretary-general, state president (head of state), prime minister (head of government), chairman of the National Assembly and head of the party secretariat – are only open to those who have served a 5-year term on the 16-member Political Bureau of the Central Committee (Politburo), the highest political body in Vietnam, the potential choices for these positions are limited.

As it transpired, Nguyen Tan Dung withdrew from the leadership contest just ahead of the electoral process, with existing party leader Nguyen Phu Trong running unopposed (AP 2016). It appeared that Nguyen Tan Dung did not have sufficient support to successfully contest the position, with increasing consolidation against the pace and extent of his reform-oriented policies, and his vulnerability for not have done enough to tackle corruption. He withdrew from the leadership contest, then, rather than embarrass both the party and his faction. The retention of Nguyen Phu Trong was seen as a compromise result, mollifying both major party factions while retaining a sense of overall party unity (see Schuler and Ostwald 2016).

In short, the leadership appeared to operate on the basis of consensus as to who would retire from the leadership group and who would be appointed from the Politburo. However, party delegates to the National Party Congress could also push for or against nominated candidates and the Central Committee, which elects the Politburo, could also overturn Politburo decisions. The Politburo enacts Central Committee decisions between (usually biannual) Central Committee meetings and functions as not only the overarching executive body of the state but also the coordinator and arbiter of party affairs between Central Committee meetings. Politburo decisions are supposed to be reached by consensus, but may be the result of compromise stemming from power plays around individual interest, ideological orientation or factional allegiances.

Reform?

The big question that is asked of Vietnam and, sometimes, within Vietnam, is whether it will reform further. In economic terms, most are happy to do business within, and with, Vietnam under present conditions, given that the country's political 'stability' compensates for its corruption and lack of openness. But further economic reform, bringing corruption under control and making business (and other) processes more transparent will likely require a more accountable political system than that currently in place. The ruling party appears to want to have the appearance of liberalisation without the substance of liberalisation, of a separation of powers and hence rule of law but in reality a 'specialisation of powers' in which various branches of government are in effect overseen by the National Assembly (Hayton 2011: 107). The party has conceded some areas of public life, but appears determined to maintain its monopoly on the control of political power.

Grievances include corruption, economic backwardness, media restrictions, and limitations on personal expression blamed on the party being 'the force leading the state and society' (Constitution of Vietnam 2013: article 4). The party operates in conjunction with, but functionally above, the Vietnam Fatherland Front, which is a 'political alliance and a voluntary union of the political organization, socio-political organizations and social organizations, and prominent individuals representing their class, social strata, ethnicity or religion and overseas Vietnamese' (article 9.1). For many, the party operates as an empty shell within which factions vie for power, irrelevant to a younger generation for whom it is only a means of protecting existing interests. Similarly, although the CPV in theory builds its base from the grassroots, local CPV branches have become more and more powerless, no longer representing local interests, and as such have become further resented by local communities. The Fatherland Front, such as it is, has similarly become empty of meaning.

While many Vietnamese are content to get on with their lives, in part due to the trade-off between oligarchic control and economic growth, there also continues to be a lack of responsiveness to local needs and desires, and such responsiveness that does occur can be very slow. Even those in the CPV who wish to see further change continue to struggle against a combination of institutional conservativism, apathy and competing interests, meaning there are 'endless rounds of coalition-building and consultation required to agree policy and get it turned into practice' (Hayton 2011: 112). Frustration with such slowness, however, could manifest in a decisive 'strong' leader as much as in open political competition. There have been some small steps towards greater openness and accountability to overcome such institutional lassitude, but a substantial change away from the current single party system towards more open political competition does not appear likely in the foreseeable future (Hayton 2011: 112).

Having noted that, 'the vested interests are taking over ... Is Vietnam's fate just to become another Southeast Asian oligarchy? It's a distinct possibility but it doesn't have to be so.' (Hayton 2011: 228). Citizens have the right to raise the alarm about abuses and inefficiency, but must not blame party leaders or their protégés for their creation or perpetuation. 'The real causes of problems like corruption, pollution and financial instability are being swept under the carpet, ignored until they turn into crises' (Hayton 2011: 226).

One area which illustrates entrenched corruption is Vietnam's education system, with competition for entry into the country's better schools often determined by bribery. So bad has the problem become that 49 per cent of Vietnamese surveyed regard their education system as corrupt or highly corrupt (Chow and Dao 2013). Similarly, while Vietnam has become an attractive place for foreign investment, business corruption continues at high levels. Petty corruption was said to have decreased in the period to 2014, but high-level corruption had increased at the same time. According to one assessment, 'the country is characterised by corruption, a weak legal infrastructure, financial unpredictability and conflicting and negative bureaucratic decision-making'(GAN 2014). 'Facilitation payments' are common, for example in the area of customs (Blancas *et al.* 2014: 17–19).

Dealing with issues such as corruption requires political will, which is difficult to achieve when decision makers are often beneficiaries of the process. Unless there is a clear political decision to address this and related problems, Vietnam is likely to become just another oligarchy in which elites enrich themselves, with a widening gap between them and the poor. In December 2012, the National Assembly passed a revised law on anti-corruption, which was seen as a sign of an intention to tackle the issue. Among other requirements, the law requires public officials to disclose their assets and income. To date, however, there have been few meaningful inroads into tackling elite corruption (Davies 2015).

As a further sign of frustration with the slow progress of reform, in 2013, 72 leading academics who were of the elite and had been CPV members signed a petition calling for far-reaching constitutional changes, which was presented by former Justice Minister Nguyen Dinh Loc to the Constitutional Amendment Committee. Referred to as the 'Petition 72', the proposed changes it asked for included multi-party elections, separation of powers and limiting the constitutional mandate of the Communist Party of Vietnam. The petition also called for the constitution to be endorsed by referendum and for the people to be recognised as citizens having allegiance only to the state, as distinct from having a dual allegiance to the CPV as conjoined to the state (Constitution of Vietnam 2013: ch. 4 section 1).

The petition also sought the constitutional recognition of human rights without requiring that this be in conjunction with a responsibility to the state, that the military be accountable to the people and not the Communist Party, and the right to private ownership of land (Son and Nicholson 2015). Unsurprisingly, when Vietnam's constitution was modified in 2013, these requested changes were not included and the overall document was regarded by reformists as offering little change. However, the simple fact of the existence of the petition, that it had been made public (and, as such, signed by a further 5,000), if not reported on in the media, and that the petitioners were able to present it and not be obviously punished was, in itself, a major step forward in terms of openness, tolerance and dissent.

Perhaps, unsurprisingly, what developments in Vietnam showed was not that there was any particular consistent model for post-Cold War political development, but that there continued to be a number of paths along which states could travel. Having begun its economic transformation before the end of the Cold War and, in some ways, prefiguring some of the pressures that brought the Soviet Union and the Cold War to an end, Vietnam appears to have planned its own future fairly carefully. There have been tension in this transformation from a centralised-economy one party state to a more open-economy one party state and, in particular, there have been real tensions between relative political closure and degrees of economic openness. But, for an elite that above all wishes to remain in control, the economic transition has been a relatively smooth one.

One might suggest that Vietnam has closely followed what has elsewhere been called the 'China model' or 'Beijing Consensus' (Ramo 2004) of development as an alternative to the neo-liberal 'Washington Consensus', with economic growth within a closed political context. The differences between the two are important. Vietnam's economic liberalisation came after China's own economic liberalisation, but it did not just follow China. Vietnam opened its economy for internally driven reasons, such as the very poor performance of its centralised economy, increasing reduction in Soviet aid and the economic pressure it faced from maintaining a large standing army in Cambodia and along its northern border with China.

Although a deeply authoritarian state, Vietnam was perhaps more liberal than China, in that it retained elements of Ho Chi Minh's more normative legacy than the ultimately more brutal legacy of Mao Zedong in China. Moreover, Vietnam was a country divided and, while it resumed unity in 1975, the southern members of the CPV were broadly more liberal in outlook than some of their more doctrinaire northern comrades, while the exuberant capitalism of the south eventually found expression throughout the whole of the country.

Importantly, too, while Vietnam has had its fair share of dissidents, it has not experienced a pro-democracy moment such as that in China's Tiananmen Square in 1989, which challenged the authority of the Chinese Communist Party, thus forcing it to close ranks even more tightly. This event has been suggested as one important reason why the CCP has concentrated authority in its Politburo over its Central Committee, whereas the CVP allocates political power more evenly between the two bodies, thus allowing for both greater internal debate within the Central Committee and some degree of balance between the two inter-linked bodies.

Having noted these distinctions, Vietnam does not appear to be moving towards further political liberalisation, much less plural electoral politics. It may do so in the future, but there is no indication that this is even a remote possibility in that part of the future which is foreseeable.

Notes

1 The Soviet Union and China had tense relations during much of the period of the American War in Vietnam, with Vietnam being drawn into that tension as well as having its own longer-term history of difficult relations with China.

2 In short, leadership by a small revolutionary body establishing a 'dictatorship of the proletariat' or one party rule on behalf of all citizens (other than anti-revolutionary groups), employing theories of collective social and economic organisation.

3 Discussions about economic reform in the Soviet Union had begun in 1985, but did not gather momentum until 1987–88.

4 Interestingly, confrontation with and lingering distrust of China, and the collapse of the Soviet Union, pushed Vietnam's political leaders to embrace, at least in part, closer relations with its former nemesis, the US (Hayton 2011: 190–1).

4   Laos

In a country in which the media remained tightly controlled and almost nothing was said in public about its secretive and autocratic government other than official statements, the crash of a military aeroplane near the Plain of Jars in north-western Laos on 17 May 2014 led to a significant shake-up of the political order of this land-locked, poverty-stricken place. In part, such a shake-up was a logical consequence of four of the fifteen Laos Politburo members on board being killed when the Antonov AN74TK-300 crashed on descent to an army commemoration ceremony in Laos' north-eastern Xieng Khouang Province.

The deaths of the group also meant the loss of much of the leadership of one of the two factions in Laos' government. However, in keeping with the lack of openness about public information, much less the ins and outs of Laos' factional politics, the official announcement of the crash said nothing about its political implications.

One initial consequence of the shift in balance of Laos' politics was that the country, previously under the overwhelming influence of Vietnam, moved a step closer to China as a key source of investment, trade and security. Another consequence was that, with a substantial reshuffle of leadership positions at the top of the Laos government, there was also a rearrangement of political leadership positions across the country's 17 provinces. For the average citizen on the street, or more commonly still in the fields, this meant little or no change to their lives, and there was little disagreement within the government over the general direction of government policy (this had been a long-standing arrangement; see Stuart-Fox 2007). But it did indicate, in a country in which politics remained a closed and tightly controlled process, that anything more than the most imperceptible movement among the political elite could have major consequences for those political actors subject to change.

This chapter considers Lao politics with a view to highlighting the increasing economic and political separation between the country's elite and its politically disenfranchised mass, its key political influences and elite rivalry, and its scope for increasing or continuing to constrain popular political participation.

The government claimed the air crash was a consequence of a technical fault, with the plane approaching the runway too low and its landing gear clipping trees on descent (IANS 2014). In Vientiane, however, there was a persistent if unofficial claim that the plane was hit by a surface-to-air missile, following eye-witnesses reporting a loud explosion before the plane crashed (Anon 2014).[1]

Among the 17 killed in the crash were the rising political star, deputy prime minister and defence minister, Lieutenant-General Douanchay Pichit. Douanchay was one of the second generation of post-1975 leaders of the Lao People's Revolutionary Party (LPRP), and was a protégé of President Choummaly Sayasone. Douanchay entered the Politburo, the inner circle of the LPRP, in 2001, being made defence minister. The position of defence minister is especially important in Lao politics given the symbiotic relationship between the Lao military and the LPRP.

Also killed was the much feared public security minister, Thongbanh Saengaphon, and Lao People's Revolutionary Party (LPRP) propaganda chief and secretary of the LPRP Central Committee Cheuang Sombounkanh. The group was at the core of a hardline, pro-Vietnam faction in Laos' government. Popular Vientiane mayor and politburo member Soukanh Mahalath was also killed in the air crash.

Laos' political trajectory

The regional empire of Lan Xang, which occupied both banks of the Mekong including Thailand's Khorat Plateau and northern Cambodia, had by the early eighteenth century broken into three kingdoms, each coming under degrees of Burmese and Thai domination and then, in the nineteenth century until 1953, French colonial occupation. Following independence, the country was riven by high levels of corruption (Stuart-Fox 1997: 148–9) and factional intrigues between royalists, neutralists and communists, and was caught up in the regional war for independence from France and then the neighbouring war for Vietnamese unification and withdrawal of US support. Conflict between factions ensued, leading to the uneasy alliances that characterised Lao politics through the early 1960s, until the US began bombing Pathet Lao targets in 1964 and internal fighting took place between rightist factions in 1965–66.

By 1968, the war in Vietnam was escalating beyond the control of the US, leading it to become more actively involved in Laos, both through its extensive bombing campaign of Pathet Lao (by then called Lao People's National Liberation Army, or LPNLA) targets and the 'Ho Chi Minh Trail' (in reality a series of trails) that ran from northern Vietnam inside or along the Lao border, into Cambodia and then southern Vietnam. By 1969, the US Central Intelligence Agency was actively arming and training Lao Hmong tribes to attack the LPNLA and Vietnam People's Army (VPA) operating in Lao territory. As part of the greater regional strategy, however, the US campaign suffered a series of setbacks in the field and was politically unpopular at home, leading to a planned withdrawal from 1972.

With reducing external military support to the Royal Lao Government, the LPRP reasserted itself, following peace accords joining in a coalition government from September 1973 but more completely dominating the coalition from the following April. However, set against the imminent fall of the republican government in neighbouring Cambodia, and the Republic of (South) Vietnam quickly succumbing to advances from the north, the LPRP forced Lao King Sisavang Vatthana to dissolve the National Assembly on 13 April 1975. Public demonstrations organised by the LPRP forced former government coalition partners to flee Vientiane on 9 May, with the 'liberation' of Vientiane and the establishment of a People's Revolutionary Administration being declared by the LPRP on 23 August. The Royal Lao Army and police were abolished, being replaced by 'workers' militias', although the façade of the previous government was maintained for a further three months. King Sisavang Vatthana was forced to abdicate on 1 December and, the following day, the LPRP proclaimed the People's Democratic Republic of Laos, formalising the party's control of the state. The LPRP wasted little time in deepening its control of the state, sending between ten and fifteen thousand people to 're-education' camps for up to 13 years, in one of which the king eventually died, reportedly from malaria, in approximately 1980 (Kremmer 1997: 196, 211).

The structure of Laos political processes is essentially unchanged since being introduced in 1975 and follows a conventional central planning ('communist') model. The party was initially part of the Indochinese Community Party (ICP), founded in 1930 with the Lao branch coming into being in 1936. A meeting of the ICP in 1951 agreed to disband and form three separate parties for each of the states of Indochina. The first iteration of the party was as the Pathet Lao, essentially a reserve force for Vietnamese Viet Minh guerrillas then fighting the colonial French, and the second as the Lao People's Party in 1955.

The country is ruled by the military, if often post-uniform, and developed powerful family and elite cliques that functioned as a coherent oligarchy. This grouping has, however, since fallen into internal dispute over the division of spoils, with what might be played out as party politics in some countries being characterised by elite factional disputes.

Laos remains a single party, nominally socialist republic, ruled by the LPRP. Confident of its hold on political power, the LPRP held its first elections in 1989. Apart from a very small number of carefully vetted non-partisan candidates, only the LPRP was allowed to contest the national elections, a situation that has remained since then. Laos National Assembly (Sapha Heng Xat) has 132 members, only four of whom were 'non-partisan', the rest being LPRP members. General policy is determined by a 49-member Central Committee, along with the Party Congress. A Politburo or secretariat (of nine people at the time of writing) of the Central Committee implements policy between (at least) biannual Central Committee plenary meetings, with major decisions being vetted by a council of ministers.

The executive president is elected by the National Assembly for a five-year term, who in turn appoints the prime minister, four deputy prime ministers (who oversee other ministers and who may also hold portfolios) and a council of ministers with the approval of the National Assembly. In reality, the process of 'election' is tightly scripted and authorised by a small group of senior figures, those with a military background tending to predominate. Elections were again due in 2016, with the expectation that there would be a gradual hand-over to the next generation of leaders, but no effective change in Laos' political style. As the party of state, the LPRP is also extensively represented in the government's bureaucracy and, as with Vietnam and Cambodia, party membership is generally regarded as a means of career advancement.

Laos is divided into 17 provinces, corresponding to four military regions (up from three). Until the mid- to late 1990s, a permit was required to travel between provinces and regions. Military Region One is headquartered in Luangprabang, Luangprabang Province, Military Region Two is headquartered in Muang Phonsavan, Xieng Khouang Province, Military Region Three is headquartered in Xeno, Savannakhet Province, and Military Region Four is headquartered in Pakxe, Champasak Province.

Village heads are elected by a locally elected committee and do not formally have to be LPRP members, although they are usually are, and are otherwise vetted by the LPRP. Given that village head authority, in which they 'govern' by village consensus, is limited, this does not present any challenge to the larger LPRP structure or administration. Village administration is, however, relatively autonomous, being formally accountable only to the (appointed) district chief and in turn to the (appointed) provincial governor and thence, in a quite removed manner, to the prime minister (UN 2005: 7–8). Corruption at the village head level is relatively limited, given that village heads can be voted out of office at each biannual election. It has been suggested that, at least at the village level, Laos does have some degree of direct democracy, with a more limited ability to accept or reject LPRP regional candidates for the National Assembly.

At a local level, political society is still organised at village level, with the village headman being the principal political representative and arbitrator between ordinary people and medium echelons of government. The village headman holds his position as a consequence of biannual elections and, short of losing consensus support, can be expected to maintain that position until he is no longer able to fulfil its functions. However, there are examples of village chiefs losing their positions because they attempted to enrich themselves and their families through their position, so there is a degree of accountability for ordinary Lao people. The village chief is virtually always a member of the LPRP, so there is a direct connection between the party and community life.

Family and village life is further organised by mutually reinforcing communal values, which tended to be typical of societies in transition from being agrarian-based and premodern to urbanised. Even in the larger urban centres, the fundamental administrative unit is still based on the village, or local community, so the model pertains across the state and not just to villages as such. Transgression of village rules can result in expulsion from the village, although redemption and forgiveness is also a marked characteristic of such situations.

At the more overtly political level, the 'government intelligence' network is extensive. That is, with everyone knowing more or less what everyone else is doing, there is little scope for anti-social, much less anti-government, behaviour. Similarly, although the law is technically quite strict in a number of matters, in fact its application is fairly lax. It depends more on whether or not there is a belief that a person has acted outside the bounds of socially acceptable behaviour rather than whether any actual crime has been committed. Of course, this does allow considerable scope for abuse, especially with reference to relatively low-level corruption. But in general there tends to be pretty much a 'live and let live' approach to formal social organisation.

In theory, Laos' constitution guarantees a number of rights and liberties to the Lao people, notably under Article 44, including speech, media and assembly. However, this is constrained by Article 47, which notes that they also have 'the obligation to respect the Constitution and the laws, to observe labour discipline, [and comply with] the regulations relating to social life and public order' (Lao PDR 2003).

The government checks that have been especially noticeable in the more troubled parts of Laos are not especially oppressive of ordinary people. There is, almost as a matter of course, a certain official brusqueness and arrogance in the starchy bureaucracy of authoritarian officialdom. The general – if not specific – lack of oppression in part tends to stem from the predominant influence of Theravada Buddhism on everyday life (Evans 1998: 49–70), which is manifested in Sangha (Buddhist clergy) involvement with and support for ordinary people, and the government's explicit respect for Buddhism and the Sangha, without being a sufficient explanation. That is, if the Lao government allows most people to live without interfering too much in their daily lives, that situation seems to be reasonably well accepted.

The Lao government's broad sense of acceptability also in large part stems from the loosening of its formerly fairly strict, orthodox Leninist policies that derived directly from the Communist Party of Vietnam and, before that, from the Soviet Union. Since the Soviet Union has ceased to exist and Vietnam has, since 1987, moved towards opening its economy, Laos too has moved towards a less centrally planned, more free market economy. This was, in any case, still largely irrelevant to a society that was very significantly subsistence-oriented and in which illicit cross-border trade was a fact of economic life. However, Laos' return to economic growth, its increase in foreign currency reserves and the slow shift towards creating an industrial base are all signs that there are positive, if still modest, economic outcomes available to the Lao people.

The international community, too, has had a very significant impact on Laos. Thailand was in the process of attempting to reassert its economic, if not political, hegemony over Laos while the international aid agencies had a significant presence in Vientiane. However, development outside Vientiane and a few other major towns appears to have been so limited that it is almost non-existent. Village life has been little touched by 'development'.

Orientation

Along with Vietnam, which itself was a Soviet client state, the Soviet Union was Laos' main external sponsor and Laos was firmly entrenched in the Soviet camp from 1975 until the end of the Cold War. The then Soviet Union was a key contributor to the development of Laos. In particular, it was the mainstay behind the development of Laos' military forces (Stuart-Fox 1997: 177–8) and was its key trading and diplomatic partner, providing up to 60 per cent of Laos' external assistance into the late 1980s. All of this placed Laos firmly within the Soviet-aligned Cold War camp.

The end of the Cold War, or the period leading up to it, impacted on Laos differently to many other countries. Where a number of other formerly communist countries transitioned towards democracy, or at least had a change of regime, Laos' LPRP further entrenched itself in power, but reconfigured its economy towards an increasingly open market on one hand and sought new trading partners on the other.

After a fall-out with China following the latter's invasion of Vietnam in 1978, Laos' relations with China were normalised in 1988. In 1997, when Thailand was hit by the Asian financial crisis of that year, Laos turned further towards China for assistance. China's position as a competitor for Laos' attention, including increasing its military assistance, has been established since that time.

From the end of the 1980s, Laos has moved closer to China, and also the ASEAN states, notably Thailand, to help rescue its flailing economy. In a bid to bolster trade with neighbouring Thailand, in 1991 construction started on a bridge between Nong Khai in Thailand and Vientiane Prefecture (south of Vientiane proper), opened in 1994. The bridge, funded by Australia's official aid program, has been a major success in terms of flow of people and trade, and in helping to open Laos to both Thailand and other countries that trade with Thailand. Its success led to a second bridge being opened further south in 2007, to Savannakhet, and a road over the Annamite Cordillera to central Vietnam. A third bridge was opened in 2011 at Thakhek, leading to a further road that crosses the Annamite Cordillera to Vietnam. A fourth bridge was opened in 2013 at Ban Houayxay near the border junction with Thailand and Myanmar in what, for its opium production, used to be known as the 'Golden Triangle'.

Economy

As with Vietnam, following the revolution of 1975 Laos steadily moved towards a socialist economy. It instituted agricultural cooperatives in May 1978, although it suspended the program the following July after widespread opposition to it. A three-year economic plan also failed to produce economic benefits, with a further five-year economic plan being instituted in 1981. As the LPRP's economic policies failed, it turned to economic policies first enunciated by Laos' 'neutralists'. Following the lead of the then Soviet Union's own withdrawal of support from Vietnam, by 1988 Vietnam had withdrawn the last of its own troops from Laos. Increasingly confident of its position as the only meaningful power in the state, the LPRP held elections for the Supreme People's Assembly in 1989.

While Soviet assistance began to decline from 1989, there has, since the end of the Cold War, been considerable and again growing Russian involvement with Laos. This has included trade and technical assistance, at least in part by way of countering China's growing challenge to Russia's former superpower status. In 2014, Laos and Russia announced that they were continuing to deepen their relationship, including investments, preferential trade arrangements and visa-free entry (*Vientiane Times* 2014a).

Despite being one of the world's five remaining 'communist' states, since the 1990s, like Vietnam and China, Laos has been a largely free market state controlled by an autocratic political party. After the failed economic experiments of the early communist years, it has seen economic growth since 1991, with a drop in 1998 due to the Asian financial crisis, well into the twenty-first century. However, despite this growth, starting from a very low base, Laos remains a least developed state, with a per capita GDP of just over US$1,700 a year and almost a quarter of its population living in absolute poverty (World Bank 2015b).

As with the militaries of other countries that began as guerrilla units, Laos' military is in part self-supporting through its own business ventures. Military businesses have included logging (Smith 2010), shipping – with a port facility in Vietnam owned and operated by the Lao military – tourism, construction, trade, and light manufacturing (see Funston 2001: 136).

This history of military business was increased after the Soviet Union began to reduce military aid to its allies in the late 1980s (IBP 2009: 72). As trade flows between provinces, or to neighbouring countries, local officials, the most senior of whom are also military officers, regularly skim a proportion of the value. Similarly, business conducted through state owned enterprises, usually operated by military officers, is rarely as transparent as their books would indicate, providing considerable scope for skimming or transferring funds to private accounts. Indicating the scope for using SOEs as a source of illicit income, credit growth ran at 50 per cent per annum until 2015, with a high level of non-performing loans (increasing from 3 per cent to 8 per cent, according to WBG 2015: 11), and with a disproportionate amount of that credit relative to performance going to state-owned or military-linked enterprises. The privatisation of SOEs, while seen as a mechanism to improve their efficiency, often means that such businesses end up being owned by the military officers who previously ran them as managers.

Bribes also continue to be commonplace at lower levels, including at border crossings and in processing conventional business and personal matters through government agencies. According to the World Bank (2012a), '[B]usiness transactions and investments are still carried out in an opaque manner. Laos, while politically very stable, remains a poorly regulated economy with limited rule of law. Corruption, patronage and a weak legal system are a drag on economic development.'

Although nominally 'communist', Lao politics now functions primarily as a means of allocating patronage and opportunities to make money, often through corrupt means.

Despite a public anti-drugs campaign, at the time of writing Laos was the world's third largest producer of opium and a major producer of methamphetamines. It was also a prime source of illegal logging. Transparency International lists Laos as among the world's most corrupt countries, in 2013 placing it at 140 on a list of 177 countries surveyed (Transparency International 2013: 4). According to a Radio Free Asia report, quoting two anonymous Laos officials: 'When many companies bid, they give bribes to officials behind the scene. "I have money, you have projects. Let's go to have lunch together." That's the way it is in Laos' (Radio Free Asia 2009). The winning 'bids' for large construction contracts can then be sold on to foreign companies, netting millions of dollars in profits.

According to long-time Laos watcher, Martin Stuart-Fox:

> The pervasiveness of corruption is due in large part to the example set by political leaders. Members of the Politburo and their families have become excessively rich. They have built vast villas, drive luxury cars, and hold lavish parties. Marriages between children of the political elite are occasions for the display of wealth, with political favours paid off in the form of envelopes stuffed with cash. Children of the elite are immune to the law in a country where legal disputes are often decided on the basis of who pays the judge the biggest bribe.
>
> (Stuart-Fox 2011)

Some corruption is simply about making life more pleasant for political leaders, such as the state funding of the construction of roads to private homes while other more travelled roads remain unpaved. In April 2015, the Ministry of Public Works and Transport approved 400 million kip (approximately US$50,000) to build a 600-metre-long road to the home of Politburo member and chairman of the Lao Anti-Corruption Organization and Government Inspection Authority, Bounthong Chitmany (Radio Free Asia 2015). This was less than a year after Bounthong announced that around USD$150 million had been lost to corruption in the previous two years.

According to Bounthong, the authority has investigated more than 300 cases since 2012. Bounthong said that the main corrupt activities included abuse of power for personal benefit, bribery, forgery of documents, illegally modifying technical standards and designs, and delaying document approval for personal gain: 'The corruption activities in the country are circulating in these five ways, with the abuse of power and delaying document approval the most widespread among them' (*Shanghai Daily* 2014).

Some corruption was, however, more venal than simply paving a road to one's house. The governor of northern Laos' Xieng Khouang Province, Somkod Mengnormek, illegally took land leased to a restaurant owner who had built a restaurant on it and sold it to the country's central bank for US$2 million for the bank to be able to build a new branch on (Souksavanh 2015).

Stability around this state of affairs was likely to follow a generational change in the leadership of the LPRP at the 2016 party congress. There was expected to be a shift away from very old men whose principle experiences were formed by warfare to a somewhat younger class of technocrats and military-business people whose interests were shaped by self-interested opportunity as much as survival.

The country's free market status was reconfirmed by LPRP Secretary-General and Lao President Choummaly Sayasone on 22 March 2015, the sixtieth anniversary of the establishment of the LPRP, when he repeatedly referred to the 'state-managed market-orientated economy' and noted that the LPRP had 'liberalized old ways of thinking towards a realistic analysis of the situation' while pursuing socialist directives (Palatino 2015). Translated, this meant minor reforms to a more or less free market economy with a single party government – 'centrally based democratic principle' – that allowed considerable opportunity for the elite to continue to enrich themselves through privileged economic access.

While around three-quarters of Laos' employment remains in agriculture, often at or just above subsistence levels, the country has experienced economic growth, if from an exceptionally low base, since the 1980s. Parallel with Vietnam, Laos has, since 1986, allowed an increasingly open market under its 'New Economic Mechanism'. Foreign investment in mining (primarily gold, copper, silver and coal) accounts for more than half of export income, with coal-generated electricity and hydroelectricity also becoming major sources of export income. However, the state controls the allocation of private contracts, which are often managed by or passed through the hands of senior party and government officials, in many cases at prices lower than true market value. Either these are then either managed with the state as a silent partner, or the contracts are sold on at a considerable profit.

As the twenty-first century unfolded, Laos' economy continued to grow at above 7 per cent and the country's elite further embraced the opportunities presented by a controlled form of capitalism. This form of 'developmentalism' – economic development within a tightly controlled political environment based on five-year plans – was consistent with the economic and political models chosen by a number of the country's neighbours within the ASEAN sphere and by China. Forestry, agriculture and electricity from dams contributed around half of the country's GDP, with the US$1.3 billion Nam Theun 2 Dam opened in 2010 generating electricity for Thailand. With mountainous terrain and high rainfall, Laos had committed itself to becoming a hydroelectricity exporter, with some 25 further electricity-generating dams either in operation or under construction as of 2014 (*Vientiane Times* 2014b). Laos also planned to integrate its economy more closely with those of its neighbours, in part by establishing further transport links, including a train line between the Thai border, Savannakhet and Lao Bao on the Vietnamese border, extending the line to the port city of Danang (providing the land-locked country with almost direct port access), a train line to Yunnan province in southern China and the three new 'friendship' bridges connecting road transport to Thailand, with one running through to China, along with a main road through to Kunming in China.

In 2013, moving closer to a neo-liberal economic model along the lines of that of China and Vietnam, Laos joined the World Trade Organization in a bid to further bolster foreign investment. Based on this growth, Laos was expected to move out of 'least developed' country status by 2020. However, there was no sign that the country's leaders had any intention of allowing it to liberalise politically, much less democratise. As noted by a specialist research group: 'The political climate in Laos will remain stable over the coming years, as the country's only legal political party, the Lao People's Revolutionary Party (LPRP), will maintain its tight grip on power' (BMI Research 2015).

Having shifted towards more market-oriented policies in the 1990s, the now free market 'communist' state of Laos has been described by some insiders as a 'narco-kleptocracy' as a result of high-level corruption and elite involvement in the drugs trade. The country having been formally and somewhat optimistically declared 'opium-free' in 2006 (it was significantly reduced but not eradicated), opium production has since been reported to have rapidly resumed, with 762 tonnes of opium being produced, refined into an estimated 76 tonnes of heroin, in 2014 (UNODC 2014).

Vietnam and China

Vietnam has, since 1975, been deeply influential in Lao politics, in particular through official party and military-to-military links. However, China has been increasingly asserting influence in what has, at times, been called the 'keystone state' of mainland Southeast Asia (Dommen 1985; see also McNamara 1995: 35, 36–8).

Given the influence of Vietnam on the LPRP, in 1977 Laos quickly formalised its relations with the newly unified state through a 25-year Treaty of Friendship. Vietnam maintained a military presence in Laos until the early 1980s. When China invaded Vietnam in December 1978 in response to Vietnam's invasion of Cambodia, Laos, also sharing a northern border with China, sided with Vietnam. The following year, Vietnam requested that Laos end its relations with China, leading to Laos' further international isolation. Relations between Laos and China began to warm again, however, with the visit to Laos of Chinese premier Li Peng in 1990.

The crash of the military Antonov with almost half the Politburo on board in 2014 was, at the time, linked to the suspicious death, in the middle of 2013, of the deputy defence minister, 45-year-old Major-General Sannhahak Phomivane. Phomivane was the son of Kaysone Phomivane, head of the LPRP from 1955 until 1992 and Prime Minister from 1975 until 1991. The elder Phomivane was a close Vietnamese ally. The younger Phomivane, also pro-Vietnam, was officially said to have died within a couple of days of contracting dengue fever. However, dengue is rarely fatal when first contracted, especially for a fit man. Phomivane's death was in turn seen within the context of the 'resignation for family reasons', in 2010, of Prime Minister Bouasone Bouphavanh. Bouphavanh, who was said to have been pushed out of office as a result of excessive personal and family corruption, also led the Lao government's then ascendant pro-China faction. Having noted that, there was also the view that his ouster could have been a result of regional factions and patron–client networks being played out (Stuart-Fox 2011).

In the competition for strategic and economic influence in Laos, Vietnam retains a historical advantage and strong links to, if not control over, Laos' government. That Vietnam was to assist Laos in the planned rewriting of its constitution indicated the continuing influence that Vietnam had with its smaller neighbour (VNS 2015).

However, China dwarfs Vietnam in every other sense. As a consequence, as Laos' pro-Vietnam leaders pass from the political scene, Laos has been moving closer to China. Following China's setback with the ousting of Bouphavanh, the suspicious death of Phomivane took Laos a step closer to China. With the 2014 deaths of the expected next President and other key figures in the hardline pro-Vietnam faction, China's position in Laos looked stronger.

While the Lao government was not necessarily noted for its violence since the effective end of anti-communist rebellion in the 1980s and crackdown on ethnic Hmong until the early 1990s, it did not tolerate dissent, or anything that could be construed as dissent. This was well illustrated by the abduction and presumed murder of sustainable development civil society activist Sombath Somphone in 2013. Somphone's last recorded movements, captured on CCTV, were of him being stopped at a police post and taken into an unmarked vehicle. The government immediately denied any knowledge of Somphone's whereabouts and has maintained a policy of silence on the matter despite extensive expressions of international concern.

Human Rights Watch noted that, since 2009, nine other people planning a pro-democracy protest had been similarly abducted and not seen again (HRW 2015).

Beyond such abductions, the Lao government has also placed tighter restriction on the activities of NGOs, including strict requirements for notification and permission to receive or spend international development aid, tighter controls on permitted work and further restrictions on speech or activities that contradict peace and social order as defined by the government (HRW 2015). Although Laos is moving towards becoming a regime based on laws passed by the legislature, it still also operates on the basis of presidential decrees which are not open to scrutiny and often serve short-term political purposes.

Among others who have suffered official systematic persecution in Laos are the country's ethnic Hmong (or Miao) population. The Hmong were relatively recent arrivals in Laos, migrating from southern China to the highlands of Laos, Vietnam, Thailand and Burma from the late eighteenth and early nineteenth centuries at the height of suppression and assimilation by the Han Qing (Manchu) Dynasty. The Hmong lived primarily in the highlands, remaining separate from the predominant lowland Lao (Lao Loum), initially rebelling against French occupation but later growing poppies for the lucrative French trade in opium. Soon after Laos' independence, US soldiers and Central Intelligence Agency operatives trained Hmong to fight against the Pathet Lao, ending their support for the Hmong when the US withdrew remaining forces from Indochina in 1975. Reprisals against anti-communist forces were initially severe, with the Hmong bearing the brunt of much of the crackdown. Perhaps 100,000 of a population of 400,000 or so Hmong were killed (Hamilton-Merritt 1999: 337–460).

Following the conclusion of the Hong war, Hmong communities were relocated by the government to resettlement camps, usually near the road between Vang Vieng and Luang Prabang. Mortality rates, especially among infants and children, in these poorly serviced areas was said to be high. Into the early twenty-first century, this area remained somewhat insecure due to continuing banditry and low-level insurgency. Many of the thousands of Hmong who had fled into Thailand at the end of the war were forced to return to Laos, despite protests by the United Nations High Commissioner for Refugees and a refusal by the Lao government to allow access by the UNHCR to the repatriated Hmong (UNHCR 2009).

A major issue of contention between the Lao government and the Hmong was, not surprisingly given international opprobrium, the cultivation and sale of opium. There was a certain level of official involvement in the opium and heroin trade, helping Laos maintain its position as the world's third largest illegal opium producer after Myanmar and Afghanistan. It was not at all clear whether the government's stated opposition to opium cultivation was genuine, given that opium (and, on a ratio of about 10:1, estimated heroin) production in Myanmar's Shan State and Laos increased between 2013 and 2014 from 61,700 to 63,800 hectares under cultivation, producing some 762 tonnes of opium (UNODC 2014: 3). 'Data collected during helicopter flights and satellite image analysis indicated that poppy cultivation in 2014 also continued to be a phenomenon linked to villages in peripheral, difficult-to-access locations, far from population and market centres' (UNODC 2014: 17). As in Myanmar, it was quite likely that local military officers involved in the drug trade were simply trying to put their competitors out of business. A further related issue was that of the trans-shipment of heroin from Myanmar through to Cambodia and Vietnam. The nature of the linkages between Myanmar and Laos were not clear, but again it seems that there was a significant degree of official involvement. This was especially so in relation to the trans-shipment to Cambodia and Vietnam, where there were close political and military links.

Some of this opium production had earlier been linked to Hmong tribespeople, who had long refused to submit to central government authority. However, in March 2004, formal Hmong anti-government activity ended when around 700 Hmong fighters and their families surrendered to the government. The surrender followed an intensification of the government's campaign to end the Hmong insurgency, especially in the Xieng Khouang Special Zone, and to dispel the last vestiges of the US-founded 'secret army'. About 300 people surrendered near Luang Prabang, and a further 400 surrendered in Xieng Khouang. While opium production dropped from its peak in 1998 to an all-time low in 2007, it returned to growth from then until 2012, with 2013 being climatically unfavourable, and again a return to growth in 2014 (UNODC 2014: 22, 26), in part reflecting the increase in the price of opium from US$200 per kilogram in 2002 to around $1,800 per kilogram in 2014.

Beyond the Hmong and active dissidents, Laos appears to have a relatively more relaxed approach to official–social relations than many other countries. Where in countries in which the military retained a close role in social administration there could be seen to be a more or less wanton abuse of power, in Laos this is less prominent, with more open relations between low-level officials and ordinary people going about their business. In part this could be explained by the predominance of Theravada Buddhism, which seems to have a moderating influence on Lao social life, and the continued and active link to and respect for the Sangha (monkhood), the joining of which, for many Lao boys and young men, remains a rite of passage.

Conclusion

While Laos allows a degree of political participation at the local level, its larger political structures remain closed to ordinary participation. Membership of the LPRP is critical for economic advancement, and having served in the army, particularly at senior officer level, appears to be a guarantee of economic success. There are strong incentives for Laos to increasingly open itself to outside influences, in particular through trade, and it has increasingly done this with regard to its neighbours. But, as a land-locked country, Laos is also restricted as an exporter and, starting from a base of least developed status, there remain huge gaps between the capabilities of most ordinary Lao and the country's military, political and economic elite.

With such a strong, vested interest in maintaining the political status quo and with the military retaining such a tight grip on the country, Laos is unlikely to move towards political openness at any time in the foreseeable future. However, coming from a very poor and previously constrained socio-economic and political environment, with greater freedoms to engage in (usually small-scale) business and to travel, and with the relatively high price paid for open dissent, there does not in any case appear to be great appetite for imminent political change.

Note

1 Having noted that, and despite having upgraded its domestic air fleet, Laos had an at best patchy air safety record, with a fatal aircraft crash each in 2013, 2014 and 2015, and around 30 similar crashes dating back to the 1950s.

5   Cambodia

Cambodia is, or was, in theory, a democracy and the country continues to pay lip-service to electoral processes by holding regular, if deeply unfair, elections. But while Cambodia does hold regular elections, the outcome of those elections has, since 1998, been entirely predictable, with the process being used to confirm Hun Sen as prime minister and the Cambodian People's Party (CPP) as the only genuinely available choice for government. How this situation came about was, in effect, in part a reversal of what was intended to be one of the first positive outcomes of the end of the Cold War.

More successfully, since 1997, Cambodia has been a country, if not entirely at peace, then no longer at war. Cambodia's civil war had a long internal history, in many respects having its origins in the character of the country's anti-colonial movement. But, by the late 1980s, while the country had distinct factions based on local goals and grievances, Cambodia was also a site for a war by proxy between Russia supporting the Vietnamese-backed CPP, China supporting the Khmer Rouge (formally the Communist Party of Kampuchea), led by Pol Pot (Saloth Sar), and the US and Thailand supporting pro-royalist and pro-republican forces.

If significantly more secure than it has been for decades, Cambodia has not become a beacon for the triumphalist 'end of history' claims of the period in which it transitioned to electoral politics (the key example of which is Fukuyama 1992). Having agreed to become a more or less functioning democracy as part of a UN-brokered peace agreement in 1991, it is now difficult to view Cambodia as other than a corrupt dominant party state, under the functional rule of one person, which may struggle with internal power plays in a post-Hun Sen future.

Authoritarianism's recent past

Cambodia and Singapore (both at 3.33) are regarded as authoritarian states in terms of political participation (EIU 2014). Both could be considered as 'flawed democracies' if the overwhelming criterion for assessment was the holding of regular elections. However, while Singapore employs judicial sanctions to silence its critics and opposition, its bureaucracy is relatively responsive, if not entirely separate from the dominant political party. In Cambodia, on the other hand, not only are judicial measures used to stifle opposition, but extrajudicial measures have also been regularly employed, along with high levels of overtly corrupt state-patronage and a state bureaucratic system that continues to reflect the lack of distinction between the party and the state that characterises 'communist' states, and which is at the origins of Cambodia's post-Khmer Rouge state-building project.

Arbitrary violence had already become a trademark of the Khmer Rouge (as it had with other Cambodian political and military groups), with disobedience being judged as treason punishable by death (see, for example, Kiernan 1985: 375–80, 384–93; Chandler 1992: 128–39). Cambodia's small educated class either was killed in the period 1975–78, or fled.

Eventually the Khmer Rouge began to devour itself; in particular the central group in Phnom Penh began turning on its members in the eastern zone, who were believed to have been excessively influenced by Vietnam (Vickery, in Chandler and Kiernan 1983: 128–30; 1985: 330–7; Kiernan 1993: 192). As the Khmer Rouge program of producing surpluses led to economic failure, tens of thousands more who questioned the policy direction were purged from the party ranks and murdered (Kiernan 1985: 392). As the purges began to take hold, Khmer Rouge soldiers and commanders in the east began to desert, fleeing across the border into Vietnam (Kiernan, in Chandler and Kiernan 1983: 136–211). Cambodia's total death toll, from disease, starvation and murder, between April 1975 and December 1978/January 1979, is variously estimated at up to two million, from a population of six million. It was, both proportionately and in absolute terms, one of the worst genocides in modern history (see also Kiernan 1996).

In 1978, for reasons that had to do with historical animosity, ideological conflict, probably an attempt to divert attention from internal problems (Kiernan 1985: 393), and possibly the sanity of its leadership, the Khmer Rouge launched a series of border attacks against the recently unified and battle-hardened Vietnam. The border disputes had begun in 1975 over Vietnamese claims to islands in the Gulf of Thailand, occupation of which had been formalised by the French during the colonial period. These claims were not accepted by Cambodia and, under the Khmer Rouge, there were now moves to have the islands returned (Chanda 1986: 12–13). There was also the lingering animosity over that part of south-eastern Cambodia that had been incorporated into Vietnam some 200–400 years before. So much a part of the Khmer 'nation' was this region of Khmer Krom that it was considered normal by the Khmer Rouge that Brother Number Three, Ieng Sary, was born not in Cambodia but in this Vietnamese-'occupied' territory. Similarly, ethnic Vietnamese living in Cambodia were increasingly persecuted, with large numbers being killed from 1975 until the Khmer Rouge was effectively finished as a military force in much of the country in 1979.

The period between 1985 and 1991 saw continued civil war in Cambodia, largely led by the discredited Khmer Rouge. Despite the convenience of the UN not recognising its formal legitimacy, the continued existence of the Khmer Rouge in turn domestically (if not internationally) assisted with legitimising the post-1978, Vietnam-backed, People's Republic of Kampuchea as a viable and somewhat more humane alternative. Throughout this period and, especially, following the transition to becoming the State of Cambodia and beginning to open its economy in 1989, Hun Sen took on an more pragmatic rather than ideological approach to state-building. In particular he increasingly avoided allowing rigid communist ideology to dictate state economic and social policy, with Buddhism becoming both the state religion and, again, extremely popular, the beginnings of small capitalism.

While Cambodia's factions had agreed to elections supervised by the UN Transitional Administration in Cambodia (UNTAC) to be held in 1993, the period between the peace agreement and the elections was marked by a high level of political violence, including political assassinations. While most violence came from the marginalised Khmer Rouge, the CPP was also responsible for attacks against opposition party members. During this

UNTAC period, Hun Sen manoeuvred to thwart the UN in its intention to reorient the Cambodian state away the Cambodian People's Party, thus ensuring his functional grip on practical power.

When the royalist National United Front for an Independent, Neutral, Peaceful, and Cooperative Cambodia (FUNCINPEC) party won 58 of the 120 available seats, the CPP, with 51 seats, refused to concede defeat. Ten seats also went to the Buddhist Liberal Democratic Party (BLDP) and one to the pro-Sihanouk Movement for the National Liberation of Kampuchea (Moulinaka). Instead of recognising FUNCINPEC's victory as a result of its plurality, the CPP insisted on a power-sharing arrangement, in which the prime ministership was twinned between FUNCINPEC leader Prince Norodom Ranariddh as 'first Prime Minister' and Hun Sen as 'second Prime Minister'. The CPP received 16 ministries, with FUNCINPEC taking 13, the rest being allocated to the BLDP and Moulinaka, which joined the CPP in coalition.

Despite the unwieldiness of this arrangement, the situation remained largely stable until the Khmer Rouge began to disintegrate. The edges of the Khmer Rouge had been breaking away for some time, but the pace of disintegration accelerated in 1996 and into 1997. With Chinese support declining, being militarily isolated, and Vietnamese-backed attacks and the UN limiting the Khmer Rouge's activity on the ground, the Khmer Rouge leadership began to disintegrate. Thousands of Khmer Rouge troops surrendered in 1994, and in 1996 Khmer Rouge Brother Number Three and former Minister for Foreign Affairs Ieng Sary broke away to form the democratic National Union Movement.

This was the most significant blow, as Ieng Sary was the Khmer Rouge's third-in-command (and Pol Pot's brother-in-law). When Ieng Sary defected to the government, he took 10,000 troops with him, significantly weakening the by-now struggling organisation. Ieng Sary already occupied Pailin in the west of Cambodia, and troops under his command had clashed with troops under the command of Pol Pot and former commander of the Khmer Rouge army and Brother Number Five, Ta Mok. In exchange for his defection, Ieng Sary was given effective warlord control over Pailin. The disintegration of the Khmer Rouge was compounded by its structure as an organisation of quasi-autonomous groups led by regional warlords. As the strategic situation of the remaining Khmer Rouge became more desperate, the various groups began to act more independently. It was only a matter of time before individual leaders began to make their own deals with the government (Thayer 1998).

The disintegration of the Khmer Rouge was played out in the idiosyncratic style of that notorious organisation. Upon learning that fighters had entered into negotiations with Ranariddh in order to defect, in March 1997, Pol Pot ordered one of their leaders executed. This was Khmer Rouge 'Defence Minister' Son Sen – Pol Pot's lifelong friend – as well as his wife, nine children and three other family members (Schanberg 1997). By this stage, Pol Pot was clearly losing control of the organisation and, in a bid to save themselves, the remaining senior leadership arrested Pol Pot.

Pol Pot was put through a show trial for the killings and sentenced to life imprisonment. This split at the most senior levels of the Khmer Rouge led to rebellion within the ranks, with the Khmer Rouge's senior military leader Ta Mok taking Pol Pot as his prisoner, along with several hundred loyal soldiers who followed him voluntarily, further into the jungles of Anlong Veng in Cambodia's north-west. By April 1998, Ta Mok suggested that he could hand over Pol Pot in exchange for his own freedom. But on 15 April 1998 Pol Pot, who had long been sick, died (Thayer 1998). No autopsy was carried out on his body. No one knows whether he died of heart failure, as claimed, whether he committed suicide before being handed over to government authorities, or whether, the proposed exchange-for-freedom deal being rejected, Ta Mok decided that Pol Pot had outlived his usefulness and killed him the night before he was due to be handed over to an international war crimes tribunal.

The rest of the Khmer Rouge leadership followed the remaining members by taking up government offers of amnesty or, in rare cases where they did not surrender, being captured (or handed over). In December 1998, Nuon Chea, Brother Number Two and Khmer Rouge second in command, and the former head of state of Kampuchea from 1975 until 1979, Khieu Samphan, returned to Cambodia from Thailand and were in the interim granted an effective amnesty. This was despite widespread calls both within and without Cambodia for a trial to account for their involvement in Cambodia's killings. People on the street were saying they wanted the former Khmer Rouge leaders to be tried, even if it meant re-opening the old conflict. 'I want peace,' said one young Cambodian who had been a small child when he and his family were sent to the fields in 1975. 'But I also want justice. Without justice there is no real peace.'[1]

Nuon Chea was later identified by Deuch, the former chief of the S-21 (Tuol Sleng) interrogation centre in Phnom Penh, as being primarily responsible for the vast numbers of killings conducted at the prison. Hun Sen told the Cambodian people that a trial could re-open the now ended conflict with the remaining Khmer Rouge. The pair and their families then left Phnom Penh for Ieng Sary's stronghold of Pailin. Around 2,000 troops loyal to Ta Mok formally joined the Royal Cambodian Army in February 1999, and just a few days later Ta Mok was arrested near the Thai border, his Thai hosts having handed him over to Cambodian authorities. By 2004, the General Prosecutor had begun proceedings so that Nuon Chea and Ieng Sary would eventually face charges in relation to killings during the Khmer Rouge era.

The end of the Cold War and agreement to allow UN intervention in 1991 to help end the country's long-running, proxy-driven civil war saw the re-establishment of Cambodia's monarchy and electoral parliamentary politics. Yet despite attempts by the UN to create a plural political model, it ultimately foundered on the underlying solidity of the institutions that had preceded it and which maintained state control through its interregnum. After what looked like a promising start, the CPP under the leadership of Hun Sen refused to hand power to the electorally victorious royalist FUNCINPEC party. With the army on side, Hun Sen simply refused to budge, forcing FUNCINPEC into a dysfunctional power-sharing arrangement, in which the state bureaucracy often answered to two ministers in each portfolio but often finally to one, that of the CPP.

This partially workable situation remained until 1997 when, with the final military dissolution of the Khmer Rouge, both FUNCINPEC and the CPP began recruiting former Khmer Rouge cadres. This quickly led to a showdown between the two parties (Thayer 2011; 1998).

Both FUNCINPEC and the CPP recognised that whoever salvaged what remained of the Khmer Rouge would be in a strategically stronger position vis-à-vis the other in any future competition. Both sides rushed to recruit Khmer Rouge leaders and their troops, with FUNCINPEC appearing to have a slight advantage. With tensions mounting, longer-term intentions becoming increasingly clear and time running out for the CPP to secure its pre-existing advantage, on 5–6 July 1997 it struck, staging what has been described as, and to some extent amounted to, a 'coup'[2] (*Phnom Penh Post* 1997).

Over two days, there was heavy fighting, particularly at the Taing Krassang military base and Phnom Penh airport.

The CPP had pushed FUNCINPEC out of government and consolidated its control over demobilised Khmer Rouge troops. More than 100 people, mostly pro-FUNCINPEC supporters, were killed, often execution-style, in the 'coup', with around 60,000 Cambodians fleeing towards the western border (Kingsbury 2005b: 24–6). When the fighting settled, the CPP had come out victorious, with Ranariddh fleeing to Paris. FUNCINPEC and its supporters had retreated to the north and west of the country, to what had previously been Khmer Rouge territory. Limited resistance continued in the north until August of that year. By 1998, the north and west were opened to travel[3] and FUNCINPEC supporters were returning from remote parts of the country, in July of that year contesting national elections amidst widespread allegations of electoral fraud (ICG 1998).

Despite forces loyal to Ranariddh continuing limited military activity from the north-west of the country, the CPP quickly consolidated power, with Hun Sen appointing Ung Huot as co-Prime Minister. However, peace was restored and elections, albeit deeply flawed, were held in 1998, with Hun Sen returning to the prime ministership alone.

The 1997 'coup' marked the ascent of dominant party politics in Cambodia. To most outsiders, it appeared that, following the coup, the still relatively young Hun Sen enjoyed unrivalled control over both the Cambodian People's Party and the state. The CPP still had to contest elections, but its domination of the media, state institutions and the country's public service, and the personalisation of political power, e.g. Hun Sen's name being used as a prefix for state facilities such as high schools, helped ensure that it remained at the forefront of most people's consciousness. If it did not, local CPP cadres were adept at applying pressure, including physical violence, to persuade voters of the 'correct' course of action.

Violence marred opposition political rallies, with a hand grenade being thrown into a rally in Phnom Penh in 1997, killing 16 people, and with violence breaking out at polling stations the following year. In 2003, a judge and a FUNCINPEC politician were murdered in elections that returned the CPP 73 of the 123 parliamentary seats, less than the two-thirds of seats required to form government. In order to formalise the political process, the CPP entered into an unequal coalition with FUNCINPEC in 2004. It was this move which consolidated Hun Sen's personal grip on power, especially after CPP 'conservative faction' rival and former 'Number One' member of the CPP Chea Sim was sent into a short exile in neighbouring Thailand and most of his key allies were removed from office.

It was instructive that among the key FUNCINPEC allies were those that Hun Sen had sided with when there was an alleged coup plot against him in 1994. However, the move against Chea Sim and his colleagues exposed a factionalism within the CPP that had previously been carefully hidden (Thayer 2014a).

Even the millions of land mines, which continued to plague Cambodia, were slowly being cleared. Cambodia's inclusion into the Association of Southeast Asian Nations in May 1999 and its readmission to the United Nations in November 1999 appeared to confirm, at least on the surface, that the country was moving towards being on a stable, if largely unaccountable, political footing.

Thus the politics of Cambodia have, in the post-Cold War period, reflected not the triumph of democracy but the hard reality of power politics and confirmation that, all too often, 'political power grows out of the barrel of a gun' (Mao 1938: 224). Such a lesson is apposite, given Hun Sen's political origins as a guerrilla fighter and later an officer with the Khmer Rouge,[4] which was deeply influenced by Mao Zedong's approach to politics.

Regime structure

Having again assumed sole power in 1998, the Cambodian People's Party, personified by PM Hun Sen, had increased its grip on the country's political process while continuing to marginalise its divided and somewhat incoherent opposition. Despite the end of the country's devastating civil war, Cambodia continued to be influenced by and reactive to its regional neighbours (increasingly China), while largely isolating itself from external or, indeed, even internal accountability.

The institutions of state that continue to dominate Cambodia were put in place by Vietnam following its invasion and removal of the Khmer Rouge in December 1978 and the creation of the subsequent People's Republic of Kampuchea, replacing 'Democratic Kampuchea'. Democratic Kampuchea – Cambodia under the Khmer Rouge – had done away with most state institutions, including the courts and legal system (replaced with 'People's Courts'), and most institutions of government but for a small, strict, top-down organisational structure. There was a 250-member Kampuchean People's Representative Assembly which, theoretically, appointed the executive branch, but the (brief and vague) constitution of that period was silent on significant organisational and institutional matters, which complemented its radical agrarian and theoretically egalitarian organisational model.

While in some sense a successor party to the Eastern Zone faction that had broken away from the Khmer Rouge, the party developed by Heng Samrin and inherited by Hun Sen was a creation of the Vietnamese Communist Party which had put it in power. The Vietnamese Communist Party was created in 1976 when the Workers' Party of North Vietnam was merged with the People's Revolutionary Party of South Vietnam as the Communist Party of Vietnam. The name change formalised the unified country as a one party state in which all institutions were loyal to the party. The political structure and party established by the Vietnamese followed a highly centralised state apparatus employing the techniques of Leninist top-down authority, Soviet-style institutional bureaucracy and, despite formally denying it, elements of Confucian ethics and order. This structure had a deep impact upon the creation of Cambodia as a post-Khmer Rouge state and left an indelible mark on the structure and psychology of the CPP.

The machinery of the Cambodian state, in which there was no effective distinction between the state, its institutions and the party, ensured that central control remained pervasive. Bureaucratic officials, who had as a class been largely wiped out by the Khmer Rouge, were rebuilt through local education and being sent for training to Soviet Bloc states. By the time Hun Sen assumed leadership of the party, in 1985, it had a well-established political structure that permeated the reconstructed institutions of what was a more conventional Soviet-era socialist state.

As a result of the Paris peace agreement, from 1993 the state was established as a constitutional monarchy, with the King as head of state but without exercising any executive authority. In October 2004, Cambodia's long-serving head of state, King Norodom Sihanouk, abdicated, appointing his son Norodom Sihamoni as his successor. Sihanouk had served through all but a brief period of Cambodia's post-colonial history variously as king, prince or prime minister. His tenure had seen Cambodia gain independence and become embroiled in the Indochina War, seen him ousted in a US-backed republican coup, endured the nightmare of the Khmer Rouge era, Vietnamese occupation and civil war, and, finally, witnessed transition to an open voting system in which the country's real ruler only accepted election results on his own terms.

Between Sihanouk's advancing years and declining health, and ultimate inability to influence real political power, he decided to stop. His son, Sihamoni, a former ballet dancer, ballet teacher and ambassador to UNESCO, has since been Cambodia's King and head of state. His older brother Ranariddh somewhat ineffectually led a political party, until he was ousted in an internal coup in 2006 (re-elected as leader in 2015); five of his other siblings had been killed by the Khmer Rouge. Sihamoni was therefore handed the throne by his father, rather than wait until he died and allow the seemingly permanent Prime Minister, Hun Sen, to choose the monarch or end the monarchy. Sihanouk died of a heart attack in 2012, just two weeks shy of his ninetieth birthday.

During the king's absence or incapacitation, the chairman of the National Assembly (which was then a unicameral parliament), acts as head of state. The National Assembly itself comprised 120 members elected from 21 provinces, with a Council of Ministers (cabinet) formed by the government. In a practical sense, the two-thirds of seats required to form government under the new Constitution meant that virtually all elected governments would be coalitions.

At a provincial level, where most Cambodians live, local governors preside over provincial governments. Provincial governors and chiefs of districts are appointed by the Prime Minister using a quota system. Chiefs of communes and village headmen are directly elected by their constituency.

Cambodia's judiciary, rebuilt from the *tabula rasa* left in 1978, remains susceptible to government influence. This has been most notable in the trials of former Khmer Rouge leaders Nuon Chea (Brother Number Two) and former Khmer Rouge President Khieu Samphan. The trials, conducted by the Trial Chamber of the Extraordinary Chambers in the Courts of Cambodia (ECCC), began in 2008 and took seven years to conclude (Cohen *et al.* 2015). Both were sentenced to life imprisonment for crimes against humanity. It was widely believed, however, that the delay in arresting the pair (and other Khmer Rouge leaders) and holding the trials meant that much evidence from the Khmer Rouge period would not come to light, in particular implicating members of the successor CPP government, notably (until 1977) Khmer Rouge Eastern Region Battalion Commander Hun Sen.

Cambodia's judicial system, formalised under the UN transitional arrangements, was based on three tiers: the regular court, the Appeals Court and a Supreme Court. Judges were to be appointed, promoted and dismissed by a Supreme Council of the Magistracy, consisting of a representative of the Minister of Justice, the President of the Supreme Court, the President of the Appeals Court, and three elected judges, each with a five-year mandate. The Council was chaired by the King, but was widely seen as politically compromised. A Constitutional Council was intended to interpret the Constitution and laws passed by the National Assembly and, after it was formed in July 1998, comprised nine members who have a nine-year mandate. Three of the members were to be appointed by the king, three by the National Assembly and three by the Supreme Council of the Magistracy.

Despite the theoretical separation of powers between the executive and the judiciary, 'instead of enshrining an independent judicial system, embodying the separation of powers, the Cambodian government of today has preferred to cement its control and codified the politicisation of judicial decision-making through its three judicial laws' (IBAHRI 2015b). The composition of the courts was also widely regarded within Cambodia as favourable to the CPP, while the courts also require Ministry of Justice and relevant departmental permission to prosecute civil servants, including members of the police force.

In 2014 the lack of separation of powers was codified with the passage of three new laws which enhanced the direct authority of the Minister of Justice over the judiciary:

> The scope of the Minister of Justice's power over the judiciary – including a vast amount of official influence over judicial budgets, resources, training, appointments, promotions, tenure and removal – is now legitimised by the three new laws and is inconsistent with international standards.
>
> (IBAHRI 2015a: 7)

As a result, 'Corrupt influence – political and financial – appears to be exerted at will over all judicial activities' (IBAHRI 2015a: 7).

A 'culture of impunity' has been, as a result, allowed to flourish in Cambodia, especially among government officials. For example, police and soldiers were implicated in a spate of kidnappings in 1999 and 2000, while Hun Sen's wife, Bun Rany, was alleged to have ordered the killing in 1999 of Hun Sen's lover, the dancer Piseth Pilika. Both Hun Sen and his wife rejected the allegations, and charges against Bun Rany were not laid.

The logic of this process is that, as the pyramid of power narrows towards the top, power is concentrated in the hands of an individual leader. In other Leninist systems this has given rise to the cult of personality, such as of Lenin, Stalin, Mao Zedong, Ho Chi Minh, Fidel Castro and various lesser political lights. This concentration of power, however, fits neatly into traditional Cambodian conceptions of power, which is concentrated at the 'exemplary centre' of the political mandala. In this sense, Hun Sen brought together the logic of the traditional with the modern, in both cases managing to largely sidestep popular accountability. The processes of democracy, for Hun Sen, remained superficial. By way of illustration, Hun Sen has consistently said that he will remain in power until such time as he decides to leave, most recently suggesting that this will be at the age of 74 (Radio Free Asia 2013), which would take his premiership to 2027.

Dissent within the party was initially muted by the Vietnamese Party's insistence that the CPP not divide, that party loyalty was more important than the niceties of decision-making by committee, and later by Hun Sen's personal military following. His personal bodyguard and officers loyal directly to him, and the troops they command, easily comprised the single most powerful force in the country, and most Cambodians recognised the efficacy if not the legitimacy of rule through the exercise of military power.

Since 1985, Hun Sen has been able to remain as Cambodia's Prime Minister (with the interregnum as 'second' Prime Minister). In achieving this, Hun Sen has used personal influence and patronage to maintain his support base intact and to manipulate and blind-side his political opponents. Hun Sen and the CPP have also used intimidation, coercion and violence to neutralise or remove serious challenges (Thayer 2015b). Yet to suggest that Hun Sen has relied solely on corruption and intimidation to maintain office would be incorrect. He is also remarkably popular with significant sections of the Cambodian population, especially in rural areas, where his style of communication and his patronage of local development projects has often been well received.

Development

Over three decades, Hun Sen's ability to use personal influence and patronage to keep his support base intact and to manipulate those opposed to his rule has been associated with a keen reading of Cambodia's political environment, and with the specific tactics he has brought to bear in managing both those under him as well as those opposed to his continuing tenure. That he has also been able to reach out to and communicate well with the rural poor has provided a genuine electoral support base. Without this it would be much more difficult for him to sustain any sense of legitimacy, even among his client network, and his highly personalised rule.

One of the ways in which Hun Sen has maintained power is through his control of the Cambodian military. Unlike most other countries where the Minister of Defence has line responsibility for the military, or where the head of state is the (nominal) supreme commander, in Cambodia the prime minister is, in effect, the military commander in chief. Cambodia's senior political leaders with military responsibilities are Hun Sen loyalists, and Hun Sen also protects himself with a praetorian guard, which is also used to quell political dissent (Meisburger 2014).

There is no doubt, though, that at base, when patronage and populist appeal have not been enough, Hun Sen has also been quite willing to use intimidation, coercion and violence to neutralise or remove threats to this rule, both before and notably during and after the events of 1997 (see Thayer 2015b). Hun Sen has managed to maintain a relatively high level of political stability – with the events of 1997 being a key exception – despite Cambodia's internal post-conflict fragility. He has, in this sense, weathered all challenges to his preeminent position.

One of the supposed trade-offs in developing countries has been, or has been argued to be, limited political openness for growth through political stability. In the period since 1997, Cambodia's economy has grown significantly, at 8 per cent between 2004 and 2012 and maintaining a rate of around 6 to 7 per cent since then (World Bank 2015a). The proportion of the population living in absolute poverty has dropped from more than half to around 20 per cent, with the biggest drop between 53 per cent in 2004 to just under 24 per cent in 2009 (World Bank 2014). There remain, however, significant pockets of poverty, particularly in the north and north-east, and a large and growing gap in wealth between the country's poorest and richest.

Importantly, too, Cambodia has meaningfully improved maternal health, early child care and primary education programs in rural areas. The maternal mortality ratio per 100,000 live births fell from 472 in 2005 to 170 in 2014, with the infant mortality rate dropping from 83 per 1,000 live births in 2005 to 35 per 1,000 in 2014. Primary school admission increased from 81 percent in 2001 to 95.3 percent in 2014 (World Bank 2015a). However, malnutrition remains a problem, with 32 percent of children under five years old being stunted, four out of five Cambodians not having access to piped water and almost two-thirds having poor sanitation (World Bank 2014).

Despite growing problems with unemployment, uncontrolled corruption and continuing political violence (although perhaps reflecting the persuasive powers of the latter two), in 2008 the CPP won 90 of the parliament's 123 seats, given it the two-thirds majority required under the constitution to pass legislation. In 2012, FUNCINPEC and the Sam Rainsy party joined to form the Cambodian National Rescue Party (CNRP). Despite what were said to be widespread electoral irregularities, in the 2013 elections the CPP won just 68 seats, with the CNRP winning 55 seats.

There were large protests against what was widely claimed to have been electoral fraud, leading to the boycotting of parliament by the opposition, large-scale demonstrations and yet more violence. In mid-2014, Hun Sen banned public protests (Fuller 2014a). In November 2015, the CPP further closed down Sam Rainsy's political options by issuing an arrest warrant for him on a 2013 defamation charge while he was overseas. This move was intended to make it difficult for Rainsy to return to Cambodia and, it was thought, could effectively end his political campaigning. 'By banning the two most prominent CNRP leaders – Sam Rainsy and Kem Sokha – from politics, Hun Sen has disabled the main political opposition, at least temporarily' (Bogais 2015).

A key issue in the 2013 elections was Cambodia's seemingly out-of-control corruption. Transparency International ranked Cambodia at 160 of 177 countries, saying it had little or no budget transparency and exercised very limited control over corruption (Transparency International 2013). While there was growing impatience with official corruption, reflected in the CPP's relatively poor showing, it was also the network of corruption that allowed Hun Sen to maintain his patronage networks and thus keep himself in power, raising questions about his longevity in office (Thayer 2014a). Hun Sen and the CPP won the 1998, 2003 and 2008 elections on the back of stability, continued minor improvements in livelihoods – Human Development Indicators increased by around 20 per cent between 1998 and 2013 (UNDP 2013a) – and populist skills. In 2013, however, Hun Sen and the CPP made the obvious error of blatantly rigging that year's election results. 'This action coupled with longstanding grievances over his semi-authoritarian style of rule produced a popular backlash' (Thayer 2015b).

Following the relative closeness of results in the 2013 elections, the question was whether, if Cambodia was to have independently monitored free and fair elections in 2018, the CPP could continue to hang on to power. There was real doubt about the results of the 2013 elections and, coupled with what appeared to be Hun Sen's alienation of Cambodia's younger voters, if the people of Cambodia were to have a genuinely free and fair vote and if its results were to be recognised, the CPP would, at least, be likely to face the prospect of losing its simple majority. However, genuinely free and fair elections for Cambodia, and the prospect of the CPP losing its majority, were very far from being certain, alienated youth notwithstanding.

Despite the political instability and change in much of the rest of the region, Hun Sen has managed to stay in power for over three decades. As Thayer (2015a) has noted, Hun Sen is above all else a shrewd political tactician who uses personal influence and patronage to maintain his support base and to manipulate and destabilise his now limited opposition. There is no doubt that Hun Sen and his CPP[5] have also used intimidation, coercion and force to remove threats to this rule. Finally, Hun Sen has also enjoyed a great deal of legitimate popular support from rural peasants, to many of whom he is seen as not only a great communicator but a legitimate leader (Thayer 2015a).

According to Thayer (2015b), the greatest failing of Cambodia under Hun Sen has been his destruction of the idea of a liberal democracy in Cambodia. While there was a brief promise of such status during the elections of 1993, Cambodia has not been a 'democracy' in any meaningful sense of the term, even if it has enjoyed elements of 'liberalism' in the day-to-day lives of its citizens. Notably, electoral manipulation (particularly in 2013), a poor human rights record, official impunity for the use of extrajudicial violence, restrictions on freedom of expression and other heavy-handed policies have all cast Cambodia as a state that tolerates freedoms to the extent that they do not impose upon the political status quo. Related to this has been the effective destruction of open and competitive multi-party politics.

Despite having his origins in a communist movement and subsequent communist government, Hun Sen's political outlook has been much more oriented towards political control rather than socialism as such. When faced with the collectivism of a more or less independent trade union movement and the singularity of his own authority, Hun Sen's default position was to ensure that workers were restricted in their right to unionise and to suspend unions that were regarded as too active.

To illustrate, Cambodia had become a popular site for garment manufacturing, with garment workers being paid a union rate of US$110 a month. This put garment workers above the artificially low poverty line of $1.25 per day, but still left many families struggling to make ends meet in the higher-cost cities where manufacturing was concentrated. Importantly, too, many garment workers were paid less than the basic union rate, with $80 per month being common. When garment workers began to push for a rise to $160 per month and others such as fuel station workers began to push for a pay rise from the basic rate of $100 to $177 per month, the Cambodian government responded violently. In January 2014, a large workers' rally was attacked by police and military, with five protesters being shot dead, hundreds injured and union leaders arrested. In September, eight major fashion labels that manufacture in Cambodia said they would increase garment workers' wages (letter to Keat Chon, Chamberlain *et al.* 2014). By mid-2015, however, Hun Sen's administration was preparing legislation to effectively stop further unionisation and public protests for higher wages.

Another critical issue in Cambodia's political life is its relations with its neighbours, with more nationalist political actors, in particular the opposition Cambodia National Rescue Party, seeking to gain support through taking a strong stand on disputed border areas with Vietnam. In order not to look weak on issues of national sovereignty, the CPP has also stepped up its rhetoric on this issue. However, increasingly risking direct confrontation with Vietnam, the CPP has sought to reduce pressure by threatening and jailing some more outspoken CNRP members (ISEAS 2015a).

'Although the final chapter in his long career has yet to be written, Hun Sen still exhibits the political tactician's skills to placate the opposition' (Thayer 2015b). Since 1985, Hun Sen has gone from being the world's youngest prime minster, at the age of 33, to becoming the world's longest-serving prime minister, with, including his period as 'second Prime Minister' more than three decades in office. He has created a state-based network of patronage centred on himself, his family and his supporters, who in turn have their own patronage networks which maintain a web of obligation and duty. As with other long-term political leaders who centre power on themselves, the period following Hun Sen's premiership may include political instability (Thayer 2015b). In a post-Hun Sen environment, Cambodia would either need to find a new, compelling and relatively charismatic, clever and adept political leader in the Hun Sen mould or, more likely, would descend into a period of political squabbles and grabs at power by groups not used to not having it, and perhaps not up to the task of maintaining it.

Hun Sen may try to pass on political power to one of his children, which is not unknown in authoritarian politics. Of his five living children, Hun Manet is a 1999 West Point Academy graduate and obtained his PhD in Economics at the University of Bristol. Since 2010, Manet has been a Major General in the Royal Cambodian Armed Forces (RCAF) and became Deputy Commander of the Prime Minister's Body Guard headquarters. Given that much of Hun Sen's authority relies on the RCAF, this position may evolve to being one of political power, particularly if there is any post-Hun Sen political showdown over the transfer of power.

Notably, following the 2013 elections when Sam Rainsy and Vice President of the CNRP Kem Sokha were arguing against the officially announced results, they said that some 70 percent of the armed forces, particularly in the lower ranks, and public service voted for the CNRP. While there was no way of knowing whether or not there was that level of dissatisfaction among voters whom the CPP would otherwise expect to form the core of its voting base, it is possible that attempts by the CNRP to infiltrate and/or win the sympathy of base-level soldiers and bureaucrats could be having some impact. Alternatively, as noted by Thayer (2015b), these claims could also have been mere posturing, and a claim by other means that support for the CPP was not as solid as the CPP had claimed as a consequence of its questionable election victory.

Should political matters again turn critical in Cambodia, continued support from rank-and-file soldiers in the RCAF would be essential to regime survival, especially if the government felt compelled to dispel public demonstrations through high levels of official violence. Similarly, in any period of political turmoil or dissent, not least in what could look like a transition into a post-Hun Sen era, an alternative military figure could potentially command the loyalty of the troops and thereby seize effective political control. Hun Manet's positioning as a rising star in the RCAF and at the heart of Hun Sen's praetorian guard is, then, an important tactic in continuing to secure political power if and when Hun Sen's personal authority declines or disappears.

Manet's older brother, Hun Neng, is a former governor of Kampong Cham and currently a member of parliament, and may also be well positioned to succeed his father. To do so, however, he would probably have to rely on support from Hun Manet to secure the army behind any eventual bid for power.

Conclusion

Political accountability and transparency remain a distant goal for many Cambodians, if they think about such subjects at all. But a pattern of elections has become established, the two-thirds requirement means that compromise has become a feature of Cambodian political life, and legislative programs can sometimes be seen to reflect a wider set of norms and values, as well as having an eye to greater international engagement. Meanwhile, that symbol of state only slightly less powerful than the magnificent site at Angkor, the monarchy, has made one of its most potentially difficult transitions in a manner that is remarkable for being unremarkable. Cambodia struggled into the twenty-first century carrying a burden of serious problems common to many under-developed states, and quite a few that were specifically its own.

Cambodia has survived its post-conflict transition relatively successfully, if largely due to the imposition of an authoritarian political model. Without a clear successor to Hun Sen, it is less clear how it will manage the transition to becoming a post-authoritarian state, when that situation eventually arrives.

Notes

1 Personal conversation, Cambodia, 1998.
2 Another view of these events was put by Australian ambassador to Cambodia, Tony Kevin (1999).

3 The author was with one of the early convoys to traverse Cambodia from Siem Reap to the Thai border in July 1998, where former Khmer Rouge soldiers still 'taxed' passing traffic at road blocks.

4 During the Khmer Rouge's internal purges in 1977, as an eastern battalion commander, Hun Sen fled to Vietnam, returning with Vietnamese forces in 1978 and beginning his political rise.

5 The CPP is formally not Hun Sen's, but so complete is his control of it that it has for many years functioned as his personal political vehicle.

6 Malaysia

Brief introduction to category: soft dominant party states

A common type of authoritarian state that allows elections but precludes political change is one dominated by a single party. 'Dominant party states' are usually a result of a conservative, elite-driven trend that opposes civil society activism, and of the effective marginalisation of the poor from the political struggle (see Jones 2014 re Myanmar's future). What is important is the institutionalisation of elite-driven politics. That this is, at least in part, a reflection of political economy is not in dispute. But, rather, there are a number of other factors at play, including the effective depoliticisation of many marginalised citizens, the resonance of both 'traditional' and 'charismatic' authority, and the use of politicised state institutions in support of the dominant party.

The phenomenon of a 'dominant party state' (Suttner 2006: 277–297; Wines 2004) has three potential problems. The first is that the dominant party can institutionalise itself in office (e.g. African National Congress in South Africa, Barisan Nasional in Malaysia, People's Action Party in Singapore, Cambodian People's Party in Cambodia); this reduces accountability and hence has the potential to promote corruption, and such an outcome can become especially problematic for transitions in contexts where there is then an alliance between the dominant party and an internally focused military.

Often the state is dominated by a military with considerable capacity for its own affairs, in particular logistics, but with a culture of giving and following orders, or where there is manipulation of law enforcement agencies and the judiciary. Further, rather than having a state bureaucracy based on merit, a dominant party state may appoint on the basis of party loyalty, military affiliation or patron–client relations.

Low institutional performance may therefore be acculturated through this institutional disincentive as well as the compounding effect of the law of diminishing returns, in which if all other factors are relatively constant then continuing to add one further factor will consistently reduce returns (Samuelson and Nordhaus 2001: 10).

Linked to dominant party state status, common to states emerging from authoritarianism and low levels of institutional and social capacity is the potential reliance on the leadership of a charismatic individual (see Benda 1960). A state with a low level of institutional capacity tends to concentrate authority in a single person whose decisions, moreover with a high level of charismatic legitimacy, brook few or no challenges. As noted by Weber, while charismatic authority can be legitimate, it usually needs to transform itself beyond a popular but vaguely articulated appeal into a more concrete political model (Weber 1964: 364). In low-capacity states, institutional capacity constraints could imply reversion to such a more autocratic political model.

A state with high institutional capacity provides alternative nodes of authority and thus diffuses the concentration of authority in a single person. However, states with low levels of institutional capacity tend to rely on charismatic individuals or assertive state institutions (such as the military or dominant party), often in combination. Further to the potential for future autocracy, while there can be a high level of public support for particular political candidates and a high level of political mobilisation around the period of elections, the period between elections can be one of disengagement from the political process. This may manifest in a political disconnect except when the country is in election mode. In this situation, active representation may be limited, governments may not be responsive to particular requirements or requests and their accountability may reduce. Each of these qualities, and most importantly that of accountability, can reduce in situations of effective one party representation, where there are no viable political alternatives or where the political space comes to be dominated by a single party to the effective exclusion of others.

Moreover, civil–military relations theory suggests that militaries tend to be less accountable to civilian governments when they continue to respond to perceived internal threats (Desch 1999), meaning even a nominally civilian-controlled military may act well beyond civilian orders. This has negative connotations for Valenzuela's (1990) concern over the nature of the state that arises from a transitional process that retains military involvement.

Introduction: Malaysia

Though dominated by a single political coalition since independence in 1963, through a system of gerrymandering, vote rigging and political buy-offs, Malaysia increasingly faces real democratic challenge as well as non-partisan dissent. Having been granted independence following the quelling of the 1950s communist 'Emergency', independent Malaysia was a relatively passive actor in the Cold War, with its political processes being overwhelmingly focused on balancing its internal ethnic mix and growing opposition to the country's dominant party (or coalition) status.

With a coalition between the three largest ethnic political parties, the country's opposition has been unable, to date, to organise sufficient votes within the context of manipulated parliamentary seats to directly confront the government. With only its opposition to the United Malay National Organisation-led National Front (Barisan Nasional, or BN) government to unite it, Malaysia's non-BN alternative remains vulnerable to fundamental internal divisions that would otherwise seem to preclude it from assuming power.

In theory a parliamentary democracy, Malaysia has been ruled by the BN coalition, dominated by the United Malay National Organisation (UMNO), since achieving independence in 1963. BN was comprised of three large parties; UMNO, the Malaysian Chinese Association and the Malaysian Indian Congress, and ten smaller parties at the time of writing. For 22 years until 2003, Malaysian politics was dominated by Mahatir Mohamad, whose centralisation and personalisation of authority continues to mark Malaysia's political processes, including exercising his personal authority within and from outside the BN since he left office.

The BN has maintained itself in office through its initial popularity and being a broadly representative coalition of the main parties representing Malaysia's three main ethnic groups, through gerrymandering (having pro-government electorates with fewer voters than opposition electorates) and through other forms of vote rigging. To illustrate the effect of gerrymandering on electoral outcomes, in the 2013 general elections, UNMO received 29.45 per cent of the vote, but achieved 88, or 39.64 per cent, of the seats, while the BN won 133, or 59.91 per cent, of the 222 seats with 47.38 per cent of the vote. The opposition Pakatan Rakyat (People's Alliance, or PR) won 50.87 per cent of the vote, but achieved just 89, or 40.09 per cent, of the seats (ECM 2013).

In a country in which the judiciary is also deeply compromised and there is no meaningful separation of powers, the judicial process has been used to damage opposition figures, the most outstanding example of which is the jailing in 1999 of former deputy UMNO leader, head of the People's Justice Party (Parti Keadilan Rakyat, or PKR) and opposition leader Anwar Ibrahim on patently false charges. As if to hammer home the point, Anwar Ibrahim was again jailed on the original charges in February 2015, after the decision to quash his conviction was overturned by Malaysia's Federal Court. Notably, Ibrahim is the only person to have been convicted of the 'offence' of 'sodomy' under Malaysian law. In a country in which the judiciary has been deeply compromised following the sacking and reappointment of judges starting in 1988, this decision was widely regarded both internally and internationally as a blatant political move to silence Ibrahim, an otherwise popular political figure.

Beyond Malaysia's deeply compromised political system, it also had in place the structural preferencing of Malaysia's ethnic Malay population under what was known as the New Economic Policy (NEP). The preferencing of ethnic Malays has led to rent-seeking behaviour, in which companies and individuals use their status or resources to obtain an economic benefit, usually from the state (although in Malaysia's case also from private companies), without an approximately similar reciprocal benefit to the state or company involved.

Such rent-seeking behaviour is common, to some extent, in most economies, but in the case of Malaysia it is legislated, in the areas of education, government employment and contract-letting, and in the representation of senior positions in private companies. This reward without equivalent effort has encouraged a culture of corruption, which reached publicly scandalous levels by 2015.

Shamsul (1999: 4–9) has noted that the introduction of the NEP in 1971 eventually led to a realignment of traditional Malaysian politics away from a focus on security (exemplified by the colonial-era Internal Security Act) to the 'ethnic bargain' (which retained Malays in power), and development planning which included an 'economic bargain' which complemented the 'ethnic bargain'. The shift was towards entrepreneurialism by Malay elites on one hand, and a divergent focus on social justice on the other. While there has been an economic shift, it has come, as noted, at the expense of reciprocity and with high levels of wealth accumulation by a new economic elite, as well as the aforementioned corruption.

However, corruption and rent-seeking, both for personal profit as well as to help to ensure political stability, had become deeply ingrained in the Malaysian political system since the introduction of a system that discriminated in favour of *bumiptera* ('sons of the soil/land' – ethnic Malays) in order to quell ethnic tensions. Originating in the NEP in the 1970s following deadly anti-Chinese race riots in the capital, Kuala Lumpur, in 1969, it allowed for minimum quotas of ethnic Malays in education, government agencies and business ownership, discounts on property purchases and other economic advantages.

While the NEP was successful in lifting many Malays out of poverty between the 1970s and late 1990s, with the percentage living in poverty dropping from half of all Malays to what was claimed to be 5 per cent, increasing commercial equity eightfold, and boosting household incomes (Funston 2001: 193–4), it also not only created, in many cases, a sense of entitlement without effort but also institutionalised forms of preferencing that amounted to corruption. To illustrate, Malaysia's water privatisation program did not improve capital investment or efficiency of service, but managed to increase the wealth of key Malay stakeholders. It was thus seen as an extension of political accommodation and stability at the price of economic efficiency or equity (Tan 2015). The NEP was increasingly criticised for increasing the wealth of particular, often UMNO-linked, Malays, with less impact on the equity of wealth distribution, and for creating a culture of government-backed inefficiency.

Law

According to Human Rights Watch, while Malaysia had done away with the colonial-era Internal Security Act, which allowed the government to jail almost anyone on the flimsiest of charges, it had strengthened the Sedition Act and other repressive instruments, so that critical public commentary and public demonstrations courted arrest and detention for up to three years and the imposition of heavy fines, in turn helping to create a 'culture of fear'. In 2015, Malaysia increased its suppression of freedom of speech by increasing arrests of journalists, activists and human rights lawyers on sedition charges, along with the closure of two newspapers that had reported on the Razak corruption scandal.

This followed the on-again, off-again jailing of former deputy Prime Minister and later opposition leader Anwar Ibrahim on charges which had been shown by at least one court, and were otherwise widely acknowledged, to have been manufactured to damage if not end his political career.

The subversion of Malaysian democratic politics had, arguably, been underway since just after independence, if not before. However, its subversion received a considerable boost in 1988 when the judiciary was brought closely under the control of the government, with the sacking of several senior judges and the appointment of more amenable judges. This move spelled an end to one of the most critical features of a democratic state, that being the separation of powers between the executive and the judiciary. (The separation of powers is not spelled out in the Malaysian constitution, but is a convention in parliamentary political systems.) Following this move, the judiciary became a political tool rather than a means of seeking or finding justice.

The declaration of UMNO as an illegal organisation was a major setback for Mahatir and showed that, while he was increasingly master of his environment, there remained some important elements of the state outside his control. As a consequence, there was a series of overtly political moves that caused perhaps even more concern, particularly in international terms, than the UMNO split. In 1988 Mahatir sacked the judge responsible for organising the hearing of an appeal of the Razaleigh-Musa challenge to Matahir's leadership, Lord President of the Supreme Court Tun Salleh Abas. The ostensible reason was 'gross misbehaviour', but the real reason appeared to be Abas' unwillingness to allow a backroom deal which favoured Mahatir to be done on the appeal. A further five Supreme Court judges who supported Abas in Mahatir's attack on him were also suspended.

In all, Mahatir's challenge to the courts seriously hobbled the independence of the judiciary and blurred the basic democratic tenet of separation of state and judicial power. It also brought both the party and the state more directly under Mahatir's personal control.

Domestic tensions

Tensions between the ethnic Malay and Chinese populations, which culminated in race riots in May 1969, contributed to modifying Malaysia's earlier more liberal orientation (Crouch 1996: 24–7). The following year, internal factional battles within the UMNO led to the downfall of Prime Minister Tunku Abdul Rahman, who was succeeded by the more 'nationalist' pro-Malay Tun Abdul Razak. Following the 1969 riots internal security laws were strengthened, and, to redress Malay grievances about economic disparities, the government introduced its New Economic Policy in 1971.

Among other provisions, NEP legislation was intended to break down the Chinese commerce/Malay farmer/labourer dichotomy by shifting a greater proportion of corporate wealth into Malay hands (Crouch, 1996: 24–5; 37–8; Goldsworthy 1991: 53). Until the mid-1980s, the Barisan Nasional coalition worked well. However, by 1986–87 there were tensions over the increasingly authoritarian style of both UMNO and the Prime Minister, Mahatir, as well as within the Malaysian Chinese Association (MCA). This was exacerbated by a downturn in Malaysia's economy, including higher unemployment and increased bankruptcies, following on from an international recession and a related rise in ethnic tensions.

Hussein bin Onn became prime minister in 1976 following the death of Tun Abdul Razak. Onn's prime ministership was noted for its relative moderation and consolidation following the turmoil of 1969. However, while Onn's leadership was regarded as moderate, he still had to preside over a difficult period, including internal UMNO scandals caused by the beginning of the Malay elites' push towards entrepreneurial activity (Shamsul 1999: 5). Onn's deputy prime minister was Mahatir Mohamad, who had previously been education minister and had presided over putting down the student protests of 1974 which were led by Anwar Ibrahim.

In early 1981 Prime Minister Onn was hospitalised, and he formally resigned on 16 July, with Mahatir being elected as UMNO party President and hence as Prime Minister. While the election of Mahatir was fairly straightforward, there was a bitter factional struggle for the deputy prime ministership. The subsequent 1984 poll was complicated by the arrival of the former Muslim youth leader, and perceived Islamic moderate, Anwar Ibrahim. Anwar had been detained for almost two years from 1974 under the colonial-era Internal Security Act (ISA) for organising student demonstrations. However, Mahatir soon came to recognise Anwar's political usefulness and set up the youth organisation which Anwar headed. In 1982 Mahatir asked Anwar to stand for election. Anwar was immediately appointed deputy minister in the Prime Minister's department and in 1983, after being elected to head UMNO Youth (and automatically becoming a vice-president of UMNO), was made Minister for Youth, Sports and Culture.

Upon becoming Prime Minister, Mahatir Mohamad pushed the entrepreneurial aspect of Malaysian development with a passion, allocating the task of social justice to his deputy. Shamsul suggests that this led to the development of a grassroots-based 'new politics', of which then Deputy Prime Minister Anwar Ibrahim was seen as the head. Such 'new politics' was suggested to include a range of non-communal, non-class-based social and environmental issues that had previously been left off the traditional or entrepreneurial agenda (Shamsul 1999: 9).

Anwar Ibrahim

Despite the 'ethnic bargain' papering over communal divisions, Malaysia as a society is in some respects politically polarised, between the three major ethnic groups and between government parties and opposition parties. Even UMNO's internal politics have, from time to time, been heated. But arguably the signature moment of Malaysian politics was when Prime Minister Mahatir Mohamad and his formerly close deputy and finance minister Anwar Ibrahim fell out over Ibrahim's expressions of concern regarding excessive corruption and nepotism within UMNO.

As the Asian financial crisis of 1997 unfolded, Mahatir made comments about conspiracies by the international financial community generally and by a particular money trader to wreck the Malaysian economy. These comments were viewed negatively both within Malaysia and, especially, internationally. Mahatir then imposed controls on the repatriation of profits from Malaysia and the exchange of the Malaysian ringgit which, in the shorter term, further alarmed the international financial community, even if in the medium term Malaysia's economy stabilised. According to some reports at the time, by the time Mahatir had imposed controls on the repatriation of profits, most money that was going to leave Malaysia had already been taken out. Mahatir, entrenched in the inward-looking, protectionist and rent-seeking system, and Ibrahim, who favoured greater liberalisation, disagreed publicly about policy direction. In particular they argued over what Anwar identified as cronyism, nepotism and corruption (Jomo 2003: 721). The disagreements ranged through Cabinet as well as in public, setting the two men on a collision course (Skehan 1998; see also Fan 1999; Jomo 2003: ch. 28).

While Mahatir was overseas, during the 1997 Asian financial crisis, Ibrahim unilaterally changed some of Mahatir's policies, including around protectionism, and instituted an 18 per cent cut in government spending. Relations between the two men became bitter, and during the 1998 UMNO general assembly, a booklet was circulated entitled *50 Dalil Kenapa Anwar Tidak Boleh Jadi PM* (50 Reasons Why Anwar Cannot Become PM), which made numerous allegations against Ibrahim, including of corruption and homosexuality. Mahatir sacked Ibrahim from the deputy and finance portfolios on 2 September 1998.

The author of the booklet, Khalid Jafri, a former editor of a government-controlled newspaper, was charged with malicious publishing of false news. Ibrahim took out an injunction against distribution of the booklet. However, police were then instructed to follow up on the veracity of the allegations, with Ibrahim later being charged with corruption and interference in a police investigation. He was later charged with and convicted of homosexuality.

While an undercurrent of increasing authoritarianism has prevailed under Mahatir, the sacking and jailing of Ibrahim offered a stark reminder of how quickly benign authoritarianism was able to turn malignant. The sacking just a few days later immediately led to an upsurge in public support for Anwar, with demonstrations calling for Mahatir to resign. Following the 'pro-democracy' protests in Indonesia, protesters began calling for *reformasi* (reform) (Skehan 1998). Mahatir changed his successor to new Deputy Prime Minister Abdullah Badawi, who succeeded to the prime ministership in 2003.

Mahatir's 22 years as Prime Minister thus ended as he had characterised them: combative, insular and combining his authoritarian tendencies with fantasist delusions. Yet this period had also seen Malaysia's economy become one of Asia's 'tiger cubs'; i.e. a newly industrialising economy. His grand '2020' vision for Malaysia was manifested in 1996 in the then world's tallest building, Kuala Lumpur's Petronas Towers, and in the 'Technology Corridor' centred on the small new city of Cyberjaya.

However, 20 years of subsidisation for a loss-making national car, the Proton (see Jomo 2003: ch. 11), losses on the national steel company Perwaja, and a range of other losses on ventures that attempted to copy the Japanese/Korean model of internally self-supporting conglomerates, also marked Mahatir's rule (see Jomo 2003: ch. 20). In one sense, Malaysia appeared to prosper almost despite some of Mahatir's economic policies. And his support for ethnic Malays acquiring businesses and the privatisation of government industries did not meaningfully shift the economy towards non-Chinese ownership or control. What it did, however, was engender a sense of nepotism and corruption that became the prime focus of Mahatir's immediate successor, Abdullah Badawi, and which entangled the subsequent political successor, Najib Razak.

Badawi was a relatively popular prime minister and made some moves towards addressing Malaysia's growing concerns with high levels of corruption. However, he inherited the leadership at a time when public discontent, overwhelmingly inherited from Mahatir, was growing faster than he could placate it. After just six years in office, which was a short term based on Mahatir's precedent, a worse than expected showing by the BN government in the 2009 elections, in which it lost its two-thirds majority, led him to resign. He was replaced by Najib Razak, who appeared to have less of a concern for addressing issues of corruption.

The media

The government's high degree of direct and indirect control over the media also assists its ability to paint itself in a favourable light and the opposition poorly. UMNO controlled the country's largest newspaper groups and commercial television stations through its wholly owned Media Prima Berhad. The group has equity interests in TV3, 8TV, ntv7 and TV9, as well as almost total ownership of New Straits Times Press (Malaysia) Berhad (NSTP), Malaysia's largest publisher with three national newspapers, the *New Straits Times*, *Berita Harian* and *Harian Metro*, along with three radio stations (see Hamin and Mangsor 2013).

Beyond 'legacy' media, Media Prima also has a significant online presence, although this is challenged by independent online news outlets such as Malaysia Kini. The BN government also exercises direct influence over the two state-owned television stations and 34 radio stations (see Kenyon and Marjoribanks 2007).

Other means of control over the media has taken place through criminal charges being laid over the 'malicious' publication of 'false news'. Under such an offence, the publisher, printer, editor and author (journalist) are all liable, as in a defamation case. There remains extensive censorship in media, with numerous foreign media outlets or programs and publications being banned. Printing presses must be licensed in Malaysia, and licences can be withdrawn at any time. Journalists regularly receive calls from the Prime Minister's Office regarding their reporting of 'sensitive' issues (Frater 2015; BBC 2015a).

One of the issues that the government and the media gained much exposure from was the issue of *hudud*, or what were claimed to be Islamic forms of punishment for breaching *syariah* (Islamic law). While UMNO was formally in favour of *hudud*, it had not adopted it in deference to its BN alliance with the Malaysian Chinese Association and (predominantly Hindu) Malaysian Indian Congress (MIC). However, the opposition Islamic Mandate Party (Parti Amanat se-Islam, or PAS) was publicly in favour of introducing *hudud*, which acted as one of the barriers to opposition unity.

The issues of *hudud*, and whether to make Malaysia an Islamic state, have waxed and waned since PAS won the Kelantan state legislature in 1990. A more accommodative approach to Malaysian politics ended when PAS President Fadzil Noor died in June 2002.

Noor had been critical to the issues of the development of *hudud*, and to PAS's taking the lead of the Anagkatan Perpaduan Ummah (APU, or People's Unity Front) and later the BA coalition.

PAS was a member of a multi-ethnic, multi-religious coalition, Pakatan Rakyat (People's Pact/Alliance), including the Parti Keadilan Rakayt (People's Justice Party) of Anwar Ibrahim and the Chinese-dominated Democratic Action Party (DAP). Within Pakatan, and among its supporters, there remain fears that should PAS achieve political power it would attempt to implement what others might perceive as Draconian laws under the provisions of *hudud*. PAS leader Nik Aziz acknowledged that DAP was opposed to *hudud* and wanted PAS to reject it, saying that was the main difference between the parties (Tarmizi 2014, writing in *Harakah*[1]). There was, however, no intention to introduce *hudud* legislation into the Malaysian parliament, although in-principle legislation was intended to be introduced into the state parliament of Kelantan, which has a PAS-dominated Pakatan Rakyat majority (Ahmad 2014). The spectre of *hudud* law in Malaysia in the past caused non-Muslim voters to desert the PAS and any party associated with it. 'Under *hudud*, a convicted thief's limb could be amputated and adulterers stoned, for example' (Ahmad 2014). There is, however, no mechanism for enabling *hudud* at the state level, given that the police and courts are national rather than state bodies.

Corruption

As noted above, Malaysia's culture of rent-seeking spurred on by the NEP assisted the development of a culture of nepotism and corruption which has come to mark much of the government's dealings, contract-letting and preferential treatment of particular private businesses. Such corruption was openly discussed by Anwar Ibrahim, which led to his sacking, and was openly addressed by Mahatir's successor Badawi. But the issue came to a head in 2015 with the '1MDB' scandal which directly implicated Prime Minister Najib Razak in the 're-allocation' of more than US$1 billion into personally controlled bank accounts. As this scandal broke, UMNO fell upon itself, with factions aligning around more or less pro- and anti-corruption factions.

While UMNO had not been immune to divisions, allegations of corruption and other scandals, it had never been so internally divided as over the corruption scandal that faced Prime Minister Razak in 2015 and into 2016. Razak was alleged by the *Wall Street Journal* to have had, in personal bank accounts or accounts he controlled, some $700 million that had been siphoned off from the state investment and development agency, 1 Malaysian Development Berhad (1MDB). That figure was later revised to over $1 billion (Hope and Wright 2016).

As members of UMNO began to question Razak, he hit back, sacking four ministers, including the Deputy Prime Minister Muhyiddin Yassin. Yassin had openly disapproved of Razak's handling of the allegations. UMNO Deputy President Shafie Apdal was also removed from his position for questioning Razak's alleged involvement in the affair. Public institutions which began to investigate the issue were also compromised, with the government sabotaging their investigations by removing, reassigning and harassing key officials in those institutions (Monitor 2015: 8). Among those sacked was the attorney-general, Abdul Gani Patail, in July 2015 for attempting to investigate the claims. Bank Negara Malaysia was also blocked by the newly appointed attorney-general, Mohamad Apandi Ali, from investigating the issue.

Razak also sacked Patail for being part of a task force involving the attorney-general's office, the Malaysian Central Bank, the Malaysian Anti-Corruption Commission (MACC) and the Royal Malaysian Police, which was believed to have been preparing corruption charges against Razak. Several other senior officers involved in the investigation were also investigated by the police and transferred (Lopez 2015). The blogs Sarawak Report, The Edge Financial Daily and The Edge Weekly were also closed down for extensively reporting the issue, although the latter two managed to re-open.

While the allegations of corruption were not proven at the time of writing, the affair appeared to indicate a clear split among Malaysia's ruling classes. Razak's response was to try to invoke Islamic and feudal Malay notions of loyalty, which tended to leave most party members unimpressed (Saat 2015). The event also signals a new low in Razak's personal popularity, with just 23 per cent of peninsula Malaysians supporting the Prime Minister (Malaysiakini 2015). However, while deep cleavages emerged over this issue, Razak appears to retain majority support among UMNO/Barisan Nasional parliamentarians and is likely to pick up support from PAS after its own internal split.

In February 2016, Najib Razak's hand-picked replacement attorney-general, Mohamed Apandi Ali, cleared the Prime Minister of any wrong-doing and instructed the MACC to close its investigation. Ali said that a 'personal donation' of $680 million had been returned to the previously unidentified Saudi royal family, which was named as its donor. 'The evidence as a whole does not disclose any conflict of interest or corrupt practices on the part of the prime minister,' Ali said (Abas and Aziz 2016).

One of the immediate consequences of this corruption scandal, apart from damaging Razak's personal credibility, was that it weakened already fragile confidence in the Malaysian economy. The Malaysian stock market dropped by 9 per cent in response to the crisis and falling commodity prices, while the Malaysian currency, the ringgit, fell, by 20 per cent against the US dollar (BBC 2015b). The Malaysian government responded by pump-priming the economy, spending US$4.6 billion in the stock market and cutting taxes. However, for the 2016 budget, the government increased higher-income taxes and the goods and services tax.

One area of Malaysia's economy that was not seriously addressed, however, and probably could not be in the face of declining value of resource exports, was government debt, which stood stubbornly high at just under 53 per cent of GDP in 2015, having remained at around or above this level since the impact of the global financial crisis hit in 2009, and having been above 40 per cent of GDP in the years before that. This high debt ratio was a legacy of high levels of government spending on subsidies for poorer Malaysians, but also reflected relatively high levels of investment in areas of the Malaysian economy which had subsequently underperformed (Trading Economics 2015).

The corruption allegations against Razak appeared to concern his perceived need to build up a 'war chest' in order to fight elections in which BN's political supremacy could be challenged. According to Transparency International, Malaysia is 'highly vulnerable' to various forms of government-related corruption (Transparency International 2015a). In 2014, before the Razak corruption scandal, Malaysia was rated at 52 of 175 countries (Transparency International 2013).

Political Islamism

Malaysia's explicitly Islamist political party, Parti Amanat se-Islam (PAS, Islamic Mandate Party) has long been caught in a contest between its avowed purpose of promoting the idea of Malaysia as an Islamic state and debates about how such a policy would manifest in practice, and its desire for political success and associated alliance with non-Islamic political parties. In part, this competition reflects a fundamental division within the party between its more conservative, rural-based constituents in 'heartland' areas such as Kelantan, and more progressive or accommodative and predominantly urban members and their leadership. This division, at base over whether Malaysia should become an Islamic state and, if so, how that would manifest, including its impact upon Malaysia's large minority of non-Muslims, has tested not just the party but also its opposition coalition with non-Muslim parties.[2]

Malaysia's Opposition Pakatan Rakyat, formed in 2008, finally collapsed in August 2015 under the weight of contradictions between PAS's commitment to an Islamic state and its coalition commitment to a plural, democratic Malaysia. This followed general disquiet over possible interpretations of an Islamic state in practice, which was exploited by Malaysia's BN government, exacerbating tensions within the opposition coalition and alienating more moderate potential voters. The division between PAS, the Chinese-dominated DAP and the PKR seemed entrenched.

In spite of Razak's fragile leadership and fall in public standing, 'PR's collapse has resuscitated, and perhaps even bolstered, the UMNO-led Barisan Nasional's foothold in Malaysian politics, its own internal politicking notwithstanding' (Izzuddin 2015).

Among those most likely to split from the PR coalition were the upper echelons of PAS, following the removal of moderates from the party in 2015 in response to discontent over the party's increasingly hardline position, which had led to a fall in PAS votes by 2 per cent in 2013. Thousands of more moderate and progressive PAS members split from the party in 2015 to form the National Trust Party (Parti Amanah Negara, or PAN), which was previously the leftist National Workers' Party. The remnant of PAS changed its name to Parti Islam se-Malaysia, being redefined as an Islamist party when it handed over majority control to the break-away PAN.

PAN was more likely to find an accommodation with PKR (down 1 per cent in 2013) and DAP (up 10 per cent in 2013), but its split caused a backlash from PAS. With more conservative leaders of UMNO sharing often similar, although not identical, world views, such a realignment looked quite possible. If it occurred, however, the remnant PAS would be effectively swallowed up by BN and cease to have a meaningful existence in its own right, apart from in those few geographic areas where its more dominant members held regional sway.

Bersih

In response to Malaysia's elite corruption and closed politics, and the inability of the opposition to present a coherent alternative to the BN government, in late 2006 a number of non-government and civil society organisations banded together to form a coalition demanding fundamental reform of Malaysia's political and economic system. This grouping, known as the Coalition for Clean and Fair Elections (Gabungan Pilihanraya Bersih dan Adil, commonly referred to as 'Bersih'/'Clean') has since grown to include 84 constituent organisations and to become a significant force outside, but influential on, the mainstream of Malaysian politics.

In particular, Bersih has campaigned on a platform of calling for genuinely free and fair elections, including an end to Malaysia's notorious gerrymandering system and other forms of electoral corruption. Bersih held its first rally, in Kuala Lumpur, in 2007 and was credited with having been partially responsible for the fall in the BN's vote in the 2008 elections.

Having been identified as associated with or supporting particular opposition political parties, Bersih relaunched itself in 2010, now solely based on civil society groups. In particular, Bersih broke its direct links with PKR and PAS.

Following subsequent rallies at which government officers used water cannon and tear gas, and the establishment of an international support network, in 2011 the BN government establish a Parliamentary Select Committee to look into Bersih's demands, including, among others, reforming the electoral roll and postal ballot system, the use of indelible ink (to mark a voter's finger) so that voters could only vote once, a minimum 21-day campaign period, access to mass media for all parties and an end to corruption.

The committee handed down a report which contained recommendations that were passed by the Dewan Rakyat (House of Representatives). However, a more critical minority report was rejected by the House Speaker (Mokhtar 2012). Notably, a number of critical issues, including addressing electoral fraud and long timelines for proposed changes, were found wanting by Bersih, which staged a further demonstration in April 2012. Bersih called for the resignation of the existing Electoral Commission members and the introduction of international election observers, along with its previous demands. Subsequent demonstrations, including in August 2015 calling for the resignation of Prime Minister Najib Razak, were again met by police use of water cannon and tear gas (see *New Straits Times* 2015).

Conclusion

Malaysia's rigid political system had, into the twenty-first century, shown itself to be sclerotic, dysfunctional and brittle. In order to balance tensions between the country's ethnic groups, they were at once bound by a coalition in government and, less successfully, in opposition, but within a model that preferenced ethnic Malays. As a positive discrimination measure this worked moderately well, but it did encourage, among other things, a relatively high degree of rent-seeking behaviour and ultimately the acceptance of increasing levels of both financial and political corruption.

The scandal involving Prime Minister Razak is but the latest and most high-profile of many corruption allegations that have been levelled over many years. Former Prime Minister Mahatir Mohamad had become deeply critical of Razak's alleged behaviour, resigning from UMNO in protest. UMNO was divided in its loyalty, although not sufficiently so to force a change of leadership, allowing time for Razak to shore up his political position by whatever means necessary. That this meant the government using repressive measures was not surprising, but what it did do was establish a precedent for such alleged levels of political behaviour to be accepted as being within the arsenal of tools available to future BN leaders.

With the government being deeply entrenched in the rent-seeking system and related corruption, it sought by a range of repressive means to retain its political authority. It has retained its electoral majority, but not without high levels of electoral fraud, vote rigging and gerrymandering of electoral boundaries. In a free and fair election process, it is quite possible that the ruling BN would be challenged for its majority control of parliament.

The problem, however, is that even if the BN could have its absolute majority challenged in a free and fair political process – of which there is little likelihood in the foreseeable future – the opposition remains at best loosely aligned and often incoherent. There remain fundamental differences of outlook between Malaysia's Chinese and Malay communities, manifested in the fall-out with the DAP and PAS. The split within PAS did offer some hope of a more moderate PAN re-joining with the DAP and PKR in a more cohesive coalition, if with the ethnic Malay community further divided in its political loyalties and a division opening up between urban and rural Malays.

Malaysia's standing as a middle-income country does not appear to be fundamentally threatened by either corruption or political repression, even if both do hold back some of the country's economic potential. Moreover, while it is likely that the opposition might again cohere and organisations such as Bersih continue to highlight the BN government's short-comings, there is no sign of imminent political change.

Notes

1 *Harakah* is the official newspaper of PAS.
2 Based on discussions with senior PAS leaders in Kuala Lumpur in 2014.

7 Singapore

Singapore is a highly successful dominant party state in which the façade of elections is legitimised by relatively high levels of average and median income. Despite having a low corruption index perception rating (7, according to TPI, on a scale of 175) (Transparency International 2015b), Singapore's oligarchy benefits financially from its functional one party status, while there is little separation between the party and the state or the executive and the judiciary. The state and its dominant party, the People's Action Party (PAP), employ a compromised judiciary to hobble the viability of likely political opposition. Singapore has also developed a sense of dynastic politics, as manifested in the political leadership of Lee Hsien Loong, who was groomed to eventually succeed his father, former Prime Minister Lee Kuan Yew.

Singapore's political consistency has continued regardless of changes going on around it, marking it as one of the most politically stable – if politically limited – countries in the world. The only change that can be discerned in its political orientation is away from its non-aligned and socialist-oriented status in its first years towards a closer strategic relationship with the United States, including the training of Singaporean military personnel and the supply of arms, and an open capitalist economy, if led in many instances by state-owned industries.

Singapore has been a remarkable success story, having been expelled from Malaysia in 1965 following a series of heated ideological arguments. It went on, from that low political and economic point, to elevate itself from the ranks of developing country status to among one of the world's more prosperous and stable, if tightly controlled, societies. In part, this success can be attributed to a high level of consistent economic planning, made available as a consequence of the continuity of its political leadership. In significant part, too, Singapore's success can be attributed to its 'developmental state' approach to economic planning, where the state is an active economic actor and in which the government has directed the orientation of economic growth (Pereira 2008).

Singapore has also benefitted from having a population that has traditionally placed a high value on education, hard work and personal enterprise. That this population has been relatively small, largely cohesive and geographically compact has assisted Singapore in taking advantage of its early nineteenth century origins as an entrepôt city, located at the key intersection of one of the world's two major shipping routes, between Europe and the Middle East and East Asia.

Finally, as an industrialising and financial centre, Singapore was well placed to take advantage of the 'spill-over' effect of the rise of the Japanese economy, following the 'flying geese' model of dynamic comparative advantage (Akamatsu 1962; Kasahara 2004). As post-war Japan quickly transitioned through levels of technological development, it shed or shifted off-shore industries it sought to replace, as well as increasingly engaging in regional trade, benefitting from the comparative economic advantages of its regional neighbours. The rise of the 'Four Tigers' – Singapore, Hong Kong, Taiwan and South Korea – can be in significant part understood as a product of this 'flying geese' phenomenon. With its own entrepreneurial advantages, and having been established as a port and trading city, like others in the region before it (e.g. Melaka), Singapore has enjoyed the economic benefits of the confluence of these important contributing factors.

Political organisation

As a compact city state, Singapore has been dominated, since 1959, by the People's Action Party. The PAP was led, from independence, by the bright, charismatic and determined Lee Kuan Yew, for three decades (1959–90) initially under self-administration, then in merger with Malaysia (1963) and finally as an independent state (1965).

The incorporation of Singapore into Malaysia in 1963 had been opposed by both Indonesia and the Philippines, as well as by Singapore's own Socialist Front (Barisan Socialis, or BS). Lee campaigned, in part, on a platform that said that 'a vote for the Barisan is a vote for Sukarno'[1] (Lee 1998: 53). However, after the elections there were serious tensions in the relationship between Singapore and the rest of Malaysia. Lee insisted on using the title 'Prime Minister', which irked non-Singaporean Malaysians whose Prime Minister, Tunku Abdul Rahman, resided in Kuala Lumpur.

Lee further led aspirations on the part of the PAP to achieve government in Kuala Lumpur. This was the beginning of what became Malaysia's primary opposition party, the Singapore-linked Democratic Action Party (DAP). The Malaysian Chinese Association, a party in the Malaysian government's Alliance with the United Malay National Organisation (UMNO), had earlier sent organisers to Singapore to oppose Lee, which also created tension. There were further ideological differences, with concern over what Lee acknowledged as Singapore's pursuit of perceived socialist-oriented policies (Lee 1998: 51). There was also real concern over Lee's refusal to allow Singapore to become financially or politically subservient to Kuala Lumpur.

Most importantly, however, in the tensions between Singapore and the rest of Malaysia, there was a long-standing fear among ethnic Malays that the inclusion of Singapore into the Federation would help to establish an ethnic Chinese majority in Malaysia. It could not, as only 42 per cent of Malaysians at that time were ethnic Chinese. But with ethnic Indians the balance would have been enough to tip the ethnic scales away from Malay domination. Conversely, Lee Kuan Yew claimed that rather than aim to establish a multiracial society, the dominant Malaysian party, UMNO, was intent on establishing a politically Malay-dominated society. After the Malaysian general election of 1964 resulted in the defeat of PAP candidates on the Malay Peninsula, the five ministerial members of parliament representing Singapore were moved to the opposition benches 'to join seven others already there' (Lee 1998: 54).

In July 1964, events began to come to a head, with Chinese–Malay riots in Singapore. Over the course of three days, at least 23 people were killed, with a further 454 injured. Lee later blamed UMNO for being behind the riots to gather Malay support in Singapore and to consolidate support for UMNO on the Peninsula. There were further clashes in August. In December, Malaysian Prime Minister Tunku Abdul Rahman told Lee that the constitutional arrangement which included Singapore in the Federation should be changed. Trade was to be independent but defence would remain Kuala Lumpur's responsibility, to which Singapore would contribute. Lee countered with the idea that the Malaysian and Singaporean governments should operate independently within their respective spheres of influence. 'Not surprisingly, we made no progress with the "rearrangements" . . . What was suitable for Singapore was not suitable for Malaysia and vice versa. Merger had been a mistake' (Lee 1998: 56–7). After ordering financial arrangements for its central bank, on 9 August 1965 Lee Kuan Yew announced in an emotional speech that Singapore had separated itself from Malaysia. At the same time, a similar, and irrevocable, announcement was made in Kuala Lumpur.

One factor that assisted the consolidation of power by the PAP was the 'siege mentality' engendered by the government by way of supporting Singapore's economic development, and, to some extent, by its changed security environment following the withdrawal of British forces in 1971.

Singapore's political limitations

As early as 1960, Lee Kuan Yew had indicated that he did not think that democracy, in the conventional sense of 'one person, one vote', was suitable for developing countries, within which he included Singapore. He said that he believed for a government to at least give the impression it was effective it must be seen as enduring. In this sense, an effective government, according to Lee, could not be subject to the vagaries of the electoral process:

> If I were in authority in Singapore indefinitely without having to ask those who are governed whether they like what is being done, then I have not the slightest doubt that I could govern much more effectively in their interests.
>
> (Quoted in Josey 1970: 8–10)

These words, uttered in a radio interview in 1960, turned out to be prophetic.

From 1965, the PAP increased its use of the intelligence apparatus to watch the opposition. The following year, when Chia Thye Poh was elected as a candidate for the Barisan Socialis, he accused the ruling PAP of harassing BS leaders. In response, Chia was arrested and jailed under the Internal Security Act until 1989. Even then, he was held under house arrest on Sentosa Island for a further two years and was thereafter banned from writing or publishing, travelling overseas without government permission, or belonging to any organisation (Chee 1998: 241–7). Following the arrest and detention of Chia, the BS withdrew from the parliamentary process, citing the impossibility of participating in the political environment while the PAP exercised regressive measures against duly elected members.

The by-elections of 1967, caused by BS resignations from the Assembly, gave the PAP 49 of the 51 available seats. In 1968 all 51 PAP candidates were returned unopposed. Singapore had started with 13 political parties contesting the 1959 elections, and by 1970 a dozen parties were still registered, although only one, the PAP, was viable. From then on the PAP overwhelmingly dominated the political landscape.

Singapore's unicameral parliamentary democracy has a maximum life of five years, although elections have generally been held more frequently, helping to maintain the façade of democracy. A largely ceremonial president heads the state, while real power resides in the hands of the majority party of parliament. The PAP has always held the majority of seats, from 1968 to 1981 holding all seats.

While it is open to debate whether the PAP under Lee governed 'in the interests' of all Singaporeans, it is true that Singapore did achieve remarkable economic development under his rule. The primary policy used to achieve this was a high level of government investment in and support for private industry, based on a high level of (enforced) savings (Low and Quan 1992: 15–27). It is also true that, in practice, Lee and the PAP did not have to ask Singapore's people whether they liked what was being done. When some announced that they did not, in fact, like what was being done, they tended to be persecuted by the state through a variety of non-democratic means.

> With control of various organs of government in the hands of the dominant party or family, individuals participating in opposition politics are vulnerable to various methods that undermine their pursuit of public office. These include public vilification, lack of recourse to action against attacks, defamation suits against critics of government members, contempt of court charges for criticism of the legal process, vigorous tax audits and police surveillance, among many others.
>
> (Lingle 1996: 22)

From the 1980s onwards, Lee promoted the idea of Chinese culture and 'Chinese values' as being at the centre of Singapore's national identity, as well as introducing institutional advantages for ethnic Chinese Singaporeans in education, the civil service and the military. Having started with a more integrated ethnic orientation, Lee went on to separately identify specific ethnic groups through the creation of race-based self-help groups, ethnic quotas in access to public housing and other measures (Barr 2015a). Lee also went on to develop his views on autocratic government, citing what he called 'Chinese values' and then the more plural 'Asian values'. He interspersed this term with the more ethnically specific term 'Confucian values', which he regarded as more culturally authentic and more closely fitting with Singapore's predominantly ethnic Chinese population.

Within this idea, Lee identified loyalty to and the dominance of the group, respect for authority and a paternalistic decision making process. Lee's understanding of Confucianism reflected the reinterpretation of Confucius under the Sung Dynasty, which wished to re-impose authoritarian rule in China. In so far as Lee was criticised for this position, he defended himself and his political style by denigrating the circumstances and values of Western states, for example highlighting Australia's relative declining status or the US' crime rate, sometimes to the point of caricature.

In 1990, Lee handed the prime ministership to Goh Chock Tong, but retained the number two position under the title of Senior Minister Without Portfolio and, as chairman of the PAP, was seen to still control events in Singapore. Goh was regarded as a capable administrator, but was in reality just filling in while Lee's son, Lee Hsien Loong, was being groomed for the prime ministership. According to Barr (2014), with Lee Kuan Yew as Senior Minister and Lee Hsien Loong as Deputy Prime Minister they were able to outmanoeuvre and defeat Goh within Cabinet in 1996. Goh managed to carry on as a figurehead Prime Minister until 2004.

Lee Junior has proven to be a relatively competent administrator. His career path was an unusually smooth one. In 1971 he was awarded the highly prestigious President's Scholarship and, upon completion of his degree (Cambridge, Honours First Class, Mathematics and a Diploma in Computer Science) and entering the army, the similarly prestigious Singapore Armed Forces Overseas Scholarship, with which he earned an MA in Public Administration at Harvard University. Lee was quickly promoted to the rank of Brigadier-General, before entering politics in 1984, aged 32, where he was quickly appointed by his father as Minister of Trade and Industry and Defence.

Upon Lee Senior's retirement in 1990, Lee Junior was appointed as Deputy Prime Minister, but in 1992 fell ill with lymphoma, which was successfully treated, allowing him to return to public life. Upon remission from his illness, Lee assumed more political responsibility and again was again seen to be on the path to eventual prime ministership, which he assumed in 2004.

When Lee Kuan Yew died, in March 2013, there was some nervousness that the person who had been at the helm of Singapore's growth from a third world outpost to a first world economic power was no longer there. The reality, however, was that, despite his central role as a political strategist and the fact that he did have a strong vision for Singapore, no state-building project is the work of one person and Singapore had a plethora of talented economic architects. More importantly, Lee had long previously handed over the reins of power, stepping back slowly through the roles of Senior Minister and Minister Mentor, formally retiring in 2011.

Maintenance of power

Methods of maintaining PAP political control have been various, but three key points stand out as gross breaches of conventional democratic parliamentary behaviour. The first was the gerrymandering of electoral boundaries. In this process, electoral boundaries of unsafe or challenged seats are reconfigured to isolate polling booths that return a strong anti-government vote. The effect of this was to incorporate those anti-government areas into more strongly pro-government electorates, hence diluting the anti-government ratio of the vote, or fragmenting the growth of anti-government sentiment within a particular area.

The second key method for the government to maintain political control through the electoral process has been to change the electoral rules just prior to elections, and sometimes after election campaigns had already commenced. For example, Singapore began as a one-person per-seat parliamentary system, but later introduced Group Representational Constituencies, a multi-person per-seat system in which the successful team takes all seats. This system required a particular ethnic mix of candidates for certain seats, the ostensible intention being to guarantee proportional ethnic representation in the parliament. However, the short notice with which this requirement was introduced and the organisational difficulties associated with standing a predetermined number of ethnically specific people in a particular seat, presented major hurdles for opposition candidates to overcome. Under a conventional parliamentary system, if an individual candidate drops out he or she only invalidates their own candidature. Under the Singaporean system, if an individual candidate drops out of a multi-candidate team, the whole team is invalidated. Since 1988, the government has changed most single-seat constituencies into Group Representational Constituencies (GRCs), often announcing changes just before elections. To illustrate, 19 per cent of voters had their electorate status changed in June 2015, just ahead of the September 2015 elections, which effectively precluded opposition organisation.

The third main method of maintaining political control was by instilling a degree of circumspection into the electorate. Residents' Committees (RCs) were used as a means of surveillance of disgruntled citizens and as a conduit for threats of loss of access to government services. An extension of this was that constituencies that voted away from the government were warned that their vote could earn them *en masse* a loss of government services. The RCs and the government-organised and -funded Community Development Councils acted, in effect, like the grassroots or local branches of the PAP (Ang 2013). As with other government-established 'social' organisations, RCs come under the purview of the 'People's Association', which is chaired by the Prime Minister.

These RCs were formed in the numerous tower blocks which dominate much of Singapore's architectural landscape, which themselves lend a 'Brave New World' feel to the physical infrastructure of the city. Although not formally founded as a part of the PAP, the chairman of each committee is usually a PAP member or is otherwise linked to the network of patronage within the PAP. RCs are used for various purposes, including fundraising and as a means of 'vote buying' at election time. In this sense, there is a parallel between the RCs and village or neighbourhood committees in communist states or under the New Order government of Indonesia. Participation in RCs is encouraged by inducements, such as enhanced ease of access to municipal services (for example, educational facilities), and through localised public works (for example, footbridges, street beautification, local infrastructure maintenance). A negative inducement for staying away from RC meetings is increased difficulty of access to municipal services or, on a wider scale, a loss or relocation of public works.

As with most single or dominant party states, active participation in RCs or membership in the PAP by individuals in the civil service had a tendency to smooth career paths. Alternatively, non-participation in RCs or the PAP, or, worse, opposition, quickly leads to the discovery of a 'glass ceiling' to professional development. Loss of employment was not uncommon for government opponents. An employee so affected cannot, in most cases, appeal to their union because there are few independent trade unions. Of the 82 unions that exist in Singapore, 72 are affiliated with the National Trade Union Congress (NTUC), which is closely linked to the government (Han 2012). The NTUC originated as supporting the PAP in its bid for independence and it has become common for NTUC leaders to also hold senior positions within the PAP, including becoming members of parliament or ministers. Most unions are poorly patronised, comprising just 15 per cent of the working population of three million (of which almost 1.5 million are foreign workers) (MoM 2015).

Judiciary

Beyond this, Singapore's use and abuse of its judicial system (and previously extrajudicial methods) to restrict or repress political opponents had become a well-honed art under the prime ministership of Lee Kuan Yew and have continued to be used under his successors. Although Singapore claims to derive its political processes from Britain, its practices are very far from those of a functioning democracy in which all people are regarded as equal before the law and the law is applied in an even-handed manner. The use of the law for political purposes would not be a tool available to the government under the conventions of the Westminster parliamentary system, nor under any system which accepted the necessity of maintaining a separation of the roles and influences of the political executive and the judiciary – the so-called 'separation of powers'. However, under the Singaporean system there is no effective separation of powers and, as a consequence, judges often hand down decisions based less on law than on political expediency.

Subordinate Court judges and magistrates, as with public prosecutors, have their area of operation determined by the Legal Service Commission. The Commission allocates judicial responsibilities and has the authority to transfer judges from the bench to non-judicial duties as a matter of bureaucratic decision making. The appointment of new Supreme Court judges requires the recommendation of the Prime Minister in consultation with the Chief Justice. Subordinate court judges are appointed on the recommendation of the Chief Justice. According to the United States State Department, 'Some judicial officials, especially Supreme Court judges, have ties to the ruling party and its leaders' (US State Department 2005). The Singaporean Constitution also allows the Prime Minister or the Chief Justice to convene a tribunal for the purpose of removing a judge on the grounds of misbehaviour or inability, although this has not been used.

What this means in a practical sense is that for a legal worker to be appointed to a judgeship he or she must be accepted as trustworthy by the PAP. Future promotion depends on continuing to satisfy political as well as legal requirements. One judge who handed down a decision contrary to the interests of the government was quickly transferred into a bureaucratic position, from which he soon resigned. The lesson to other judges about failure to comply with government wishes was clear.

Beyond the threat and reward system of having judges hand down politically desirable decisions, and the appointment of 'suitable' candidates in the first place, is a type of legal hegemony. What this means in practice is that there developed a kind of culture or world-view which regards the PAP as not only the legitimate government of Singapore but also the 'natural' government of Singapore, and that there could not really be an alternative. As a consequence, opposition figures and other critics are not seen as 'legitimate' political participants but trouble-makers intent on accidentally or intentionally arousing antagonism and ill will. In a political society that so highly values – or has imposed – order, critics of the government are implicitly culpable. In this sense, the letter or even the meaning of the law is less important than the 'common sense' of the judge as understood from a peculiarly pro-PAP perspective.

While judicial appointments are usually made on the basis of 'suitable' but otherwise anonymous candidates, it is not always so. In particular, there was the case where a long-time law school friend of Lee Kuan Yew was appointed to the High Court Bench and, within a year, was elevated to the position of Chief Justice, the most important legal position in the country. Lai Kew Chai had not practised law for 20 years (spending much of the intervening time in business in Malaysia), and both his initial appointment and his quick rise to power shocked even Singapore's compromised legal fraternity. Not only was Lai a friend of Lee Kuan Yew, but he had formerly been employed as a lawyer with the Lee family legal firm, Lee and Lee. His appointment was a fairly blatant example of achieving pro-Lee/PAP political outcomes from ostensibly legally unbiased situations. To say that the judiciary in Singapore is corrupt or unduly influenced by external powers is to risk being charged with contempt of court. In 1995 Dr Christopher Lingle and the *International Herald Tribune* were sued for contempt of court (as well as through a related defamation case) for suggesting that Singapore's courts were politically influenced. The use of the charge of 'contempt of court' did not diminish over time, with blogger Alex Au being convicted of contempt of court in 2015 for claiming that a judge had manipulated the dates of a constitutional challenge so the effect of one trial would have an impact on the hearing of another (CPJ 2015).

Democratic challenge?

There was a thought that, after so long almost entirely dominated by the PAP, the 2015 elections might start to show the beginning of an opening of Singapore's political space.

Eight parties, including what appeared to be a somewhat resurgent Workers' Party, and a handful of independent candidates contested the elections, making it the most contested in Singapore's political history.

Singapore's 2011 elections had given to a rising tide of disenchantment with the country's open policy on guest workers, with the country of three million hosting a million foreign workers. There were consequent complaints of overcrowding, particularly on public transport and, following the global financial crisis, a wide gap between rich and poor (at 0.464 in 2015, about a third greater than the OECD average), and rising housing prices (Chong 2015). In 2011 the income gap was shown to be widening, with the Gini Index at 0.473, increasing the following year to 0.478 (MoF 2015). With the PAP's relatively poor showing of just 60.1 per cent of the vote in the 2011 elections, there was a high degree of expectation that it would perform even worse in 2015.

Ahead of the 2015 elections, on the evening of 8 September, Lee Hsien Loong addressed a PAP rally with what was a speech marked by a lack of fluency, calm and confidence. It was the pleading speech of a political leader who appeared to be panicking, made all the worse by focusing on the issues on which the government had performed poorly – housing, incomes and working conditions, public transport. Audience responses were, unsurprisingly with so little to be inspired by, less than rapturous, (Lee 2015). It seemed as though the PAP – and in particular its leader – could be in real political trouble.

It could be argued that, with such dominance of electoral politics in Singapore, the PAP leaders had slipped into a sense of complacency around having to win elections. The party's tactics of using defamation actions and other legal actions to silence or bankrupt opposition figures and civil society leaders was tried and tested, but managing the media and threatening constituencies with loss of housing and other welfare benefits were ceasing to be as effective as they once were.

PAP returns

Despite getting off to a shaky start, a series of corrective policies, including universal health care and greater access to public housing (which had only a marginal impact on income inequality), added to the fiftieth anniversary of Singapore's independence, and a celebration of the achievements of Lee Kuan Yew made 2015 the perfect time to hold the elections (Chong 2015; Barr 2015c). Along with the PAP's usual political manipulation, threats and extensive criticisms of opposition candidates (Barr 2015b), this was enough to convince voters to return to the governing party.

On 11 September 2015, the people of Singapore went to the polls and, despite little material change in their lives, returned the PAP with a 10 per cent swing towards the party, taking its overall vote to a convincing 70 per cent. Opposition parties, which had hoped to capitalise on their 2011 performance, went backwards, with the number of opposition parliamentarians being reduced from seven to six (with all opposition seats being won by the Workers' Party), and with the PAP securing 83 of 89 seats.

The result was a devastating and bitter blow to Singapore's opposition, particularly its leading figures who had campaigned long and hard against what they reasonably regarded as the injustices of Singapore's largely closed political system. Singapore Democratic Party leader Chee Soon Juan did particularly poorly, failing to win a seat after again being allowed to contest the elections. Chee had been jailed and bankrupted by the government on charges of speaking without a permit and defamation, yet continued to come back strongly. Despite his somewhat heroic political attempts, they increasingly appeared to be quixotic, with even the metaphorical windmills being charged at only increasing their own resilience while remaining elusive as targets.

As Barr (2015b) noted, the importance of these elections was twofold. In the first instance, while the percentage of the vote was not the highest the PAP had ever received and the number of opposition parliamentarians had on earlier occasions been lower, this was the first time that every one of Singapore's seats had been contested. That the PAP did so well overall when the competition was more challenging confirmed the PAP as the consistent, if not 'natural', party of government.

Secondly, after the setbacks of 2011 and the use of the Internet to circumvent restrictions on more conventional communications channels, the PAP still managed to sell its message sufficiently convincingly to woo a substantial majority of voters. The elections were also a major test for Lee Hsien Loong, who, following the elections of 2011 which showed the PAP could not take Singapore's political outcomes for granted, was under increasing scrutiny as perhaps not being up to the task of carrying on his father's legacy. In short, the PAP had to make a real effort to win over voters.

Barr suggests that the PAP leadership had learned from what might be taken as complacency and had relearned 'how to do politics', including recognising that it could no longer take the PAP's status as the party of government – or Singapore's voters – for granted. Not only did it ramp up reforms around health care and housing, but it promoted these reforms so that both potential recipients as well as other voters were well aware of what was being made available to them by this new, 'listening and responding', government.

But beyond this, and despite popular grumblings, Singaporean voters did not, it seemed, sufficiently trust opposition figures to be able to deliver. Having increasingly become used to long-term rising standards of living and opposition policies that were marked by their disunity and, to some extent, incoherence, voting for the PAP represented a flight to security. The idea of stepping away from state managerialism, which had come to define the lives of two generations of Singaporeans, appeared to be more than many could accept. What Singaporean voters did respond to, however, was an orientation towards more populist and redistributive policies. This meant that for the PAP to maintain its return to relative political security would mean at least sustaining and perhaps extending such policies (see Chong 2016).

Conclusion

The results of the 2015 elections showed that, with just a modicum of political effort, as well as its other, less 'free and fair' tactics, the PAP could continue not just to win but to dominate Singapore's political landscape. From its control of constituencies, right down to where people lived, through to its various mechanisms for exclusion and punishment, its control over the media, its manipulation of electoral boundaries and, perhaps more than anything else, its overall economic success, it seemed unlikely that the people of Singapore would easily be able or, perhaps, want to abandon the comfort and security of the PAP's known quantity.

Even if there were to be a more cohesive, coherent and respectable opposition, rather than a fragmented plethora of opposition parties with varying messages and sensibilities, it would still struggle to make a significant dent in the PAP's stranglehold over Singaporean politics. Ordinarily, for such a political grip to be broken, Singapore would have to face a crisis of the type that would leave its government unable to respond and would drive not just its voters but its elite towards an alternative.

Such a crisis does not appear likely in the foreseeable future and Singapore's elite, so closely intertwined with the PAP, seems to be determinedly opposed to the idea of cutting off its own life support system. Perhaps a third of Singaporeans might continue to vote against the government, for ideological, personal or group reasons. But, with the PAP's management of electoral boundaries to suit itself, even this number is unlikely to find sufficient concentration, in more than a handful of seats, to actually win. And then there would be the much greater challenge of assembling enough such seats to be able to seriously challenge the PAP as the party of government.

It may be that Lee Hsien Loong is not the political strategist that his father was, but he continues to benefit from a generation of politicians who received their own tutelage from Lee Senior, who continue to advise Lee Junior, along with his own direct benefit of having been Lee Senior's son. It may be that when Lee Hsien Loong looks to retirement he may not be able to bequeath the entirety of his father's political legacy to his own family. But the system established by Lee Kuan Yew is likely to persist into the indefinite future. In a world full of change, and with everything that it means for a failure of substantive democratic process, little of substance is likely to change in Singapore for the foreseeable future.

Note

1 Indonesia's President Sukarno led the 'Confrontation' over the establishment of the state of Malaysia.

8   Brunei

Brunei, formally Brunei Darussalam, is a tiny state on the north coast of the island of Borneo,[1] almost entirely dependent on oil, and ruled by a monarchy that stretches back 600 years in its current line. Brunei is, functionally, an absolute monarchy, in which the Sultan has in effect complete political power over all matters. While he may take advice from the Legislative Council or ministers – both of which he appoints – he is not obliged to do so.

Brunei is one of just six such monarchies in the world (Saudi Arabia, Qatar, Oman, Swaziland and Vatican City being the other five, although the list could arguably also include Morocco). Brunei did have a restricted Legislative Council from 1959 until 1984 which was reconvened in 2004. It comprises 33 members hand-picked by the monarch, Sultan Hassanal Bolkiah Mu'izzaddin Waddaulah, who has ruled since 1968. In 2006, the Sultan amended the constitution to make himself infallible under Bruneian law.

This situation has meant not only that the Sultan has been able to run the tiny country as a personal fiefdom but that he has been able to accrue a large proportion of the considerable wealth of the country for his personal use. In one sense, the Sultan runs Brunei in a way that has changed very little over the past 600 years. The major change has been that the Sultan, and his administration, runs the state with a relatively high degree of social support. However, to the extent that Brunei has flirted with notions of representative politics, that came and went in the period between the late 1950s and early 1960s. It has not since been allowed to recur.

As a monarchy, Brunei has weathered the changes that have gone on around it, being physically reduced in extent and existing as a British protectorate, but emerging again in the later twentieth century as an independent Sultanate. It has survived the larger political changes, of democratisation and the post-Cold War era, supported by its 'non-interfering'[2] ASEAN fellow members, geographically wrapped in a sympathetic Malaysia and feted for its extensive oil and gas deposits.

State formation

The current area of Brunei, of less than 6,000 square kilometres, is what was left after a British adventurer, the 'white rajah', James Brooke, carved out increasing sections of the state for his own administration and, he had hoped, exploitation in the mid-nineteenth century. Initially aligned with the Sultan to fight regional piracy and then in suppressing a rebellion, Brooke secured large areas of land in a number of tranches as payment, eventually assuming control over most of the area of the historic Sultanate (Runciman 1960: chs II–VI).

The territory controlled by Brooke became the British protectorate of Sarawak and eventually a state of Malaysia, with the rump state of Brunei remaining. Because of the piecemeal way in which Brunei had been carved up by Brooke, including his control of the town of Limbang, the remnant state of Brunei exists in two geographically distinct areas separated, just a few kilometres apart, by the 'Limbang Corridor'. Brunei dropped its long-standing claim to the Limbang Corridor in 2009 in exchange for two Malaysian-controlled hydrocarbon blocks in the South China Sea (Masli 2009).

Brunei would have struggled to continue to exist, and perhaps would have been unviable, as an independent state if it were not for the discovery of oil and gas. Following initial drilling in 1899, commercial flows of oil were discovered by Royal Dutch Shell at Seria, Brunei, in 1929. By 1940 the flow of oil had grown to six million barrels per year. Off-shore drilling commenced in 1959 with the South West Ampa gas field being discovered in 1963, and with new off-shore oil fields coming on line from the 1970s (BSP 2015a). At the time of writing, Brunei Shell Petroleum operated more than a thousand producing wells (BSP 2105b), and Brunei was Southeast Asia's third largest oil producer and the world's fourth largest liquid natural gas producer.

As Britain moved to decolonise, Brunei's status as a protectorate was put in the mix with Sarawak and Sabah as possible states in a new Malaysian federation. Domestic self-rule commenced in 1959, and in 1962 Brunei was formally invited to join in the Federation of Malaysia, which its Sultan Omar Ali Saifuddin III initially supported. However, there was popular opposition to the move by the Partai Rakyat Brunei (Brunei People's Party, or PRB) which had won all 16 elected seats in the 33-seat legislature in the 1962 elections. The PRB favoured making Brunei a constitutional monarchy, which would have significantly limited the powers of the Sultan, and opposed federation with Malaysia under the terms offered (see Majid 2007: ch. 3).

The PRB proposed that it should only join in federation with Malaysia if Brunei could be combined with the territories of Sarawak and Sabah. The Sultan rejected the proposal to amalgamate with the other northern territories, given it would considerably weaken his power, and delayed the opening of the legislature. In response, the PRB's armed wing, the Tentera Nasional Kalimantan Utara (North Kalimantan National Army, or TNKU) rose in rebellion (Ibrahim 2013). The TNKU was supported by Sukarno's Indonesia with limited training (Majid 2007: 78) and its uprising has been viewed by some as representing one of the opening stages of the Indonesia–Malaysia 'Konfrontasi' (Confrontation) over British colonialism and Malaysian independence (Majid 2007: 137–8, 141–2).

Planning for the rebellion was known about in advance and, with the government at the ready, was put down within days by the Brunei police and British Gurkhas, marines, commandos and other troops (Jackson 2008: ch. 15), with the PRB being outlawed. In response to the uprising, the Sultan decided against joining the Malaysian Federation, in part through fear of further negative reaction from the people of Brunei, instead remaining independent (Majid 2007: 131–2). On British advice, in 1962 the Sultan suspended the constitution and declared a State of Emergency, ruling under emergency powers, renewed every two years until 2004. Emergency powers conferred upon the Sultan the capacity to:

> make any Orders whatsoever which he considers desirable in the public interest; and [to] prescribe penalties which may be imposed for any offence against any such Order, and [to] provide for the trial by any court of persons guilty of such offences.
>
> (CBD 1959: 83.3)

The British army continues to retain a light infantry Gurkha battalion in Brunei as a praetorian guard to protect the Sultan and his family. Its base is at Seria, in the west of Brunei, where it also protects a major oil installation, and where it conducts a jungle warfare training school. The Royal Brunei Armed Forces also comprises four battalions which are employed both for defensive purposes and to assist the Royal Brunei Police in maintaining law and order.

With the option of joining the Malaysian federation still on offer, the proposed reduction of monarchical powers under the Malaysian federation finally decided the Sultan against joining with Malaysia. Instead, the Sultan chose self-rule under British protection until 1984, when the colony achieved full independence. To mark the occasion, Sultan Bolkiah, one of the world's richest men with a personal wealth estimated to be up to US$20 billion, built a new palace, the Istana Nurul Iman, which houses government ministries as well as the royal family. The palace is reported to have 1,788 rooms and a 110 car garage. If this is correct, however, it would still not accommodate what has been described as probably the world's largest collection of more than 5,000 luxury cars (Remmell 2013). The cost of its construction has been estimated at around $1.4 billion, and it is the largest occupied palace in the world (Bartholomew 1990; Boulos 2014).

Brunei enjoys a high per capita GDP for its population of around 430,000, based on oil export income and, increasingly, an oil-based sovereign wealth fund, rather than wider economic development. About 90 per cent of Brunei's export income and more than half its GDP is based on oil, with that and associated industries employing about a quarter of the workforce. Brunei's known oil reserves are expected to be close to being depleted by the mid-2030s (Vanderklippe 2015), meaning that, short of the unlikely possibility of developing a viable non-oil economy, Brunei and its people will rely on returns from the country's sovereign wealth fund. Brunei continues to have a high degree of social protection including free health care and education, with most workers employed in the public sector, based on its high per capita GDP.[3] Brunei is widely characterised as a 'welfare monarchy', with this arrangement being a key mechanism in sustaining the legitimacy of non-participatory political structure.

Conventional modernisation theory (e.g. Huntington 1968) would imply that the monarchy is trapped in a bind of having to be and be seen to be benevolent but, as a consequence, seeing the rise of a well-educated middle class which would be likely to want more direct inclusion in the running of government. However, like some Middle Eastern Gulf states, Brunei has evolved as a non-traditional model of political development through both repression of dissent and relative generosity, the latter of which has enhanced what Weber referred to as 'traditional' political legitimacy (Weber 1958).

As long as most of Brunei's citizens are relatively wealthy there is little compelling reason to seek a high-risk push for political change. However, if Brunei is unable to diversify its economy, oil revenue declines as expected and the sovereign wealth fund is unable to meet the continuing government expenditures, the current Sultan's successor could face greater domestic political challenges than the Sultan has himself so far faced.

Governance

Formally independent since 1984, Brunei functions under the restrictive state ideology of *Melayu Islam Beraja* (MIB, or Malay Islamic Monarchy). MIB is 'a blend of Malay language, culture and Malay customs, the teaching of Islamic laws and values and the monarchy system which must be esteemed and practiced by all' (IBP 2008: 123). Islam is the official and state religion of Brunei; MIB opposes the concept of secularism. According to Brunei's then education minister, Awang Abu Bakar, speaking at a compulsorily attended lecture at the Sultan Sharif Ali Islamic University in the capital, Bandar Seri Begawan: 'MIB was not a slogan but a system regulating the way of life' (Rajak 2014). Despite the introduction of a strict interpretation of sharia, the MIC claims that: 'Brunei Darussalam as an Islamic nation honours everything which embodies Islam in a moderate way' (IBP 2008: 123). This 'moderate way' was unilaterally changed by the Sultan to a strict version of sharia in 2014.

The MIB situates the Sultan as the centre of the nation and of Islam, with Friday attendance at mosques around the country, as well as visiting public works, symbolising his own piety. The Sultan promotes the idea of clean government, which, in theory, extends to members of the royal family. Brunei officially had a zero-tolerance policy towards corruption, but was ranked 38 of 175 countries on the Transparency International corruption perception index in 2013 (Transparency International 2013), which was an improvement from forty-fourth position in 2011 (no assessment was available for Brunei in 2014). However, a perception of 'clean government' was deeply compromised by a long-running legal battle between the state and the Sultan's youngest brother and former finance minister and chairman of the Brunei Investment Agency, Prince Jefri. This related to embezzlement charges dating back to 1998 concerning the unexplained loss of US$15 billion.

Despite being pursued by the Bruneian state, the Prince Jefri saga has been held up internationally as a profound exception to Brunei's claim to having a 'zero-tolerance' policy towards corruption. In 2000, in a private agreement, Prince Jefri handed over his extensive personal assets, including 500 properties (including luxury hotels), 2,000 cars, five luxury boats, nine aircraft (including his personal Boeing 747) and an art collection of approximately 100 paintings worthy of a high-level national gallery, to the state. Prince Jefri was also the subject of accusations of maintaining a harem, which were detailed in a book by one of his mistresses, Jillian Lauren (2010). The Prince had a statue made of himself making love to his then fiancée Micha Raines (a photo of which was publically leaked), which further compromised notions of royal propriety.

In 2009 Prince Jefri returned to Brunei from exile, having faced extensive legal battles over financial matters in the UK and the US (Maremont 2009). As Prince Jefri fought legal battles from Brunei, continuing legal cases against him within Brunei were settled in 2010, with all charges but one being found against him, requiring his surrender of most of his remaining possessions. In keeping with protecting the image of the royal family, the trial judge strictly limited what could be mentioned in the case (Gregorian 2010).

Tellingly, in 2015, the Sultan also openly criticised the Royal Brunei Police for corruption, noting that in 2014 only 21 per cent of criminal cases were resolved and that police had been involved in corrupt and other criminal practices. He said that police officers had been involved in the prohibited drinking of alcohol, gambling, bribery, intentional loss of evidence and smuggling. 'Many criminal cases cannot be brought to court because the files have gone missing' the Sultan said. 'Why are they missing or lost? Were these made to disappear deliberately to dispose of material evidence or simply due to the carelessness of the investigating officers?' (Bandial 2015).

In terms of governance, the Sultan is supported by five 'consultative' councils, each of which are appointed by the Sultan and which he heads. They include the Privy Council, which advises on constitutional and customary issues, the Council of Succession (which is effectively passive as succession is determined by the constitution), and the Religious Council, which advises on matters pertaining to Islam. Members of the Religious Council include ministers, a deputy minister, *pengiran cheteria* (first minister with blood ties to the royal family), *pehin manteris* ('life minister', minister for life), state *mufti* (Muslim legal expert), legal attorney (represented by the Attorney General), *Syarie* (Islamic) Chief Justice and others as appointed by the Sultan, who is also the Official State Religious Head. Brunei's legal system is based on that inherited from the United Kingdom, employing common law but much of which is now codified, combined with a separate Islamic court system dealing with matters of Islamic law. There is also the Council of Ministers and the Legislative Council.

In one sense, this parallels the Malaysian Barisan Nasional government's approach of absorbing potential discontents into the governing structure before they become a challenge to the status quo. As part of the 'welfare monarchy', the monarchy has developed a skilled professional and administrative class with relatively high levels of institutional capacity.

Rather than liberalise, in 2004 the Sultan amended the constitution to give himself even greater powers, including clarification of royal powers which further entrenched him as an absolute monarch and above the law in both official and personal capacities. At the same time, the constitutional amendments weakened the powers of the Legislative Council, including the requirement for it to be consulted and to give consent before the passing of new laws. The council remains entirely appointed and meets only once a year, in March, to discuss budgetary matters.

In 2004, the Sultan reintroduced a limited, appointed 21-person Legislative Council. At that time, there was no discussion of the election of council members, with the Sultan saying 'Its existence is not designed to spark chaos and apprehension among the community. Any mistake carries risk that takes time to ameliorate. As such, we begin this process with caution' (BBC 2004). So cautious was the Sultan that, more than a decade later, there had been expansion of the council, but there was still no discussion of making it formally representative. It appears that the intention is to retain the current structure, more or less, indefinitely.

The Legislative Council has, since 2004, been expanded to 36 members, including five indirectly elected representatives of village councils and the Council of (nine) Ministers, all appointed by the Sultan. The Sultan occupies the posts of Prime Minister, Defence Minister and Finance Minister and still determines all policy. 'The reform efforts of Sultan Hassanal Bolkiah Mu'izzaddin Waddaulah have been largely superficial and are designed to attract foreign investment. The unicameral Legislative Council has no political standing independent of the Sultan' (Freedom House 2014a).

The Legislative Council does vote on matters before it, but 'supreme executive authority' remains vested in and exercised by the Sultan, ministers appointed by the Sultan, or the Legislative Council acting on his orders (CBD 1959: 3.4.1, 2, 3, 4). While the Sultan may take advice from his ministers, he is not obliged to follow that advice or, indeed, to consult with ministers or the Legislative Council where he thinks it appropriate not to do so (CBD 1959: 18.2, 3a, b, c). The Sultan 'may act in opposition to the advice given to him by the majority of the Members of the Council of Ministers if he shall, in any case, consider it right so to do' (CBD 1959: 19.1).

The Sultan's eldest son, Crown Prince Haji Al-Muhtadee Billah, was appointed as senior minister in 2005 and has increasing deputised for his father, in part in order to ensure a smooth succession. The Sultan has been grooming the Crown Prince since 1998, introducing him to official duties including as acting Sultan when his father is overseas, as a General in the Brunei Armed Forces and as Deputy Inspector General of the approximately 4,400-strong Royal Brunei Police Force. His father awarded the Crown Prince an honorary doctorate in 2006 (BDPMO 2102). Loyalty of and control over the armed forces and police will remain critical to Muhtadee's succession as Brunei's thirtieth Sultan. The first son of the Crown Prince, Abdul Muntaqim, born 2007, is next in line to succeed Muhtadee to Brunei's throne.

The other family member who holds a prominent position in the state administration is the Sultan's brother, Prince Mohamad Bolkiah, as Minister for Foreign Affairs and Trade. In such an environment, not only is political activity limited but such limitations are actively imposed. There is very little transparency of political processes, with Transparency International ranking Brunei at 44 of 183 countries.

Despite the promise of elections in 2004, no elections have been scheduled and Brunei technically continues to be ruled under the State of Emergency. Brunei had three legal political parties, each of which supported a constitutional monarchy with an elected legislature. In 2007 the People's Awareness Party was disbanded by a government agency, and the Brunei National Solidarity Party was forced, without explanation, to deregister the following year. The National Development Party continues to exist, but remains largely inactive.

The Brunei National Democratic Party was formed in 1985, calling for free elections and an end to emergency rule, but was deregistered in 1988 under legislation in which it is an offence to challenge the authority of the Sultan. Under continuing emergency powers, freedom of association and assembly are restricted; no more than ten people can assemble at any one time without a government permit, while individuals may be detained for up to two years without trial. Brunei's constitution does not make any reference to political parties or elections, and only discusses voting within the context of the Legislative Council (CBD 1959: amend. art. 43).

While the Sultan can be critical, for example in relation to corruption, there are very limited opportunities for citizens to represent their concerns or issues to the government, other than circuitously through village councils. Brunei also practices a high degree of censorship, with media licences able to be revoked at any time and the country's main newspaper, the *Borneo Bulletin*, being controlled by the Sultan's family. 'The private press is either owned or controlled by the royal family, or exercises self-censorship on political and religious matters' (BBC 2013). Freedom House identifies Brunei as, in political terms, 'not free' (Freedom House 2014a). The government has the power to arbitrarily shut down media outlets and, under the 2005 Sedition Act, may jail journalists for up to three years for criticising the Sultan or the royal family, 'to raise discontent or disaffection', or to 'promote feelings of ill-will or hostility between different classes of the population of Brunei Darussalam' (AI 2009: 4). Newspapers are required to renew their licence to publish each year. Brunei ranked 121 of 181 countries on the Reporters Without Borders Press Freedom Index, placing it in the second most restricted of five categories (RWP 2015).

Against a backdrop of relatively high standards of living and generous social services, the official state religion of Shaf'i Islam was made increasingly strict in 2014, when the Sultan unilaterally introduced a literalist interpretation of sharia,[4] further limiting already restrictive social freedoms. This new interpretation of sharia included the adoption of strict sharia punishments, including whipping, amputation of hands for theft and stoning to death for illicit sex (such as adultery and homosexuality) and apostasy (abandoning Islam). The strict new laws were to be introduced in three phases into 2015.

The new laws, known as *hudud* ('restriction' on crimes against God), include failure to observe call to prayers being punishable with fines or even jail. Other crimes, including adultery, alcohol consumption and homosexuality, are punishable with flogging, amputation and stoning to death, punishments to be phased in between 2014 and 2016. Even where a woman is pregnant following being raped, she may still be subject to the adultery laws. The new laws could also apply to all people in Brunei and not just its majority Muslims. The Sultan hit back at international criticism of the laws, saying 'people outside of Brunei should respect us in the same way that we respect them' (*Daily Mail* 2014).

The Sultan's demand for respect, unfortunately, assumes that the rest of the world agrees that the orders of an individual hold sway beyond his direct political domain, and reflects the internalisation of an autocratic approach that is otherwise not always shared. Whether or not people beyond Brunei's borders respect its more recent interpretation of sharia, especially at a time when its application has come under critical scrutiny in other countries, is at best a moot point. For the people of Brunei, however, given they are not able to freely decide on whether or not they wish to employ an archaic legal code, at least public displays of 'respect' are a given.

The new laws were introduced by the Sultan under his guise as 'protector' of Islam in Brunei, which is part of the national ideology and which shores up the Sultan's popularity with the majority (approximately two-thirds) ethnic Malay Muslims.

Already an observant Islamic state, this further unilateral move towards a more strict interpretation of sharia reflected the arbitrary decision making available to an absolute monarch. The shift represents an interpretation of Islam dominant in Saudi Arabia seeking to increase its external influence. It also indicates, as an alternative to modernist politics, Islam's capacity to act as a wider legal and political vehicle in place of liberal pluralism.

This shift towards what is portrayed as 'true Islam' is directly linked to the Sultan's rule, so support for 'true Islam' also implies support for the monarchy, and vice-versa. Conversely, opposition to monarchical rule implies opposition to Islam which, in a predominantly and officially Muslim country, is untenable in a practical sense. The move towards a more strict interpretation of sharia has been interpreted by some observers as shoring up both the ageing Sultan's personal rule, especially given that his own lifestyle is widely regarded as self-indulgently lavish, and that of his successor, and as an attempt to attract increased foreign investment from religiously similar states in the Middle East, in particular from the Islamic banking sector (Liljas 2014).

The real question for Brunei's Sultan, for Brunei's monarchy more generally and, indeed, for its people, is what will happen when existing and presumed hydrocarbon deposits have been exhausted. The country will have income from its sovereign wealth fund, but this is unlikely to sustain the country at its current rates of expenditure. In 2015, Brunei's sovereign wealth fund was estimated to be worth about $40 billion, while the country had an annual GDP of $17 billion. At a 5 per cent rate of return from the sovereign wealth fund, on the balance at the time of writing, this would mean that Brunei's GDP would be reduced to two billion dollars a year. Even if the sovereign wealth fund was able to be doubled before the oil and gas ran out, it would still only produce less than a quarter of current income. Assuming careful management and no collapse in global investment, the sovereign wealth fund should, however, be able to continue to comfortably cover Brunei's annual budget of under $400 million a year (down from over $700 million).

This tightened economic environment may, however, imply further restrictions on government expenditure, especially in regard to its generous social welfare program.

If the 'social welfare bargain' that the Sultan has implicitly struck with the people of Brunei is no longer able to be sustained, there then may be greater pressure for a much higher degree of accountability and, potentially, for political change. In the interim, the Sultan, and his successor, will have to balance wider public expectations against the introduction of the more strict interpretation of sharia and its possible impact upon ordinary Bruneians.

Notes

1 The name 'Borneo' derives from 'Brunei', the historical Sultanate which, at its peak in the sixteenth century, once covered much of the north of the island.
2 'Non-interference' in the sovereign affairs of another ASEAN state is the foundational principle of ASEAN.
3 Around US$40,000, although fluctuating, depending on the price of oil.
4 While the Shaf'i school of Islamic jurisprudence is not commonly regarded as the most strict and fundamentalist (a position which is usually ascribed to the Hanbali school), it does remain very formal in its interpretation of the Holy Quran and the *Hadiths* (supposed verbatim reports of the Prophet Mohammad on various subjects).

9 Myanmar

Brief introduction to category: transitional states

The process of political transition implies that the old order is disappearing, but it does not imply the speed at which, or extent to which, it might change. Recognising a transition might therefore overstate the extent of change. In some cases, an existing political order may simply re-invent itself, or pretend to do so, to gain advantage. At least as commonly, the existing political order will be divided and there will be a contest within it to see which possible iteration of future possibilities succeeds. Very often, the outcome is not a clear victory for one faction or another, but a jumble in which compromise dominates but many other elements may remain ambiguous.

In capturing and compiling the key points made by other scholars on political transitions, Valenzuela (1990) noted there are, broadly, two phases to political transitions away from authoritarianism. The first is that there is a crisis within the authoritarian regime that leads to the option of an alternative in which free and fair elections are considered viable (see also Collier and Collier 1991 on 'critical junctures'). Myanmar had free elections, if within particular constitutional constraints, in November 2015. The reform process that led to these elections in many respects reflected the outcome of Valenzuela's understanding of 'crisis' within this particular authoritarian regime.

As noted by Karl (2005: 16), political transitions are periods of great uncertainty, in which sometimes unrecognised or poorly understood forces can suddenly and often unexpectedly come into play. Myanmar has been undergoing momentous changes, but it would be an error to assume that the process of change would in a deterministic way lead to that much overused, sometimes poorly analysed and almost always underspecified term, 'democracy', much less its 'consolidation' (there being no scholarly agreement on what constitutes 'consolidation'; see Linz 1990: 158; see also O'Donnell 1996: 34, 38–40 on the failure of teleological democratic assumptions; Carothers 2010: 78).

It is an anecdotally common although relatively poorly documented phenomenon that newly liberated/post-authoritarian states experience a strong upsurge in popular (and sometimes quite unrealistic) expectations prior to, during and immediately after such transitions. A common problem with not being able to meet such high and often unrealistic expectations is that popular support may quickly turn to popular disenchantment.

Notably, popular disappointment may be able to be manipulated by political actors not positively disposed towards new, post-election regimes, manifesting as protests, riots or other destructive action. While peaceful protests are a legitimate part of a plural democratic process, the state's security institutions, in particular the army, can and sometimes do react in ways that reflect their previous acculturation, which is to apply force rather heavily and often indiscriminately, which in turn leads to greater disenchantment and backlash. Conversely, democratically elected leaders may retreat to authoritarian methods in the face of increasing political disenchantment set against a low institutional base and capacity from which to deliver (e.g. see Kingsbury 2009a: 21–3).

The ability or otherwise of the state's security services to moderate their responses to public protest commonly reflects the political experience and sensibilities of their political leaders. Political leaders with a history of repression may respond by ordering security services to take strong anti-protest action. The subsequent social and political polarisation could, in turn, produce further repressive measures which, as can be approximately seen from a number of case studies, has been the model for a decline of new democracies in the face of scarcity and low capacity, resulting in a return to authoritarianism and/or autocracy.

Introduction: Myanmar

On 8 November 2015, the people of Myanmar went to the polls to elect a new government. As voters queued in the early morning, there was a sense of apprehension about how the day would play out, what the result would be and whether there would again be a military intervention. What was extraordinary about this event was that it happened at all, and further that it happened in such a conventional and ultimately widely accepted way.

Despite extensive but largely minor and inconsequential irregularities (e.g. see Mon 2015) and some pre-election intimidation and political violence, the electoral process proceeded in a generally free manner and its results were widely regarded as a legitimate expression of the will of Myanmar's people. Votes were cast across most parts of the country in a relatively orderly manner. The voter turnout rate was approximately 80 per cent, consistent with votes polled against voter registration lists at polling stations inspected by the Australian observer team.[1]

Around 33.5 million people were registered to vote, with a further four million being unable to register due to disbarment on grounds of loss of citizenship (ethnic Rohingyas), being in conflict or other insecure zones, being overseas (especially guest workers in Thailand), or in some cases being in internally displaced persons (IDP) camps (Jacob 2015).

An assessment by the Australian observer mission concluded that while the electoral process was generally sound, the prospect for democracy in Myanmar remained undermined by structural issues. The current constitution was drafted by the military regime without public consultation, and allocates 25 per cent of legislative seats to the military (preventing constitutional reform without military approval), barred the leader of the most popular political party from becoming President, and establishes a supra-parliamentary role for the military's National Defence and Security Council (Kingsbury 2015).

The elections confirmed that Myanmar was a state in transition, from a deeply authoritarian form of government to a more liberal, if not quite democratic, form of government. Myanmar was not alone in Southeast Asia in undergoing such a transition but it was the most recent example, as well as representing a move away from an extreme form of authoritarianism.

Myanmar has been described as 'a country of ill-fitting ethnic nationalities crammed into one state united only by a long-gone colonial power . . . sharing little common memory and only a vague vision of integration into one society' (Badgley 2004: 17–18). This has meant that a number of ethnic groups have wanted to separate from the state or come to a very different constitutional arrangement about their relationship with the state. This has, in turn, been used by the military to justify its involvement in Myanmar's domestic politics. This military involvement in politics has in turn subverted civilian political processes, which the country was in the process of trying to re-establish.

As with most transitions, the path taken by Myanmar was marked by limitations, sidesteps and failures. The key limitations to Myanmar's transition from deep authoritarianism were the retention of its military in government and its having veto power on further constitutional change, the transitional party of government until the election of a new government in 2016 having been born of the military, and the constitutional restriction on the country's most popular political figure, Aung San Suu Kyi, becoming its President.

A sidestep in the transitional process could be seen to be the ouster of the pro-reconciliation chairman of Myanmar's ruling military front, United Solidarity and Development Party (USDP), and Speaker of parliament, Shwe Mann, in August 2015, ahead of Myanmar's general elections, and the use of the military and police to ensure that change occurred without dissent. This indicated that military hardliners who controlled the USDP could attempt to continue to rule through forming a coalition government to keep out the otherwise popular, reformist National League for Democracy (NLD), headed by Nobel Laureate Aung San Suu Kyi.

Shwe Mann had angered many members of the USDP with his highly personalised political style, his expressions of interest in running for the presidency and his closeness to Suu Kyi and the NLD, referring to Suu Kyi as an 'ally' (Matsui 2015). In particular, Shwe Mann angered Myanmar's military when he supported a bid to amend the constitution to limit the military's political role (Zaw and Slodkowski 2015). In the arcane world of Myanmar's military-political world, having a personalised political style has not been unusual. President Thein Sein's own political approach had put him at the centre of Myanmar's military-political factions, pursuing a substantial economic reform agenda, from which regime cronies have benefited, and a cautious political agenda.

Tensions between factions within the USDP came to a boil in the first week of August 2015 when the majority of a group of around 150 officers who retired from military service to run as USDP candidates were left off the party list. There had been rumours of tensions between Thein Sein and Shwe Mann throughout the first half of 2015 and it appeared that Thein Sein had at least given his blessing for, if not orchestrated, Shwe Mann's ouster. Given that a number of Shwe Mann's supporters in the parliament were also removed from their posts, the move looked like a purge more than an action against a single individual. With armed soldiers and police surrounding USDP headquarters, the move against Shwe Mann certainly had the public appearance of a purge (Fuller 2015).

Shwe Mann was subsequently under pressure to resign his parliamentary position, with moves being made by his opponents to see if it was possible to legally oust him. Prior to Myanmar's move towards openness, he would more likely have been arrested and jailed for an indeterminate period. This had happened to one of his predecessors, former Prime Minister, former intelligence head and architect of the original reform process, Khin Nyunt. Shwe Mann's removal came when he was not present, at an emergency meeting of the USDP on 12 August. 'His speeches used to receive thunderous applause from members of parliament. In a sign that his reversal of political fortunes is all but complete, his statement that day was met with near silence' (Matsui 2015).

Some believed that the extent to which Myanmar had liberalised prior to the elections was the extent to which it would be allowed to do so for the foreseeable future. In the shadowy world of Myanmar's military politics, the entry into active politics of retiring ministers Lieutenant-General Wai Lwin and Lieutenant-General Thet Naing Win could have suggested that the army wanted to continue to be directly involved in politics. As Matsui (2015) noted, Shwe Mann's 'fall from power underscores an enduring reality of Myanmar politics: The military continues to hold all the cards.'

Ahead of the elections, in October 2015, the government signed a ceasefire agreement with eight of the country's non-state armed groups. However, seven, including the most powerful of them, refused to sign the ceasefire agreement, arguing that it only locked in place existing inequalities and did nothing to substantively address their underlying concerns. The failure to include the most powerful armed groups in the ceasefire agreement reflected a 'take it or leave it' approach to ceasefire negotiations by Myanmar's military.

This meant that the elections could not proceed in affected areas and, as it turned out, even in most areas where armed groups had signed ceasefires. In response to the refusal of some groups to sign the ceasefire agreement, the military stepped up its attacks against the non-signatory groups, especially the Shan State North Army and the Kachin Independence Arm. It also meant that, while Myanmar faced internal unrest, the military could continue to justify its role in internal politics.

Why 'reform'?

The question has been asked: what prompted Myanmar's military leaders to move away from their complete domination of the political process towards a more representative, ostensibly civilian one? A likely answer has been that, in the latter years of the military regime, it had experienced a series of crises which undermined confidence in the ability of the state to continue as it was, with unwanted consequences for its entrenched politico-economic elites.

There have, clearly, been moments when the sense of specific crisis has been worse and when it has been less pronounced. However, it would be difficult to claim that the regime had not experienced a broad-based crisis of legitimacy following the long collapse of its economy, the public rejection of its military government demonstrated by the overwhelmingly anti-regime election results of 1990, and the state's inability to adequately address the devastating effects of Cyclone Nargis in 2008. (Taylor proposes that the crisis which spurred the constitutional changes came in the first decade of the twenty-first century, culminating in the 2010 elections; see Taylor 2012: 231–2.)

Given the interlinked nature of the critical problems that have beset Myanmar's military regime, especially between 1987 and 2008, it is possible to refer to it as having experienced a sequential or interlinked series of crises. The key moments in these interlinked crises began in 1987 with the demonetisation of the three highest banknotes, which made worthless around 56 per cent of money in circulation. Around the same time, at the request of then President New Win, the UN formally declared Myanmar to have 'least developed status', confirming what most of its citizens already experienced.

In the protest that followed the currency change, at least 2,000 unarmed protesters were shot dead by soldiers. In response to the crisis, there was a split within the military and the then ruling Burmese Socialist Program Party was dissolved (reappearing as the largely inconsequential National Unity Party). A faction of the armed forces announced that it had taken power under the guise of the State Law and Order Restoration Council (SLORC), suspending the constitution and declaring martial law. Subsequent protests led to the killing of thousands more protesters during August 1988.

The crisis which led to the creation of the SLORC triggered elections, held in May 1990. These elections were overwhelmingly won by the opposition NLD, which took 392 of 485 seats in parliament. However, the regime refused to acknowledge the results, killing hundreds more protesters, banning the NLD and closing universities. Under house arrest, in 1991, NLD leader Aung San Suu Kyi was awarded the Nobel Peace Prize. The following year, further protests in Mandalay led to hundreds more being killed. While these issues ebbed and flowed in intensity, the regime could be said, by this stage, to be operating in something akin to 'crisis management mode'.

It was in this state of crisis management mode that, in November 1997, the SLORC was dissolved, replaced by the State Peace and Development Council (SPDC). The SPDC retained many of the authoritarian features of the SLORC, but some members of it recognised that the authoritarian state model was becoming untenable. This was particularly so in light of economic sanctions placed on the country by some of the world's larger economies.

Consistent with Valenzuela's theory of transition, in response to these crises, in 2003, then Prime Minister Khin Nyunt outlined a plan to slowly move away from formal military control. However, reflecting O'Donnell's qualifications about transitions (1996), in November 2003, disagreement among the military elite resulted in Khin Nyunt, being sacked as Prime Minister and jailed. This resulted in a reassertion of hardline military control, notably with the crushing of the 2007 'Saffron Revolution'. However, the devastating impact of Cyclone Nargis in May 2008, which left at least 140,000 (and probably many more) dead, often because of state inaction, highlighted the regime's inability to manage the state's affairs and raised the prospect of external intervention (Daalder and Stares 2008). Myanmar's military government was again in a state of crisis.

While the regime was already edging towards some sort of reform process, particularly around liberalising its economy, it was this crisis of capacity that can be proposed as the final part of the larger sequential crises. A new constitution, voted on as the country was still reeling from the impact of the cyclone, allowed the regime to recommit to a 'Roadmap to Discipline-Flourishing Democracy', as initially formulated by Khin Nyunt.

When Aung San Suu Kyi announced before the World Economic Forum in Naypyitaw in June 2013 that she would seek election as President following the bicameral legislature (Hluttaw) elections in 2015, the world's media reported this event as further confirmation of Myanmar's transition from authoritarianism to democracy (Sein 2013; Fuller 2013). Her statement followed by-elections in April 2012, in which Suu Kyi's NLD stood candidates and in which it won 43 of the 44 seats it contested in the country's lower house (Pyithu Hluttaw). According to three senior government advisers interviewed for this chapter, the USDP did not actively contest the 2012 by-elections, in order to help ensure what looked like the NLD's apparent crushing victory. This was by way of further bolstering the regime's increasingly positive international credentials without making more than a symbolic gesture towards political openness at this time (see Bunte 2011 on military consolidation within the transition).

Part of the transition that might have allowed Suu Kyi to be elected as President involved changing Myanmar's constitution, which barred such election on the grounds of having an immediate family member who must 'not owe allegiance to a foreign power, not be a subject of a foreign power or citizen of a foreign country' (*Constitution of the Republic of the Union of Myanmar* 2008, ch. 3, section 59f). Suu Kyi's sons are citizens of the United Kingdom. There was mixed but insufficient government support for changing this aspect of the constitution (Fuller 2014b; Poling, Nguyen and Weatherby 2014).

Seeming to assume, relatively uncritically, the fundamental correctness of the 'transitions' paradigm that authoritarian states evolve towards more liberal, democratic models (Rustow 1970; O'Donnell and Schmitter 1986; see also O'Donnell, Schmitter and Whitehead 1986), the international community eased economic pressure on Myanmar and softened its tightly restrictive political conditions (US State Department 2013; EU 2013; DFAT 2013). However, that Myanmar's political changes would result, teleologically, in 'democracy' was less than given. (Radio Free Asia 2012b). Reflecting the definition of democracy as developed by Di Palma (1990: 13) and Linz and Stepan (1996: 5), this then goes to Valenzuela's second phase of political transition, when free and fair elections – and related conditions – have been instituted and legitimised as 'the only game in town'. The November 2015 elections appeared to confirm that tendency, although they remained a long way from being consolidated as such.

Consistent with O'Donnell and Schmitter (1986) and Dahl (1989: 250–1), some of the conditions under which such a political transition can occur, as identified by Valenzuela, can be summarised and assessed as follows:

1   The authoritarian regime is removed quickly: In Myanmar's case, however, this has been a gradual rather than a quick process and one which will remain incomplete for the foreseeable future.
2   The outgoing regime is repudiated by supporters as well as opponents: There has been no repudiation of the former regime or significant elements of it, which, moreover, continued in power until the 2016 government was appointed, and continued thereafter to have significant inclusion in a 'government of national unity'. According to Deputy Defence Minister Brigadier-General (ret.) Aung Thaw, 'The government is leading the democratisation. The Defense Services are pro-actively participating in the process' (Marshall and Szep 2012).

    There was, however, a process of sidelining anti-reform actors from senior positions in the military, formally known as the Tatmadaw (Royal Force), and the government, with the pro-reform faction appearing to have the upper hand in this intra-institutional competition. The cabinet reshuffle of August 2012 saw 11 new ministers appointed. Conservative retired General Kyaw Hsan was demoted from the post of Information Minister to the Ministry of Cooperatives. Two other former generals also retired. This reshuffle followed the retirement in July 2012 of conservative Vice-President Tin Aung Myint-Oo. The reshuffle of July 2013 saw the 'resignation' of some ministers, others demoted and the appointment of five academics in place of military officers as deputy ministers.
3   Former members of the outgoing order support or participate as accepted actors in the subsequent electoral process: This was the case in the 2015 elections, with the Tatmadaw-proxy Union Solidarity and Development Party (USDP) contesting most Hluttaw (legislative) seats.

4   The transitional phase to elections is handled by a civilian rather than military provisional government: Myanmar's transitional USDP government was not provisional but fully constituted and was overwhelmingly dominated by former military officers and military-aligned members. The military continued to play an active role in government, with three constitutionally allocated ministries appointed by the military commander-in-chief: Defence, Home Affairs and Border Affairs.

5   The military concerns itself with external security matters: The Tatmadaw continued to have a minimal external security focus, remaining overwhelmingly focused on internal security issues. Further, its heavy-handedness in doing so, including extensive human rights abuses (Adams 2013), had in many cases exacerbated internal insecurity by provoking negative militant responses. In situations where militaries have an active interest in retaining involvement in the internal affairs of state, they can (and have) intentionally provoked conflict in order to demonstrate their necessity as guardians of the state; the Tatmadaw appears to have been little different in this respect.

6   The drafting of a new democratic constitution occurs after the formation of a democratic government: Changes to Myanmar's existing constitution had been rejected by the USDP government in 2015 and the country was unlikely to have a new constitution under the in-coming government, in part because the Tatmadaw held power of veto over such matters and in part because Suu Kyi appeared to want to work with the Tatmadaw to ensure a peaceful transition, rather than push too hard against them and risk a backlash.

Although cautioning against political expectations arising out of such structural preconditions, Di Palma also noted that economic instability, a hegemonic nationalist culture and the absence of a strong, independent middle class all impeded transition from an authoritarian political model towards one that is more democratic (Di Palma 1991: 3). In this sense, Myanmar was not necessarily well positioned to advance its political reform process towards one that was democratic. These factors were all impacted upon by the dominant and continuing role of the Tatmadaw.

The Tatmadaw

At the heart of the challenges to Myanmar's reform process lay the continuing role of the Tatmadaw in critical aspects of the state's institutional life. As with other military-led transitions, there is always the subsequent issue of more recalcitrant or less change-minded officers who can act as spoilers during, or after, a transition process (see O'Donnell and Schmitter 1986: 37–47). Within the Tatmadaw and Myanmar's former government, there emerged a clear distinction between more and less reform-minded officers or former officers. Former President Thein Sein was initially seen as the most prominent 'softliner', but reverted to military type in response to proposed constitutional changes supported by 'softliner' Shwe Mann.

Myanmar's constitution remains that as passed in 2008, which among other provisions ensures that the Tatmadaw retains 25 per cent of seats in the Hluttaw, in practical terms giving it a constitutional veto. This includes a veto on whether the constitution should be amended to remove this veto power. Changing the constitution to remove the Tatmadaw's 25 per cent allocation, its exclusive appointment of one of the two Vice-Presidents or any other of a number of restrictive clauses requires 75 per cent of the

Hluttaw's vote. Blocking constitutional changes opposed by the Tatmadaw bloc in the Hluttaw would require the support of just one other Hluttaw member. The USDP was thoroughly trounced in the 2015 elections but, added to the Tatmadaw's 25 per cent of seats and an anti-NLD ethnic bloc, this meant that there would be very considerable difficulty in changing the constitution without Tatmadaw agreement.

As well as the USDP winning some seats, the constitution also provided for 12 representatives from states and regions in the 168-seat upper house, the Amyotha Hluttaw, some of whom were ambivalent towards the NLD. This positioning was based on divisions between state and regional parties and the NLD over what a number of regional ethnic groups regard as the NLD's ethnic Burman orientation. In particular, reflecting Di Palma's noted concern over a hegemonic nationalistic culture, this division included a lack of agreement about future constitutional relations between non-Burman states and regions and the central government. These factors would leave the overwhelmingly NLD-majority government short of the super-majority of 75 per cent required to change the constitution.

Beyond its 25 per cent occupation of the Hluttaw, the Tatmadaw is also constitutionally protected as a separate and autonomous entity from the government, and is exempt from civilian oversight. Article 20(b) of the constitution gives the Tatmadaw the right to appoint the Ministers of Defence, Interior and Border Affairs, helping to ensure that this exemption from civilian oversight is maintained in practice as well as in principle.

One question that has arisen is whether the government would abolish the Emergency Provisions Act, in which article 5j has broadly formulated charges that carry a prison sentence of up to seven years for anyone who prevents civil servants and army officers from carrying out their duties, or for anyone who spreads information among the public that opposes the government. The government was also opposed to abolishing the State Protection Law, in which articles 10a and 10b gives the authorities sweeping powers to detain anyone who has committed or is about to commit an act that may be considered as an 'infringement of the sovereignty and security of the Union of Burma', or as a 'threat to the peace of the people'. The National Police Chief and Home Affairs Deputy Minister, Kyaw Kyaw Htun, told the Hluttaw that the government had no intention of abolishing or amending the 1950 Emergency Provisions Act or the 1975 State Protection Law (The Irrawaddy 2013a). This then goes to Valenzuela's fifth point, concerning the orientation of the military impeding democratic change.

At least as importantly, if not more so, while the Hluttaw is the state's legislative body and oversees its day-to-day affairs, it constitutionally occupied a position *below* what amounted to Myanmar's supreme arbitrating body, as well as the core cabinet, the National Defence and Security Council (NDSC). The NDSC was announced the day after the swearing in of the new government in April 2011, which assumed parliamentary authority from the State Peace and Development Council (SPDC) and which ushered in Myanmar's apparent 'transition'. The NDSC has, in effect, assumed the SPDC's mantle as the final arbiter on Myanmar's political processes (see also Huang 2013). This then reflects Valenzuela's first, as well as fifth, point concerning the removal – or lack of removal – of the previous regime.

The NDSC comprises 11 members, ten of whom are serving or former senior Tatmadaw officers, the eleventh of whom is Myanmar's civilian Vice-President, an ethnic Shan, Dr Mauk Kham. The 2008 constitution does not define the day-to-day role of the NDSC, nor has it exercised such a day-to-day role. However, the NDSC does have the capacity to declare a state of emergency, in which it may dissolve the Hluttaw and assume all legislative, executive and judicial powers. The NDSC is chaired by President Thein Sein, with Vice-Presidents Nyan Tun[2] and Mauk Kham occupying second and third positions. The People's Assembly (lower house) Speaker General (ret.) Shwe Mann occupies fourth position on the council, followed by House of Nationalities (upper house) Speaker and presidential aspirant Lieutenant-General Khin Aung Myint.

According to two senior interviewees, the real power holder in the NDSC is the Tatmadaw's commander-in-chief, Senior General Min Aung Hlaing, supported by his deputy, Lieutenant-General Soe Win. General Hlaing has been cautious in his dealings with the government to date, balancing its requests, for example to limit military action against the Kachin Independence Army, against expectations from within the Tatmadaw (Callahan 2012: 126–27). The NDSC is completed with the inclusion of then Defence Minister Major General Hla Min, then Minister of Home Affairs Lieutenant-General Ko Ko, former Tatmadaw Director-General and former Foreign Minister Colonel (ret.) Wunna Maung Lwin, and then Border Affairs Minister Major-General Thein Htay.

In short, although Myanmar had a largely elected government taking office in March 2016, the Tatmadaw continues to play a strong role in the Hluttaw through its unelected 25 per cent allocation, and in coalition with USDP members and some ethnic parties. The Tatmadaw is also set to functionally continue to exercise the power of veto over any constitutional changes. Should this power of veto be insufficient for any reason, under chapter 11 of the constitution, the NDSC may impose martial law and dissolve the government at any time. The decision-making authority allocated to the Hluttaw is, thus, closely monitored and confined by the continuing political role of the Tatmadaw. As noted by Callahan: 'The Tatmadaw remains central to politics' (Callahan 2012: 124).

The political economy of the Tatmadaw

In light of Myanmar's significant economic reforms, paralleling or exceeding political reforms over the period 2011–13, it would be exceptionally difficult and economically counterproductive for even Myanmar's 'anti-reform' forces to completely overturn the country's reform process. While Callahan has claimed there is no clear explanation as to why the Tatmadaw has gone down the path of reform (2012: 126), Jones (2014) has suggested the answer lies in the economic self-interest of Myanmar's elites, in particular the Tatmadaw. It is reasonable to suggest that the evolution of these interests, and in particular the interests of its senior members and their families, was best served by allowing a greater degree of openness. That is particularly so where the Tatmadaw is able to exercise what might be called 'back room' political control over the longer term.

There is no doubt that Myanmar's move towards opening its economy and liberalising its politics has had a positive economic benefit to the country and, by extension, many of its key businesses. Along with the dropping of sanctions, by March 2013, commitments of foreign investment in Myanmar's economy had increased fivefold (Reuters 2013) to almost US$1.5 billion. This was matched by local investor confidence, which increased to US$1.3 billion in commitments over the same period, promising to inject much-needed capital into the still frail economy. Stepping back from processes that have allowed this level of promised investment could cause a backlash from local elites heavily invested in the opening economy and from ordinary citizens who anecdotally, in some areas at least, appeared to be seeing some economic benefits trickle down.

As a consequence of this business development, Myanmar has seen the rise of a new class of tycoons, who have taken advantage of developments in banking, building materials, construction and property, trading, mining, hotels, manufacturing, logging, marine products, transportation, the energy sector, agribusinesses, and food and beverages (Larkin 2015). Most of these tycoons were cronies of the military. Along with such non-military business tycoons who are heavily invested in the economy are members of the Tatmadaw and their families. To illustrate, while ousted Pyithu Hluttaw Speaker General (ret.) Shwe Mann had acknowledged government corruption (Myo Thant 2013) and was regarded, while in office, as one of the more 'clean' generals, his son Aung Thet Mann owned Ayeya Shwe Wa Company, which was identified as one of Myanmar's crony companies (US Embassy 2009). Shwe Mann's two other sons, Toe Naing Mann and Shwe Mann Ko Ko, owned Red Link Communications, one of Myanmar's few wireless providers. Toe Naing Mann was married to Zay Zin Latt, daughter of business tycoon Khin Shwe, who owns the Zaykabar Company, which has extensive interests in construction, property, petrol stations (under Toe Naing Mann's name) and telecommunications. 'While he may not be as notoriously corrupt as some of his colleagues, Shwe Mann has solid connections to regime business cronies' (US Embassy 2007).

Perhaps more important than the direct business interests of senior officers and their families were the Tatmadaw's two large holding companies and primary economic vehicles, the Myanmar Economic Corporation (MEC) and the Union of Myanmar Economic Holdings Limited (UMEHL). The MEC was founded in 1997 with a focus on heavy industries, initially to provide the Tatmadaw with raw construction materials. The UMEHL was established in 1990 with an initial capital base of US$1.6 billion. In 2013, the UMEHL still had investments in more than 50 diversified companies. The chairman of UMEHL was Major-General Khin Zaw Oo, heading a military-controlled board of directors. The MEC and UMEHL and their directly owned companies did not pay tax (The Irrawaddy 2011).

The UMEHL also had a partnership developing the Dawei Deep Sea Port in Launglon (Dawai Project Watch 2012), the only port allowed to load/unload containers. The UMEHL had allegedly transferred money to the Korea Kwangson Banking Cooperation in Pyongyang as well as buying arms from North Korea (Kirk 2013). It was also identified with the export of rice and other agricultural goods to Pyongyang as payment for arms (ABC 2013).

The MEC, for its own part, operated coal mines (PYO 2011b) and Dagon Brewery (AOW 2011), between 1999 and 2012 established 50 joint ventures with foreign businesses, and in 2013 owned 38 businesses outright (AOW 2012). In 2013, MECtel, a telecommunications arm of MEC, began SIM card distribution (Khine 2013), significantly reducing the cost of SIM cards in Myanmar. The MEC was dominant in the iron and steel industry (Asia Steel Construction 2013; Xinhua 2010) as well as dominating the mining of precious stones (Kyaw-Zaw 2009).

As a result of the deep involvement of these two holding companies in the Myanmar economy, any reduction in investment and trade would directly and negatively impact upon their own revenue sources. Given that the Tatmadaw is in large part self-funded, as well as providing extra benefits to officers and enlisted men, this would impact upon both the military's functional capacity and the material welfare of its members. There was, then, a direct incentive for the Tatmadaw to maintain both the tax-free status and the lack of transparency of the MEC and the UMEHL.

As with other reforming states in which the military has played both a political and an economic role (e.g. Indonesia), there has been discussion about the state directly funding all the Tatmadaw's activities. The purpose of this direct funding is twofold. In the first instance, it would remove from the Tatmadaw its focus on non-military activities, including interfering in the political process in order to protect its economic interests, as well as limiting the Tatmadaw's corrupt practices such as smuggling. In the second instance, separating the Tatmadaw from its independent source of income would limit its capacity to make decisions independently of the government. This could ultimately be used to impose reform upon it, along with determining what military activities it could engage in.

However, the cost of such funding, proposed at 15 per cent of the budget (Callahan 2012: 128), would put considerable pressure on a still weak state budget, as well as facing opposition from Tatmadaw officers who continue to directly benefit from military businesses (see Bunte 2011: 16, 25). The 'reform' process, then, makes good business sense to the country's military and business elites, and this alone seems likely to secure economic openness. It also informs the military's (preferred) lack of accountability to a civilian government.

Other reform-limiting factors

In times of political, economic and social uncertainty, there can be a retreat to one's ethnic group or calls for a return to the previous social or political order, or to a form replicating many of its features. This is usually based upon contrasting the previous period of 'stability', often portrayed as rosily hued, with current 'instability' or a sense of uncertainty. The unleashing of or support for previously constrained forces may be manipulated by anti-reform actors to create an environment or a sense of instability (Toft, Philpott and Shah 2011: 109; Holliday 2010).[3] An illustration of this was in outbreaks of anti-Muslim rioting in Lashio, and in towns from the north of Yangon up to Mandalay and in Rakhine State over much of 2013.

Anti-Muslim sentiment had long existed in Myanmar, but its expression had largely been limited by authoritarian control. The lifting of that control, combined with pent-up anti-authoritarian resentment and a growing assertion of Burmese nationalism under the cloak of 'religious respectability and moral authority', created a more enabling environment for the riots (ICG 2013: 18). The Lashio riot and other central riots were attributed by a number of senior figures close to the government to disgruntled officers opposed to reform, or to officers who felt they had lost or were losing local economic advantages as a result of economic reform. While such forces were said to include Tatmadaw hardliners, they were also associated with business interests in support of more chauvinistic elements of the Buddhist community, notably under the banner of the ultra-nationalist '969' movement (Beech 2013). However, while an International Crisis Group Report said that 'It is certainly possible that there are some influential individuals, perhaps even in powerful institutions, who may be encouraging or funding extremist movements as a result of their personal prejudices', it also argued that no evidence had been found to support assertions that the riots were intended to create conditions for a return to authoritarian rule (ICG 2013: 18–20).

As a multi-ethnic state, Myanmar has since the outset faced challenges to state cohesion by separatist organisations. It was these challenges to state cohesion that gave the Tatmadaw its primarily internal focus and which eventually led to its direct involvement in and control over Myanmar's political processes. However, while internal conflict continued to rationalise the involvement of the Tatmadaw in internal affairs as the guarantor of state unity, even that self-legitimising institution understood that continuing conflict was not a sustainable proposition for the state.

Beginning in 1989, the Tatmadaw thus began negotiating a series of ceasefire agreements with armed groups. One key mechanism for achieving these ceasefires was allowing armed groups to keep their weapons, control their own territory and engage in illegal activity such as drug production without interference (Meehan 2011). In particular, the Wa and Kokang continued to run autonomous narco-territories in the north-east of Shan State. The economy of these autonomous territories is now based primarily on production of amphetamines, which have largely replaced the more vulnerable opium.

Yet despite such ceasefires, there have continued to be clashes with some armed groups, notably in Kachin State and Shan State, in turn continuing to rationalise the Tatmadaw's internal role. To illustrate, in the lead-up to and following the 2015 elections, there was intense fighting in northern Shan State and in the north of Kachin State (DVB 2013; Eleven 2013; author communication with KIO 1 November 2015).

The existence of non-state armed groups reflects a sense of the cultural and economic divide that continues between the ethnic Burman majority and Myanmar's numerous minorities. There is a sense among many minorities that 'Burmans have always ridden roughshod over the sensibilities of other ethnicities' (*The Economist* 2013). The people of Myanmar continue to face serious poverty (ranked in the bottom quarter, at 149 on a global index of 186 states, according to UNDP 2013b). But according to one senior government adviser, the outlying ethnic minorities experience more debilitating conditions than those of the central regions (see also ADB 2012). Lack of education is arguably the biggest problem facing the ethnic minorities (Bush and Saltarelli 2000: 9–11), with claims that Burman language teachers either refuse to work in non-Burman areas or leave soon after they arrive. Without education, much less in a language they understand, minorities remain trapped in a cycle of poverty and alienation. This, in turn, pushes such groups into illegal trade, drives armed resistance to the government and continues to insinuate the military into the affairs of the state in ways that undermine its attempts to reform, potentially even under a more open electoral political system.

Conclusion

Any conclusion about Myanmar's 'uncertain' transition must be 'tentative' (to paraphrase O'Donnell and Schmitter's 1986 title). Myanmar is clearly undergoing a political transition, but it is not yet 'democratic'. The election of 2015 only partially fulfilled conventional democratic criteria. It was, in many respects, a remarkable process with an equally remarkable outcome, not least for the manner in which the Tatmadaw and USDP accepted its results. However, as noted, if one was to take a political economy approach to the transition, it was in the military's interest to do so.

But perhaps more than initial concern being expressed about the likelihood of Myanmar's transition to democracy, in keeping with O'Donnell's later cynicism regarding the teleological assumptions about such processes (O'Donnell 1996: 34–51) is the question as to how far Myanmar will be able to transition towards democracy.

Myanmar had become a more liberal state over the period following reforms initiated from 2011 and in particular during 2012; the media was relatively free, previously banned individuals were allowed to return and open political organisation was not restricted as it once had been. Even here, however, while Myanmar underwent significant economic reform, this was not protected by rule of law or conventional business practices. Some of the worst excesses of corruption had begun to be tackled and state monopolies were in the process of being dismantled. But Myanmar's economic elite, usually either part of or closely connected to the military, were best placed to take advantage of the economic reforms. For the economic elite, and the mutual and increasing enmeshment of the Tatmadaw's business interests in non-military business activities, it was simply good business sense to continue with economic reform. There was, however, somewhat less compulsion for the state and its key institution, the Tatmadaw, to allow political reform to run as freely as economic reform appeared to be.

As a consequence of the 2015 elections, the country has ended up with a significantly more representative government. The previously restricted NLD achieved a thumping majority status in the Hluttaw, winning 225 of the 330 Hluttaw seats able to be contested (of 440 in total) and 135 of 168 seats able to be contested in the 'House of Nationalities' (upper house) (of 224 in total). It was therefore able to form government, if of one that included Tatmadaw involvement. Yet despite saying that she would be 'above' the President, Suu Kyi could not run for the presidency herself.

In March 2016, Suu Kyi's close aide Htin Kyaw was elected as President. Suu Kyi was elected as 'State Counselor' – a position sometimes equated with that of Prime Minister – as well as Foreign Minister (placing her on the powerful security committee) and Minister in the President's Office.

There was also a question, among Myanmar's ethnic minorities, as to whether the country would simply exchange one dominant political group for another, with a charismatic leader who would find it difficult, if not impossible, to live up to sometimes unrealistic popular expectations. In particular, while Suu Kyi has been feted as a democratic leader she was, like her father, General Aung San, a committed nationalist. With limited institutional and financial capacity, hopes for change resulting in quick improvements in people's lives were limited. This, then, has the potential to both diminish both Suu Kyi's personal popularity and support for the NLD. Should this be reflected in public protest, there remains scope for the re-application of more authoritarian responses, if of a different type to those imposed under military-dominated rule.

But more importantly, the Tatmadaw has only begun to give up some of its ultimate power (see Bunte 2011: 24). As the state institution that also constituted itself as the state regime for over five decades, the Tatmadaw remains profoundly integrated into the fabric of the state. Both formally and informally, it controls or strongly influences and benefits from a significant proportion of the state's economy. It controls the direction and pace of change and, indeed, through the NDSC explicitly reserves to itself the right to replace any government should it deem the circumstances so warrant.

It was likely that Myanmar would continue to change and reform and increasingly wear the trappings of a democratic state, including having Suu Kyi and her colleagues in many ministerial offices. Importantly, on 16 March 2016, Myanmar's two houses of parliament elected Suu Kyi's close confidant Htin Kyaw as President, with another NLD member and a Tatmadaw member occupying deputy positions. Htin Kyaw was seen as being a trusted ally of Suu Kyi, having operated on her behalf in other roles. As important as his election was his acceptance, the following day, by Tatmadaw chief Min Aung Hlaing as the first non-military or ex-military President since 1962. Less positively, the election of the Tatmadaw candidate, former hardline military intelligence chief Myint Swe, to one of the two vice-presidential positions, indicated that the Tatmadaw intended to keep a weather eye on the country's political processes.

To the extent that Myanmar did continue to reform, for much of the transition period that reform would be that which the Tatmadaw approved, controlled and, very likely, benefited from. To suggest otherwise would be to propose a fundamental disjuncture between the actions and interests of the institution that, at the time of writing, continued to firmly control the parameters of political change.

Notes

1 The author was coordinator of the Union Aid Abroad-APHEDA election observer group, one of five international observer groups of a total of 350 international observers accredited to the election process. Importantly, more than 11,000 local election observers were also accredited (Kingsbury 2015).
2 Admiral Nyan Tun was previously the commander-in-chief of the Myanmar Navy. He was elected on 15 August 2012 to replace Tin Aung Myint Oo, who had resigned for 'personal reasons'.
3 There were also extensive examples of the anti-reform manipulation of local militant groups, with resultant high levels of communal violence and political destabilisation, in Indonesia between 1999 and 2005.

10 Thailand

Thailand is a paradoxical study in democracy and plutocracy, or legitimacy and elite control. Notably, Thailand appears to be structurally (if broadly) divided between urban-southern and northern-north-eastern political allegiances within the context of elite competition, institutionalised high-level corruption and a winner-takes-all political mentality. The question for Thailand is whether its main political parties (and their leaders) can reach across the current ideological, cultural and geographic divides and achieve government that is broadly accepted as being elected by a majority but representing all. If they stumble at this challenge, the country is more likely to retreat to a more restrictive constitution – its twentieth since 1932 – and a return to what might be termed a limited or constrained electoral process (see Pawakapan 2015c).

If not formally colonised, Thailand was, however, subject to colonial influence through the domination of its trade and influence on the transitions of its state institutions by Britain. Moreover, Britain set both the country's western and southern boundaries, much to the unhappiness in particular of those Malay Muslims who were divided from their southern counterparts who ultimately federated into the state of Malaysia. Similarly, Thailand's northern suzerain principality of Lanna remained within the modern Thai state, but the T'ai-speaking Shan State was incorporated into what was then British Burma.

In the east, France demarcated Thailand's border, primarily along the Mekong River[1] between it and what was to become Laos. One might suggest that this was a generous boundary, given that it left a significant ethnic Lao population in what was Thai territory. But it might equally be argued that the creation of this colonial boundary seized from Thailand territory that it regarded as under its suzerain authority, as indeed it also did with the setting of the Thai–Cambodian border.

Thailand began to modernise in the late nineteenth and early twentieth centuries and again from the 1930s. This modernisation had two effects. The first was to establish institutions of state, including higher education so that the state would no longer have to rely on an aristocratic class of bureaucrats. From the 1930s, it also began to transform parts of the economy from being traditionally rural and agricultural to manufacturing. Following Japan's economic rebirth in the post-World War II era and economic development in East Asia, Thailand experienced an economic boom from the mid-1980s until the mid-1990s which established it as an 'upper middle income' country with a per capita gross national income of around US$5,500 (World Bank 2015c).

The second effect of Thailand's modernisation was that it led to the rise of a professional military class, a military coup in 1932 and the consequent breaking of the country's absolute monarchy and establishment of a constitutional monarchy. From this point onwards, the military became the arbiter of state affairs, becoming entrenched in that role with the resignation, under pressure, of King Prajadhipok in 1935. A fulsome sense of this influence, and the self-regarding appropriateness of exercising it, created a propensity for the military to intervene in and regularly take over control of the political process. Indeed, the coup of 1932 was intended to further modernise Thailand, including changing its name from the externally applied 'Siam' to Thailand in 1939–45 and again from 1949.

If Thailand had 'modernised', there remained a structural interdependency between the monarchy, the military and elite economic interests. Thailand has had numerous elected governments, but one view of Thai politics is that, until the twenty-first century, they had not given real political power to Thailand's people. When it looked like Thailand might have a government that, while still elite-driven, more closely represented the interests of its rural poor and middle classes, traditional elites defaulted to military intervention to again secure their own interests.

Thailand was a staunch ally of the United States during the Cold War era (Fineman 1997), having a military government from 1932 until 1944, from 1947 until 1972, and then again from 1976 until 1982 and in 1991–92. Thailand actively supported the US in the Korean War (1950–53) and its war in Vietnam from 1964 until 1972, as well as combating its own communist insurgency (1965–83). Given the US's strategic concerns in Southeast Asia until well after the end of the Cold War, it continued to retain Thailand as a close and trusted ally, despite its tendency to have recurrent, imposed non-democratic governments.

A kingdom of coups

On 22 May 2014, Thailand underwent its twenty-first (and its twelfth successful) military coup since 1932. It has been suggested that countries with a history of military coups are more prone to having them again (Moore 2010: 132; Decalo 1976; Belkin and Schofer 2003), despite other factors that might seem to militate against such political overthrows. In Thailand, however, the option of military coups had an odd legitimacy, set against a global paradigm that condemned such overthrows of existing political processes, and which was not found in many other countries. To a large extent, this coup reflected the Thai military's deep and long involvement in Thailand's modern politics and was, in a sense, an option always available should nominally democratic processes not perform according to a particular set of established ideas.

At a time when other countries were moving away from authoritarian government towards more representative models, in 1991 Thailand underwent political upheaval when the popularly elected government of Chatichai Choonhavan was overthrown in a military coup after having challenged the country's traditional elites. While there were large-scale protests, numerous deaths and widespread human rights abuses associated with the coup and its aftermath, the subsequent return to democracy led to the formulation of the 1997 constitution, often praised as Thailand's most democratic ever. It was, however, not to last.

After having grown at around 9 per cent during the decade before, the period between 1997 and 2006 was marked by the impact of the Asian financial crisis and its consequent flow-on into civilian politics. The crisis began with an attack on the Thai currency, which was increasingly viewed as overvalued on the back of a 'bubble' economy. The economy had grown quickly, with money pouring into it from outside.

Much of this investment became speculative, moving into non-productive areas such as property investment, and sometimes into questionable loans. International demand had begun to reduce from 1996 and many companies found themselves having borrowed more than they could repay.

Suddenly, there was a view among international money traders that the value of the Thai currency, the Baht, had become greatly over-inflated. The value of the Baht fell from around 25 Baht to the US dollar prior to the crisis, losing 20 per cent between May and July 1997 when it was floated, declining to more than 40 Baht to the dollar by 1998, eventually bottoming out at 43 Bhat in 2002. As the value of the Baht fell, Thailand's foreign currency denominated debts increased proportionally, further adding to pressure to debt repayments.

In 1997, Democratic Party leader Chuan Leekpai, who had previously been elected Prime Minister after an abortive coup in 1992 but who lost the subsequent election in 1995, was again elected as Prime Minister. Chuan's main political claim was that he was Thailand's first Prime Minister not to have come from an aristocratic or military background. In that role, he called in the International Monetary Fund (IMF) to assist in bailing out and restructuring the country's ailing economy. 'Guest' workers, mostly from Myanmar, were sent back in order to limit the impact of business closures on Thai nationals. While Thailand's economy slowly recovered from its economic troubles, and although not nearly as corrupt as some of his predecessors, Chuan's second prime ministership was plagued by corruption scandals, leading his Democratic Party to be defeated in the 2001 elections.

With a population wanting a populist civilian government, the Democratic Party was trounced by the Thai Rak Thai Party, founded as the personal political vehicle of Thaksin Shinawatra, the former police officer and billionaire founder and head of the Shin Corporation. Thaksin's government launched popular poverty reduction programs and promoted small and medium-sized business. His appeal was very strongly oriented towards Thailand's urban and rural poor, notably in the north and north-east of the country. Thaksin was clearly of the elite, and was a largely self-made billionaire, but he was also from the north of the country and a relative outsider to the more established Bangkok-centred elites. He quickly worked out that, by pursuing populist policies among Thailand's rural (and some urban) dispossessed, he could command a majority voting block that would challenge the traditional elite grip on power and the economy.

Thaksin's populism had a darker side, too, with his 'war on drugs' leading to the extra-judicial killing of more than 2,000 suspected drug dealers. Thaksin's appeal to nationalism focused on abandoning a conciliatory approach to the country's disaffected Muslims in the south. This quickly led to an escalation of violence in the south and, in effect, the reignition of a conflict that had all but disappeared. Then Thaksin sold his Shin Corporation to foreign investors for over a billion dollars, without paying tax on the sale. His biggest 'crime', however, was to oppose the traditional establishment, whose patterns of patronage he had disrupted. Thaksin having been the first Thai Prime Minister to serve a full term, the Thai Rak Thai Party went to the ballot in 2005 and was overwhelmingly re-elected.

While the Thai Rak Thai Party won an absolute majority of seats, the elections did see a distinct geographical division between the pro-Thai Rak Thai north and the pro-Democrat south (Attachai 2012). Moreover, the strength of Thaksin's personal appeal in securing the winning vote enraged his opponents. A popularly elected government was acceptable to the traditional elites if it conformed to their ways of doing business. Thaksin did not, so his traditional elite opponents formed the 'People's Alliance for Democracy', which became better known as the 'Yellow Shirts', after the royal colour they identified with. Mass 'Yellow Shirt' protests against and 'Red Shirt' protests in favour of Thaksin's rule, allegations of corruption and abuse of power, and what was said to be his autocratic style, led Thaksin to call a snap election for April 2006. This election was boycotted by opposition parties and several members were elected with less than the required 20 per cent of the vote.

King Bhumibol took the unprecedented step of calling the elections 'undemocratic'. The election results were invalidated by the Constitutional Court, which ordered new elections to be held in October. Protests continued under Thaksin's caretaker government and, a month before the fresh elections were due to be held, the military staged a coup. The military declared martial law, arrested government ministers, scrapped the 1997 constitution, banned protests and restricted the media. Retired General Surayud Chulanont was appointed as Prime Minister, with a promise that new elections would be held in a year (*The Economist* 2006).

The Constitutional Court outlawed the Thai Rak Thai Party and banned its party executive, including Thaksin, from contesting further elections for five years. Thaksin's assets were frozen by the junta-appointed Assets Examination Committee and he and his wife were later charged with the corrupt purchase of landholdings while in office, with his wife and brother-in-law also being charged in 2007 with conspiring to evade taxation.

Despite the establishment's attempts to break Thaksin politically and financially, the Thai Rak Thai Party was reformed as the People's Power Party (PPP), led by Samak Sundaravej. After 17 months in self-imposed exile, in February 2008 Thaksin returned to Thailand but faced further charges, with his wife being convicted of violating stock trading and land sale laws. While Thaksin and his family had engaged in a number of profitable ventures while in office, there was a widespread view that the charges brought against them were politically motivated. In August, Thaksin and his wife both left the country, in violation of bail conditions, moving to Dubai and then Cambodia.

Thailand's sense of political crisis continued, despite elections being held at the end of 2007. The PPP formed government with five smaller parties, but Yellow Shirt protests continued, along with unsuccessful parliamentary votes of no confidence. However, Samak was forced to resign as Prime Minister after being found guilty of a 'conflict of interest' for hosting a television cooking program. Samak was succeeded in October 2008 by Thaksin's brother-in-law, Somchai Wongsawat, but he immediately ran into trouble when Yellow Shirt protesters blocked him from entering his offices, as well as blockading the airports. Two months later, the Constitutional Court ruled, controversially, that the PPP had engaged in electoral fraud, ordering the party to dissolve, in what was described by the pro-PPP 'Red Shirt' United Front for Democracy Against Dictatorship as a 'judicial coup' (Weaver 2008; see Hewison 2010 for a summary of key machinations over this period).

The minor parties that had formed government with the PPP were encouraged by the armed forces to join with the Democratic Party to form a new government. Democratic Party leader Abhisit Vejjajiva was sworn in as the new Prime Minister on 17 December 2008. Political turmoil continued, however, with Red Shirt protests forcing the cancellation of the April 2009 East Asia Summit after storming the Pattaya hotel where it was to be held (it was eventually held in October). A year later, further Red Shirt protests led to at least 87 deaths and more than 1,300 injured, and in April 2010 an army attempt to block a Red Shirt protest was met by the opposition 'Watermelon' faction within the army,[2] with automatic gunfire, hand grenades and firebombs. Grenades and bomb attacks against government offices and ministers' homes continued, with some Bangkok business districts being shut down for several weeks. Thailand was veering wildly.

To break the cycle of violence, elections were held in July 2011, with the Pheu Thai Party headed by Thaksin's sister, Yingluck, winning in a landslide. It was becoming clear that, despite claims made against Thaksin, for most Thais he had tapped into a deep-seated sense of alienation from the political process and his party, in differing guises, appeared to have a lock on majority government. Similarly, the 'old guard' alliance of the king, the military and the financial elite could no longer command a majority in an open electoral environment. In response, the Yellow Shirts, led by former deputy opposition leader Suthep Thaungsuban, maintained a campaign of destabilisation against the Pheu Thai government. Another coup seemed almost inevitable.

According to the International Crisis Group:

> The past decade has seen an intensifying cycle of election, protest and government downfall, whether at the hands of the courts or military, revealing deepening societal cleavages and elite rivalries, highlighting competing notions of legitimate authority. A looming royal succession, prohibited by law from being openly discussed, adds to the urgency.
>
> (ICG 2014)

Protests against Yingluck's prime ministership began to mount, with Yellow Shirt protesters alleging that she headed a 'parliamentary dictatorship' and presided over a corrupt government. Yingluck called a general election which was boycotted by the main opposition and invalidated by the Constitutional Court. The same court then forced Yingluck from office for an alleged administrative violation. Yingluck appointed a caretaker government amid continuing protests and, as she refused to resign, the military staged a coup.

There was little doubt that Thailand's coup was about more than removing an allegedly corrupt government. It was very much about trying to break the Shinawatra family's hold on political power and, by extension, dismantling its extensive crony networks. But it was also about ensuring that the country's more traditional elites, including the royal family (or most of it), the armed forces and allied businesses, regained political power in a way that could not again be easily overturned by something as simple as an electoral majority (Pawakapan 2015c; Jory 2014).

Parties that represented Thaksin had won each of the general elections in 2001, 2005, 2007 and 2011, each time confronting stiff establishment resistance. Indicative of the deep divisions in Thai politics, only the first of these governments was allowed to run a full term. Thaksin showed an authoritarian bent, yet his parties won each time there was a return to the polls. Under these circumstances, the ouster of Yingluck's government seemed to many – both those for and against it – almost inevitable. This time, the more active role of the military in government, the intensifying political divide and the impending royal succession have created a tightening torque of tension that might prove difficult to roll back.

There is no doubt that the turmoil that led to the 2014 coup was highly engineered, although destabilising a political environment in order to achieve a particular, if dramatic, outcome was not a novel approach to politics in Southeast Asia's political history generally and Thailand in particular. However, the consequent coup did represent a further confluence of interests that was unusual even for Thailand's sometimes fractious political environment, and which centred on the source of Thailand's political and economic hegemony, if not legitimacy, since 1946, King Bhumibol Adulyadej.

Thailand had long been dominated by a cosy elite that was linked to royal patronage and protected by the military. There were, from time to time, occasional nods in the direction of democracy, or at least electoral politics, but a less generous view might have suggested that, until the election of Thaksin Shinawatra as Prime Minister in 2001, this elite acted as a functional oligarchy and only pretended to allow ordinary Thais any say in how the country was actually run.

When push came to shove, Thaksin's elite opponents, the People's Alliance for Democracy, had their protesters on the streets, wearing Yellow Shirts, from which they derived their name, symbolising the authority of the king, which they did not explicitly have. By way of clarifying differences, although much of the pro-Thaksin Red Shirt movement was populist and driven by frustration, there were also significant elements of political sophistication and those who dared to start thinking of a Thailand that was radically reconfigured from its elite, patronage-driven past to a more genuinely democratic future (see Buchanan 2013).

The royal political economy

A critical element in the ordering of Thailand's elites, perhaps the country's key source of patronage and that which continued to underwrite the power of the monarchy (and the need for a smooth transition), is the Crown Property Bureau (CPB). The CPB is an investment arm of the Thai monarchy, but technically it neither belongs to the king nor is it a government agency. It was established, towards the end of the nineteenth century, as the Privy Purse Bureau within the Ministry of Finance, with about 15 per cent of government revenue allocated to it until the mid-1920s, declined over the following decade.

The CPB was used to develop trade infrastructure, including roads, and facilitated significant economic development, including the purchasing and development of property and supporting commerce in Bangkok, thus linking Bangkok's economic development and its beneficiaries to royal interests. Following the military coup of 1932 and the ending of absolute monarchy in Thailand, a civilian government divided up the royal properties. However, the CPB Act of 1948, at the direction of military dictator Field Marshall Plaek Phibunsongkhram, handed control of royal properties back to the monarchy, with the king appointing the CPB's operating director and board.

There has been a close, cooperative relationship between the military and the monarchy since, as well as close connections between the CPB and the military, and between the military and companies (Pasuk and Baker 2002: 107–10) which benefit from being in business with the CPB and which are in corrupt relationships with senior military officers (Ferrara 2015: 194). Indeed, it could be said that the military is the guarantor of the king's wealth and the CPB and, by extension, Thailand's elite networks, in what has been called 'despotic paternalism' (Keyes 2015: 1), in no small part for its own benefit. In 2008, *Forbes* magazine estimated the king's wealth to be in the order of US$35 billion, making him the world's richest ruler (*Forbes* 2008).

The Asian financial crisis (1997–98) hit Thailand hard, with the CPB incurring losses of around US$200 million, with no dividend income from two of its key investments, the Siam Cement Group and the Siam Commercial Bank, for five years. It survived the crisis, however, restructuring, diversifying, raising rents on larger properties and focusing on short-term investments. It also continued to enjoy, and take advantage of, the tax-free status of many of its investments. By 2015, the CPB was estimated to have increased in value from around US$1 billion to almost US$3 billion, being among Thailand's largest business conglomerates and with its directors also being directors in other large Thai corporations (Ouyyanont 2015). Having said that, the CPB controlled property valued at more than US$30 billion, and was said to be worth some $70 billion in total (Lee 2014).

A significant part of the concern with the succession of Thailand's ageing and frail king, therefore, concerned which way patronage would flow following the king's death. Crown Prince Vajirlongkorn's close relationship with Thaksin Shinawatra, himself still estimated to be worth US$1.7 billion, could see the CPB's patronage directed away from its traditional beneficiaries, those behind the Yellow Shirt movement. While Thailand's king remained active, this was troubling but perhaps not critical. The 'troubling' aspect of Thaksin's political rise was quickly dealt with by a military coup in 2006, Thaksin being voluntarily exiled in 2008. But, no sooner had the interim military regime allowed a return to a popular vote than Thaksin's sister, Yingluck Shinawatra, acting in his place, was elected as Prime Minister in 2011, employing the same policies and rising on the back of the same support base.

If Thaksin had threatened to challenge Thailand's oligarchic status quo while the king was alive, as the King became older, less well and less active, as the pivotal point in Thai political-economy, the issue of his succession became critical. It was alliances between members of the royal family and political contenders, and their significant vested interests, that ultimately shaped both the movement to oust Yingluck and, ultimately, the installation of another military government that appeared to be moving towards establishing constitutional and hence economic security for the traditional elites.

Whither the monarchy?

Thailand's political crisis reflects competition over elite access to the spoils of office, high levels of official corruption and a class division between the country's urban and rural poor and the urban middle and upper classes. But what is not openly discussed, even though it has been at the centre of Yellow Shirt calls for political change, is the future role of Thailand's monarchy and the eventual departure of King Bhumibol, whose seven decades on the throne had been the centrepiece of Thai politics.

This subject has not been raised because to do so is to commit lèse majesté – offence against royal dignity. This is a crime regularly punished by imprisonment (e.g. see Jenkins 2015), while the *International New York Times* had articles arbitrarily removed by its Thai printer four times in 2015. So harsh had Thailand's lèse majesté laws become that even the US Ambassador to Thailand was investigated by police for having discussed in a speech the issue of excessive use of lèse majesté laws.

Lèse majesté charges increased following the 2006 coup, in large part reflecting the deepening division and brittleness of Thai politics since that time, and marking a public obeisance towards the king in marked contrast to earlier and especially Cold War-era journalistic references (Pawakapan 2015a). While King Bhumibol was said to be widely respected in Thai society, in some quarters even being revered (and it was illegal to say otherwise), his immediate successor to the throne, Crown Prince Maha Vajirlongkorn, was said to be less well accepted. *The Economist* reported, in 2010 and soon after King Bhumibol was hospitalised, that Prince Vajirlongkorn was 'already widely loathed and feared' (*The Economist* 2010), not least by Thailand's traditional elites.

Few in Thailand were comfortable with the idea of Prince Vajirlongkorn becoming king. Among the country's oligarchs, a lack of trust concerning the prince's patronage preferences and his various indulgences rankled. The prince was widely known as a play-boy (Swaine 2010) who preferred the pleasures of Europe to his own country, who made 'artistic' movies and whose pet poodle, Fufu, was formally ranked as an Air Chief Marshal, sometimes wearing a military uniform. Although not a movie, video footage of the near naked Princess Srirasmi, consort of the Prince, at Air Chief Marshal Fufu the dog's 2001 birthday party, caused a major scandal when it was leaked in 2007.

The leaking of the video, following the 2006 coup, was thought to be the work of opponents of the Crown Prince who did not want to see him succeed his father to the throne. Citing corruption by members of her family, in 2014 the Crown Prince divorced the Princess and asked that she be formally stripped of her title. Fufu died in February 2015 and, following four days of Buddhist funeral rites, was formally cremated (*The Guardian* 2015). The Prince had shown a clear dislike of courtly behaviour (as illustrated by the 2001 video), but as his father's health declines has begun taking on more ceremonial roles.

By contrast, the prince's sister and second in line to the throne, Princess Sirindhorn, has been widely admired by Thais looking beyond King Bhumibol's reign, in particular by the Yellow Shirts. It has been widely suggested that this admiration is mutual and that both would like to see her ascend to the throne. Thailand's laws of succession were amended in 1974 (and reaffirmed in 1997 and 2007) to allow the succession of a direct female descendent of the king, pending the approval of the legislature. Yellow Shirt leader Suthep Thaugsuban and his protesters were said to be financially supported by those who strongly wished Princess Sirindhorn to succeed her father. In contrast to the royal yellow, some troops on the streets soon after the 2014 declaration of martial law wore purple ribbons – the princess' color.

Reflecting the division within public Thai politics, Prince Vajirlongkorn was said to be close to ousted former Prime Minister Thaksin Shinawatra. The prince even had his own praetorian guard, the Royal Guard 904 Corps, largely drawn from soldiers from the north and north-east – home of the Red Shirts and bastion of the Shinawatra clan. When the army was slow to provide protection to ousted Prime Minister Yingluck Shinawatra in 2014, the prince sent his own guard to protect her. Whether or not the prince suc-ceeded to the throne could determine whether Thaksin was granted a pardon and allowed to return to Thailand.

However, while the Shinawatra family appeared close to one side in the royal feud, many Red Shirts, often informed by more revolutionary ideas, wanted to see an end to the monarchy altogether. It was notable that, within this context, that the only element of the 2007 constitution that was retained immediately following the 2014 military coup was that section identifying the king as the head of state.

The question, then, that was not discussed was what would happen to Thailand's mon-archy once the king eventually dies. One option was that there would be a continua-tion, or even a strengthening, of the role of the royalty, with very limited democracy, as the Yellow Shirts wanted. The alternative was that the monarchy would be further made ceremonial and increasingly irrelevant or, less likely, done away with altogether, with Thailand becoming a fully democratic state, as many Red Shirts wanted. The army, firmly in political control, was unlikely to loosen its grip on power until after the king died and this question about the fundamental direction of Thai politics was able to be answered.

In seizing power so soon after its last intervention in 2006, and following its involvement in violently quelling 2010 street protests, the military, under General Prayuth Chanocha, appeared determined to learn from what it sees as its past errors. Thus, the new military regime, the National Council for Peace and Order (NCPO), moved forcefully to repress dissent and looked unlikely to relinquish power easily. An interim charter gave absolute power to the NCPO, including amnesties for its members for past and future actions. It provided no role for elected representatives or means for popular political participation. The parameters it set out for the next constitution suggested elected authority would be heavily circumscribed, given that previous efforts to overcome the influence of Thaksin and his proxies had so comprehensively failed.

On 17 April 2015, the first draft of Thailand's new Constitution, written by the NCPO appointed 36-member Constitution Drafting Committee, was completed. It 'has been framed by the coup-makers as a critical step to moving Thailand out of political paralysis' (Prashanth 2015). The new constitution was to be, when inaugurated, the country's twentieth since 1932.

A survey showed some degree of concern with what type of constitution Thailand would have once the military government had decided to relinquish power. Almost two-thirds of respondents to a survey agreed that a referendum on the new Constitution should be conducted (ISEAS 2015b). More than 10 per cent were opposed to the idea of a referendum, with just under one quarter being either unsure or not specifying an answer. If this response could be construed as hostility to the process of the new constitution, it might then roughly accord with the continuing majority opposition to the military regime and the Yellow Shirt political coalition and, at least as importantly, likely continued majority support for the Shinawatra-led rural and poor coalition.

Responding to continuing support for a genuinely democratic process, the NCPO embarked on what was described as the militarisation of Thai society, including its responses addressing small unregulated commercial activities such as street vendors and disputes over access to resources:

> The measures in question are a result of the NCPO's plan to resolve disputes over national forest areas, and exemplifies the result of the 2014 coup allowing the military to extend its power and control far into the social, economic and political life of common people.
>
> (Pawakapan 2015b)

Following the coup

After months of political turmoil, the Thai economy remained sluggish. In spite of its proclaimed anti-populism, the military had found no alternative to extensive public spending. The decade-old separatist insurgency in the Malay-Muslim-majority southern provinces ground on. The NCPO insisted it would pursue dialogue with militant leaders, but its refusal to countenance any form of special administration for the region called into question the rationale for talks (see ICG 2010 for background). A bombing at the Erawan shrine in downtown Bangkok which killed 20 people and injured scores more in August 2015 only highlighted Bangkok's sense of uncertainty.

The bombing occurred against a background of the NCPO having maintained its suspension of civil liberties, imposing media censorship and measures to remove the power of elected officials, all of which appeared to contradict its stated aim of returning Thailand to democracy, which had been deferred until at least 2017. Yet without any sign of a national consensus being formed, it seemed that Thailand would at best be allowed to have limited electoral politics, but no longer a democracy in a meaningful sense of the term. It was expected therefore that, without strong and independent institutions and a proper process of representation and accountability, the country's pattern of military-backed elite control and patron–client relations would continue to shape Thai political and economic life.

According to Ouyyanont (2014), the 2014 coup differed from previous coups in that not only did it repress dissent, centralise power, impose censorship and defer a return to electoral politics, it also focused on dismantling the political apparatus established by Thaksin Shinawatra when he was Prime Minister. By establishing a strong – some said almost authoritarian – prime ministerial regime, Thaksin sidestepped traditional power structures and the royalist influence that Duncan McCargo (2005) described as a 'network monarchy'. McCargo noted that the leading 'network' in Thailand's political economy between 1973 and Thaksin's rise to power in 2001 was centred on the palace and the king's proxies in civil office.

Ouvyanont proposed that the 'network' monarchy implied a weak state in formal institutional terms, which Thaksin (and his sister Yingluck) had attempted to counter. In doing so, the 2014 coup entrenched its authority to a greater extent than had previously occurred in Thailand's more recent coups, and may have removed the balancing role that the Thai monarchy had come to play in Thai politics (Ouvyanont 2014).

Despite the military coup showing outwards signs of control, it has also been criticised for being more a display of institutional weakness. Moreover, it may not achieve its intended goals of structural change in ways that at least provide electoral balance, if not privilege, to the country's urban elites (Jory 2015). The concentration of power in the hands of self-appointed Prime Minister General Prayuth Chan-ocha and the NCPO, a high level of repression, widespread censorship and heavy propaganda were all signs not of strength but of a lack of popular support and hence the weakness of the military regime.

Following the coup, the military junta put in place a 36-member Constitution Drafting Committee (CDC), intended to draft a new constitution which would ensure that the electoral system would fall in favour of the old centres of elite power. A draft of the constitution would allow for extra-parliamentary powers, including the military, to legally intervene in Thailand's politics, and for an unelected person to become Prime Minister with two-thirds of parliamentary support. It was also expected that the military would have a more active role in the political process even following elections (Pawakapan 2015a). Moreover, the military officers responsible for staging the 2014 coup would be granted immunity from prosecution. The proposed constitution would see only 77 of 200 senators elected, with the rest being appointed via a proportional representation system. There was little support for the proposed constitution from any of Thailand's political parties (Niyomyat 2015).

Should the proposed constitution be enacted, the proportional voting system would encourage smaller parties and coalition governments in the lower house of parliament, which would weaken it and make it less stable. The upper house would be comprised of candidates nominated by committee or selected by professional groups, including one dominated by former military figures. In order that there would be an oversight function, agencies seen as linked to traditional elites would be given new powers. The intention, clearly, was to ensure that Thailand's traditional elites retained control of both the economy and the government and that traditional networks of power, patronage and influence remained intact, while non-elite Thais were to be allowed a marginal say in the political process.

Earlier Thai constitutions had also featured an appointed prime minister and senate, along with a divided and relatively weak lower house. Such systems were unstable, leading to 25 coalition governments between 1979 and 2001. However, many non-elite Thais unhappy with their being sidelined from the active political process had felt, under the two constitutions prior to the 2014 coup that their vote could actually produce an outcome they preferred. Moreover, of the two rationales used to oust Thaksin and then his sister Yingluck, corruption could have been expected to remain endemic in Thai economic life, being part and parcel of the patron–client networks that comprise Thai political life.

On 29 October 2015, Prayuth threatened to stay on in power and to 'close the country' if 'peace and order' could not be established. In response to external expressions of concern, Prayuth's statement was quickly defended by Deputy Prime Minister Prawit Wongsuwon as not being intended to be taken literally (Wassana 2015). However, many did view Prayuth's comments as being a frank expression of his intent should there not be broad acceptance of his restrictive constitutional vision for the country.

Thailand's uncertain 'roadmap'

Following the coup, the junta said that it had what it called a 'roadmap to a return to democracy'. However, the announcement of a 'roadmap' only indicated that it would be some time before Thailand again had some form of civilian government. Although there was no clear way of knowing levels of support, it was clear from the outset that, while there had been an orchestrated campaign against Yingluck Shinawatra as Prime Minister and many were not supporters of previously ousted Prime Minister Thaksin Shinawatra, they believed she had performed better in that role. One of the concerns that many elite Thais had with Thaksin was that he let huge government contracts to his own supporters. There was less such concern with Yingluck, but more with her trying to engineer Thaksin's return to Thailand.

One question that had arisen following the coup was whether the junta was letting its own contracts to businesses associated with the army and senior officers, or to others of the traditional elite, given allegations of corruption that had been levelled against a number of junta ministers (Chachavalpongpun 2014).

In November 2015, an army Colonel and a Major were charged in connected with lèse majesté and with a corruption scandal involving an army-backed development project at Rajabhakti Park. The charges related to demanding illegal commissions worth millions of dollars in relation to the construction of the project (Wassana and Wassayos 2015). A key figure in the scandal, Suriyan, and a police Major at the centre of the affair both died while in police custody. These deaths came with claims that there had been a number of unusual 'suicides' of prisoners.

Under an eventual civilian government, there remains a question over the extent to which it will be democratically elected and, hence, politically accountable. The junta has appointed a committee to advise on political 'reforms', including rewriting the constitution. Thailand's 1997 constitution was widely regarded as its most democratic, placing the election of both houses of parliament in the hands of the voters and stipulating a series of human rights and democratic safeguards. It was criticised by a small minority, however, for removing power from previously vested interests. The replacement 2007 constitution much more narrowly prescribed Thai citizens' rights and ensured the Senate was controlled by interests aligned to more traditional sources of power. It was deadlock caused by this Senate, supported by anti-government and other vested interests, that led to the political showdown of 2013–14, the ouster of Yingluck as Prime Minister and, ultimately, the 2014 military coup.

The junta's proposed 'roadmap to democracy', then, begs the question of whether whatever political system is next put in place, in a meaningful sense, will comply with the widely prescribed definition of the term 'democracy' – sovereignty vested in all the people under a rule determined by a majority in a free, fair and transparent electoral process.

Whither democracy?

Thai politics has historically been driven by near feudal patron–client networks, in which senior political actors could switch allegiance depending on changing circumstances and with their client networks largely following along behind. This process was underwritten by Thailand's military, which has a long history of stepping in and taking power when elite feuding had become destabilising. However, the effective control of Thai politics by Thaksin Shinawatra, who came from a police rather than military background, threw out this political model. While Thaksin was of the wealthy elites himself, and became more so just prior to and following his assumption of the prime ministership in 2001, he acknowledged and gave voice to Thailand's traditionally excluded rural populations, especially of the north and north-east, and some of the urban working class.

Thai politics suddenly became functionally apolitical, along lines of top-down patron–client networks, and much more 'horizontal' and hence ideological. Party politics was at last given substance around competing visions of the state, rather than as a largely coherent elite dividing up the spoils among itself, protected by and enmeshed with the Thai military. In this sense, even when Thailand was returned to electoral politics, it was not likely to be one that represented wider group interests but rather one which reflected narrow elite interests and hence the interests of groups loyal to those particular elites.

Adjudicating above it all, but deeply a part of this system and guaranteed by the military, is the king. There is little doubt that, when he was younger, King Bhumibol was able to control the worst excesses of elite division by simply giving an order. However, in the years ahead of the 2014 coup, and since it, his capacity for any sort of meaningful decree, much less astute decision making, has diminished. With deep divisions between his son and favoured daughter, and the king himself having lost some capacity and hence authority due to the ravages of time, the royal family could be said to have lost much of its political influence. In one sense, this 'majestic control' was what General Prayuth Chan-ocha tried to impose in the days before the coup, and what some viewed as his own post-coup positioning.

However, as highly as the general might have regarded himself, others did not see him as having that final majestic quality. His commands, therefore, came across as the barked orders of someone used to giving commands and being strictly obeyed, rather than as wise advice from a respected, in some quarters even revered, father figure. Those commands being ignored, Prayuth launched his coup.

The second change, connected to this, is that while the Thai royal family would likely continue in its symbolic role, its real power is under question, which could help create a fundamentally democratic opening. It is impossible to tell what Thailand's citizens think of the royal family, given that it is illegal to conduct surveys which might ask, and answer, such questions. But it is reasonable to say that the stature and influence of the king has not been passed to his squabbling children. There was an old prophecy that the Chakri dynasty would only last for nine kings, making Bhumibol – also known as Rama IX – the last of them. It is perhaps excessive to put much store in such prophecies, but that they are widely known could help accelerate what might otherwise be a natural decline.

In the period since the 2014 coup, the military has arrested 'dissidents' for relatively short periods of 're-education' and banned public political meetings, while overt political activity has been forced underground. As the 2015 academic year drew to a close, there was some unrest among Bangkok university students, historically the source of pro-democracy protest. It is one thing for the military to crack down on the uneducated and uncultured country bumpkins who, in the Bangkok elite view, were thought to comprise the Red Shirt movement. But it is entirely another thing when the country's supposed next elite generation is being attacked.

In this respect, there is a growing distance between the military regime and even its former Yellow Shirt supporters. In the final analysis, the civilian side of politics has more in common with each other, regardless of the colour of their shirts, than they do with the military regime. There might remain a deep competition of political ideas between the 'red' and 'yellow' factions, but there is increasing agreement that this competition does not include the military.

With an historic elite increasingly recognising that it no longer remains in a 'winner takes all' position and that reverting to military coups is an unhelpful and unpalatable option, there is an incentive for agreeing to 'the rules of the game'. It may be some time before a social contract is understood to exist in Thailand, but this is the only viable alternative to an isolated elite or a more and more restive and demanding rural and working class. Thailand is, therefore, in a political situation that demands significant evolutionary change. That its politics suffer from a relatively high degree of geographic divide is unhelpful, although there remains more commitment to the idea of being 'Thai' than there is to how being 'Thai' could be politically manifested.

The military regime, meanwhile, has tried to come up with a new constitution that is all but universally regarded as illegitimate. The main problem is that the process by which it was developed was widely seen as illegitimate, so no matter what its content, it cannot be regarded as popularly acceptable.

The mood in Thailand, therefore, is one for a return to civilian politics, probably in a more negotiated environment which includes greater coherence around 'the rules of the game'. The military has worn out its welcome, even among those who initially called for its intervention, the royal family is all but finished as a political force and there is a sense that a return to electoral politics could include the sorts of compromises that have allowed it to work in a representative capacity elsewhere.

In the period following the 2014 coup, Thailand has been a long way from democracy, but the democratic sentiment is perhaps the strongest it has been. There appears to be a rejection of non-democratic actors as viable alternatives, and an acceptance of compromise of the type that implies 'government for all'. That is, perhaps, an optimistic assessment of Thailand's political future.

Notes

1 The name 'Mekong River' is a linguistic redundancy, given that the Thai word *mae* translates as 'river', and that its name is more accurately the Kong River.
2 So-called because they were 'green on the outside, but red on the inside'.

11 The Philippines

Brief introduction to category: democratising and democratic states

If Southeast Asia has reflected the full gamut of the main categories of state types, it has included within that, if somewhat fitfully, some states that have developed, or redis-covered, a commitment to forms of democracy. Democracy, in the contemporary sense, implies competitive elections devoid of fraud, with broad suffrage; civil liberties; freedom of speech, assembly and association; and the elected government having effective capacity to govern. These conditions comply with what is referred to as an 'expanded procedural minimum' of requirements (e.g. see Schmitter and Karl 1991). A more normatively desir-able substantive democracy also implies the separation of powers between the executive, legislature and judiciary, to ensure there is no undue or corrupt interference in the func-tions of the key institutions of the state.

However, as some Southeast Asian states so well demonstrate, democracy is not inevi-table, is not necessarily permanent, and includes among its practices many compromises that can raise, and have raised, the questions of at what point a democracy can be said to be such, and at what point it functionally becomes some other sort of political system.[1] Moreover, in keeping with O'Donnell's analysis (1996), there are arguably no 'consoli-dated' democracies but only a range of more or less democratic systems that are in a state of conceptual movement, democratising when heading towards more representative and accountable outcomes and tending towards more authoritarian models when heading away. Further, the outwards aspects of a state can be democratic while its internal and less publicly visible practices, such as corruption, vote-buying, intimidation and violence, may not be.

Regardless of the extent to which democracy can be said to have 'arrived' or 'con-solidated', the process is almost never a straightforward one, with numerous twists and turns, the occasional dead-end and, very often, reversals along the way. As O'Donnell and Schmitter noted, democratic transitions can be reversed by powerful vested interests (1986: 56), so the way forward is never set according to some determined formula.

Introduction: the Philippines

It used to be suggested that, due to its Spanish colonial heritage, the Philippines was more an honorary Latin American country than an Asian one. While the Philippines shared many commonalities with its archipelagic Southeast Asian neighbours, its own political trajectory appeared to also be similar to that of its Latin American counterparts. Ecuador's transition to democracy in 1979 heralded the beginning of a wave of Latin

American democratisation, as one after another of the region's military dictators was replaced by more or less democratic regimes. In 1986, the Philippines followed suit, ending the 21-year long and increasingly corrupt rule of President Ferdinand Marcos.

To some extent, the political changes in Latin America could be attributed to a shift in orientation by the United States, under the Carter administration, towards a more human rights-based approach to foreign policy. Notably, in 1977, President Jimmy Carter initiated the first of what were to become annual Country Reports on Human Rights Practices, which found serious fault with many regimes the US had previously supported, including those in Latin America and, not least, the Philippines (Ahlberg 2013: 199). These anti-authoritarian changes were also part of a wider 'third wave' of democratisation that had been sweeping parts of southern Europe and Latin American since the mid-1970s (see Huntington 1991, 1993).

As a former US colony, the Philippines had subsequently been very close to the United States, being a key regional ally during the Cold War. Until 1991, the US maintained active military bases in the Philippines, at Subic Bay and Clarke Field air force base and minor subsidiary locations. However, following the conclusion of the Cold War, the US' focus shifted away from East Asia and the Pacific. There was also growing frustration with the US within the Philippines and, with the bases agreement up for renegotiation in 1991, the Philippines Senate voted by a slim majority not to renew the base leases. The two countries have, however, maintained close military cooperation under a Visiting Forces Agreement.

While the country transitioned to 'democracy' in the 1980s, as with much else in Filipino public life, that process was as much about style as substance. The Marcos dictatorship was replaced by a return to pre-Marcos oligarchic politics in the capital, if with perhaps the development of an increasingly competent political class compared to the Marcos era. However, corruption and violence remained influential at the local level and family networks or dynasties continued to dominate the political landscape from the top to most local levels of government. High-level leadership change, however, became much more possible, even if political leadership continued to require the functional support of a majority of the elite to sustain political power.

Having noted that top leadership change was more possible, following patterns of elite reproduction (Querubin 2012), family dynasties remained the dominant political form. At each level of government, office holders were only allowed two terms. However, it was common across the Philippines for office holders not to be challenged in their first or often second terms (mayors are allowed to run for three terms), meaning less rather than greater political competition, and for such office holders to use their position to leverage the advantages of office to place other family members in succeeding positions.

The presidency of Benigno Aquino III was a case in point. Aquino was the son of former President Cory Aquino (of the Cojuanco clan, with both her own parents being highly politically connected), who in turn succeeded as a politician her husband, former Senator Benigno Aquino Jr. The Aquinos were of the Philippines' *hacienda* elite, which derived from the influence of colonial quasi-aristocratic Spanish who based their power in large land-holdings. Benigno Aquino Snr was the Speaker of the House of Representatives, while his father, Servillano Aquino, was a General under the Philippines' first recognised President, Emilio Aguinaldo (1899–1901). Benigno Aquino III's uncle, Herminio Aquino, was a former minister and a vice-presidential candidate in 2004.

This phenomenon of families controlling political power has been referred to as 'clan political enterprise' or 'clan-inclusive government'. Referring to their embeddedness in the Philippines' political process, Alim (2014) noted that: 'In many instances, local politicians are the most resistance to change'. While there has been an improvement in the performance of the political class since the Marcos era, there has since also been a decline from initial advances, with in particular a decline in leaders being elected on merit (Mendoza 2015). 'There is strong evidence suggesting that the leadership selection process in the country is already failing these meritocratic ideals. The failure stems primarily from dynastic politics' (Mendoza 2015).

The state

As with most other contemporary Southeast Asian states, the Philippines as it is known did not have a history as a state but, prior to European colonisation, was comprised of a number of maritime and highland polities. By the late fourteenth century, Islam had arrived in the archipelago, gaining its strongest hold in the south but having more limited influence towards the north of the island group.

The Spanish explorer Ferdinand Magellan was among the first Europeans to discover the archipelago, in 1521, claiming the islands for Spain. Magellan was killed at Mactan Island, near Cebu in the Visayas, after intervening in a dispute between local chieftains. Spanish colonialism of the Philippines was deeply important for three reasons: it broke down traditional polities and land ownership systems, creating a *hacienda*-type economy based on large land-holdings predominantly owned by a locally born Spanish and *mestizo* class; it subsumed local religious practices, including Islam, in the middle and northern parts of the archipelago under Roman Catholicism; and it ran up against Muslim resistance in the south of the archipelago.

The other main colonial influence in Philippines political organisation and life was that of the United States. At a time when Filipino elites were becoming restive and beginning to rebel against Spanish colonial rule, as a consequence of the Spanish–American War, the United States took possession of the archipelago from Spain in 1898. Despite initial rebellion and longer-term dissent in the Islamic south, the United States was to be the Philippines' colonial master from that time until 1946.

By the 1920s, the United States was already a fervent anti-colonial actor on the world stage, so its possession of the Philippines was anathema. It therefore readied the Philippines for independence, bequeathing an interpretation of its own model of republican government, underscored by the landed elites of the Spanish era. Oligarchic exploitation of a landless peasant class and electoral politics fuelled by corruption and violence became the norm, with consequent leftist political opposition, repression and increasing political closure. As a close US ally during the Cold War, the Philippines' intolerance of leftist dissent was encouraged, further entrenching the delegitimisation of otherwise reasonable protest against poverty, income inequality and dispossession, and a culture of corruption, violence and impunity (Muller 1985).

Political system

If to some extent more in theory than in practice, the Philippines was effectively bequeathed a US-type of government, although as a unitary rather than a federal state, with a strong focus on the *trias politica*, or separation of powers between the executive, the legislature and the judiciary. The executive branch is headed by the president, elected for a single six-year term. The term of the presidency and vice-presidency has varied, but

was standardised in 1987 at a single six-year term (as per the original 1935 constitution) after having been shortened to four years but for two terms and, under Ferdinand Marcos, three terms.

The Philippines legislature, the Congress, has a House of Representatives and a Senate. Twenty-four senators are elected from the entire country every three years for a six-year term, with a maximum of two terms in office. Having a national constituency, senators tend to have a national profile, with the Senate itself being highly centralised. Given there are relatively few senators for the size of the country and the number of parties, pre-selection for senate positions is keenly sought after and contested, with usually non-transparent deals within and between parties determining favoured candidates. Eight parties and two independent candidates were represented in the Philippines Senate following the 2013 elections. The Nacionalista Party, the Philippines' oldest political party, and the United Nationalist Alliance (UNA – translating as 'first' in Filipino), founded by two main parties and having 20 small parties in alliance, were the two biggest parties in the senate, with five seats each.

There are 250 members of the House of Representatives, from both geographic and sectoral (minority) constituencies. One of the biggest issues facing the House of Representatives is the unequal size of its electorates, which in 2013 varied from less than 17,000 inhabitants (Batanes) to almost 1.1 million inhabitants (1st District Caloocan City). More heavily populated provinces tend to be those which are least well proportionally represented. This form of 'gerrymandering' has led to disproportionate results in the Philippines' House of Representative and has fundamentally compromised the simple democratic notion of all votes having equal value.

The Philippines' local government areas are divided into autonomous regions, provinces, cities, municipalities and *barangays* (sub-municipal districts, wards or villages), each of which has an elected leader (governor, mayor, 'captain') and a legislative body. While politics at any level of Philippines public life can be brutal, politics at the sub-national levels can be especially so, with 'warlord' families often forming political dynasties to ensure that political control and its spoils are not lost. Intimidation and corruption are common in sub-national politics, and mayoralties in particular can be highly sought after and strongly competed for.[2] It is conventional practice for Filipino politicians to have personal security guards, and not uncommon for them to have teams of 'security' and indeed large, highly organised paramilitary gangs that are used as a means of enforcing law, compelling compliance with particular political or economic wishes, or attacking political rivals.

Perhaps the best known, but very far from the only, example of this violent political rivalry was carried out in 2009 by loyalists of a former Governor of the province of Maguindinao, Andal Ampatuan, whose son was attempting to succeed him against a former ally-turned- competitor, Ismael Manudadatu. Manudadatu sent a convoy of journalists and women to file his candidacy papers, believing they would be protected from attack by the Ampatuan gang. Instead, nearing the Ampatuan area, 46 people, including 12 journalists, were forced from their cars by a gang led by Andal Ampatuan Jr and summarily murdered, being buried in mass graves. Local police officers were said to have been present during the murders (Murphy 2009).

More conventionally, though, on a day-to-day basis, constituents are more commonly persuaded by promises of money or services, or through clan loyalties based on wider patron–client relationships. Violence and intimidation are primarily kept for maintaining 'law and order'. It is generally only when constituents or opponents present a real challenge or strong critique that violence and intimidation came to the political fore.[3]

The culture of 'guns, goons and gold' may have declined (Linantud 1998), but it is very far from having disappeared.

The quality of the Philippines' 'democracy' is, however, poor. 'The Philippines, in particular, got category-scores of 9.12 in civil liberties, 8.33 in electoral process and pluralism, 5.56 in political participation, 5.36 in functioning of government, and 3.13 in political culture, for an overall score of 6.30' (EIU 2014). That is to say, the Philippines is a fairly open society in terms of, for example, freedom of speech, and its electoral (voting) process is relatively clean and transparent, in large part due to the Philippines being the birthplace of NGO election observation.[4] But the 'Philippines is classified as authoritarian in political culture, its 3.13 being the lowest of all countries' as a consequence of the way in which politics is practised. 'It is a *hybrid* regime in terms of governmental functioning, with its 5.36 only good for seventh place, ahead of Vietnam (3.93), Lao PDR (3.21) and Myanmar (1.79). These are the matters where our democracy is relatively weak, according to EIU' (EIU 2014; emphasis added, indicating that the Philippines has an electoral system that only meets some of the criteria for democracy, defined as an 'expanded procedural minimum').

Communist insurgency

Central to the Philippines' Cold War orientation and its US alliance was, and to some extent continued to be, its own communist insurgency, fuelled by gross income disparities, landlessness and displacement, with violence often used to maintain an inequitable economic status quo. The origins of the communist insurgency pre-dated the Second World War and reflected a long history of such unequal social and economic relations.

A peasant group that had been demanding land reform in the 1930s, following the Japanese invasion in 1942, reconstituted itself as the Hukbong Bayan Laban sa Hapon (Anti-Japanese Peoples' Army), abbreviated in Tagalog (the common language of Luzon) as 'Hukbalahap' or the 'Huks'. Despite having fought the common Japanese enemy, leaders of the communist-influenced Huks were imprisoned by the victorious Americans in 1945, while US military police assisted private Filipino landlord armies in restricting leftist political activity, most notably for land reform. Clashes between Huks and police became more frequent and an attempted ceasefire in 1946 failed.

The Huks formally (although not actually) disbanded in 1946 in order to contest the coming elections. Under the name of the Democratic Alliance, six Huks were elected to the Philippines Congress. However, President Manuel Roxas barred them from assuming their seats (Wurfel 1988: 101), with assassination squads killing two of them (Monk 1990: 8). Meanwhile, approximately US$2 billion of economic aid from the USA was largely siphoned off by Roxas and the rest of the political elite, prefiguring the type of corruption which would become better known from the mid-1960s until the mid-1980s (Seagrave 1988: 126). Although the Huks did not present an electoral threat, Roxas declared the organisation illegal in March 1948 and refused them participation in the elections of the following year. Roxas died the month after the declaration and his successor, Elpidio Quirino, offered the Huks an amnesty. However, an effort to reach a settlement failed on both sides and quickly led to all-out conflict.

Terror was used as an instrument of state policy until 1954, with paramilitary militias being recruited for the purpose of political thuggery and the imposition of ideological conformity. In the 1950s, the civilian guards system was instituted in order to serve large landlords and local government officials, as an important part of the counter-insurgency structure. The US Army and the Philippines military learned valuable lessons in counter-insurgency as a result of these terror tactics (see Lansdale 1976: 770).

The three-sided elections of 1948 were noted for their use of guns, money, and a high level of fraud and intimidation, securing a 52 per cent majority for Quirino. 'The way in which the Liberal regime achieved power substantially affected the way it exercised power, that is, corruption bred more corruption' (Wurfel 1964: 700). In February 1950, the Huks changed their name to the Hukbong Mapagpalaya ng Bayan (People's Liberation Army) and called for the overthrow of the government. The USA stepped in to assist the Philippines government in sorting out its economic problems, in large part with a grant of US$250 million. The Philippines government failed, however, to adopt a land reform program.

Between holding out the promise of reform to disaffected land labourers and embarking on an active military campaign with the help of the United States, President Ramon Magsaysay managed to end the Huk rebellion in 1954 (Smith 1958: chs 6, 7). The US had continued its high level of military interest in the Philippines after independence, and maintained that close association until 1991.

From the American occupation until the late 1960s, the Philippines had witnessed sporadic uprisings and rebellions. None, apart from the Huk rebellion, was ever likely to directly challenge the government. But they did indicate a deep-seated sense of untenable oppression among the country's rural poor, and even its urban poor (see Sturtevant 1969, 1976). The outcome of conservative agrarian legislation, and a structural failure to implement land reform programs, was the 'proliferation throughout the archipelago in the 1960s of all those pernicious institutional practices which had triggered the Huk rebellion in the 1940s' (Monk 1990). This laid the groundwork for further radical rebellion in the late 1960s.

The ideological war came to a head when Ferdinand Marcos was elected as President in 1965. Born in 1917 in Ilocos Norte, Marcos was the illegitimate son of Ferdinand Chua, who was from the wealthiest family in the region: 'Of the top ten Chinese clans in this inner group of forty billionaire families, Ferdinand's [Chua's] clan ranked number six' (Seagrave 1988: 14, see also 22–3). While Chua never openly acknowledged Marcos as his son, he did financially assist him, including in his education. In 1939, Marcos graduated with a law degree. At the same time, he was charged with murdering Julio Nalundasan, who had defeated Marcos' nominal father, Mariano Marcos, in his bid to be elected to the Congress for Ilocos Norte. The conviction for this crime was overturned in 1940, with the assistance of President Jose Laurel, to whom Marcos became indebted as one of his 'clients'.

Marcos was elected to Congress for Ilocos Norte, the same seat formerly occupied by the person he was alleged to have killed, in 1949. Elected to the Senate in 1959, he became Senate President in 1962. Marcos stood against the incumbent Diosdado Macagpal in the 1965 elections, winning with money and nationalist slogans, and again winning in 1969.

In line with his unprecedented pork-barrelling, corruption and maladministration in his government worsened (Monk 1990: 87), while protest against a perceived loss of legitimacy grew (Wurfel 1988: 38). In particular, Marcos took what was already widespread corruption and institutionalised it through a system of patronage of which the president was the centre. This network then radiated out into a web of political, bureaucratic and business linkages through an extensive 'crony' network in which businesses were subservient to and reliant upon such patronage (see Hutchcroft 1998 for a detailed explanation of its functioning within the Philippines' banking sector).

By the beginning of the 1970s, Marcos' grip on power appeared to be slipping. To counter this, supporting the continuation of the Philippines' exploitative agrarian policies and Islamic unrest in Mindanao gave him an excuse to continue his rule unimpeded.

By the early 1970s a rising tide of nationalism, fuelled by hostility to the Vietnam War and by resentment at continued US economic dominance, saw increased student activism and an increasing challenge to central authority from the Mindanao-based Moro National Liberation Front. The name 'Moro' derived from the Spanish attribution of their word 'Moors' to denote all Muslims, with Islam having established itself among a number of indigenous ethnic groups in Mindanao, if more tenuously elsewhere in what was to become the Philippines, before the Spanish arrival. Reflecting Sino-Soviet tensions, in 1968 the Partido Kommunista ng Pilipinas (PKP, also known as the PKP-1930 or Communist Party of the Philippines-1930) split and Jose Maria Sison led a Maoist breakaway group to form the Communist Party of the Philippines (CPP), which in 1969 formed its military wing, the New People's Army (NPA). The NPA frequently clashed with government military forces, focusing its efforts in central Luzon, first around the key agrarian centres of Tarlac and Isabella, later spreading its area of operations to other rural areas. In the early years China was a source of weapons and expertise, although that support ended after 1977.

As the corruption and repression of the Marcos regime continued, many Filipinos came to view the CPP-NPA as the only viable force for overthrowing the dictator. In the mid-1980s, the NPA was believed to have some 26,000 fighters and it operated in 63 of the country's 73 provinces. A well-organised political coalition operated alongside the NPA; there was an alliance of underground groups known as the National Democratic Front, and a range of legal organisations including peasant groups, labour unions, other sectoral organisations, political parties and development groups (see Holden 2015).

The end of the Marcos regime in 1986, the end of the Cold War, and (often poorly conceived) purges within the NPA in which numerous comrades and supporters were executed all contributed to diminishing the NPA's standing. The guerrilla army's numbers shrank and it broke into several effectively independent factions (for example, the Revolutionary Proletarian Party). From the aforementioned peak strength of around 26,000 armed guerrillas in 1987, the combined strength of the remaining forces had fallen to around 6,000 by 1999.

Most of the continuing military activity from the communist-based groups appeared to be on the islands of Negros and Mindanao. 'Sparrow forces' of urban guerrillas conducted a sporadic terror campaign in Manila, including political assassinations, up until the early 1990s. Attempts at negotiating a 'peace accord' between the government and the National Democratic Front, the 'umbrella' organisation for the former CPP-NPA, foundered between 1998 and 2001. Amnesties offered by President Gloria Arroyo-Macagapal in 2007 saw 1,377 NPA members leave its ranks. The organisation continued, however, to have an active presence in most provinces and, with further peace talks under President Benigno Aquino failing in 2015, continued to regularly launch armed attacks.

'People power' or elite transition?

As a formerly close ally of the United States, and still within the US sphere of strategic interest, the Philippines experienced political changes which did not directly correspond to other changes wrought by the end of the Cold War. Rather, the political changes in the Philippines appeared to be driven primarily by the excesses of President Ferdinand Marcos and his alienation of the Philippines elite. Between his militaristic approach to addressing concerns about social inequality, his personal corruption (and its notorious flaunting by his wife, Imelda) and his riding roughshod over calls from allies for moderation, it was only a matter of time before Filipinos and in particular their dominant elites would start to look elsewhere for representation.

The Philippines underwent regime change, if only from a dictatorial to an oligarchic rather than a genuinely democratic model. Marcos had lost the support of his US backers and, eventually, the country's oligarchic elite and sections of the military. In this respect, there appeared to have been an elite pact for careful change in the Philippines (for discussion of this phenomenon, see O'Donnell and Schmitter 1986: 40–5). Capitalising on the 'political moment', elites, with the support of mass mobilisation, developed or reasserted political parties and organised political constituencies under a 'grand coalition'.

When this 'grand coalition' allowed mass mobilisation on the streets, with the blessing of the military, the process was deemed to be a 'people power' movement. There was a popular movement for change, and there were mass demonstrations of this desire for change. But it occurred because it was allowed, even encouraged, to occur rather than because 'the will of the people' had overwhelmed elite control. It had not, and in many respects Filipino politics was not too long in returning to 'business as usual'.

The critical juncture for this change was the murder of Benigno Aquino. Aquino was elected to the Philippines Senate in 1967 and soon became a vocal critic of Marcos, posing what Marcos believed to be a threat to his personal power. When Marcos declared martial law in 1972, Aquino was imprisoned on manufactured charges of murder and subversion. While in prison, Aquino started the Lakas ng Bayan (People's Power) Party, which contested the 1978 elections but was defeated by Marcos' Nacionalista Party candidates amid widespread allegations of electoral fraud.

Requiring heart surgery in 1980, after intervention by US President Jimmy Carter Aquino was sent to the US, where he was granted political exile. As Marcos' political fortunes waned, Aquino returned to the Philippines, but was assassinated as he stepped off the plane at Manila airport. His alleged killer was also shot numerous times. In 1985, 25 military personnel, including senior officers, and one civilian were charged with the assassination, but all were initially acquitted (16 later being re-tried and convicted in 1990) (PhilStar 2014). Had Aquino not been murdered, he would have been a likely contender for the Philippines' presidency (David 2014).

The main impact of Aquino's murder was to galvanise disparate anti-Marcos forces, with Aquino's widow, Corazon, becoming its figurehead leader. When snap elections were called for early 1986, Corazon Aquino was prevailed upon to run for the presidency, in tandem with Salvador Laurel, employing the electoral force of Laurel's United Nationalist Democratic Organisation (UNIDO). The subsequent elections were notable for massive fraud, violence, intimidation, coercion, and electoral disenfranchisement and election rigging. Despite Marcos claiming victory, Aquino called for a protest which, with widespread elite support, turned into a massive rally. Rejecting a power sharing arrangement and with the armed forces switching sides, Marcos fled the Philippines and Aquino was sworn in as President. This series of events returned the Philippines to electoral politics, and also to a type of oligarchic rule that had been prevalent prior to Marcos' ascension.

Corazon Aquino and attempted coups

After Marcos fled, former Defence Minister Juan Ponce Enrile, who had switched sides and helped facilitate the change away from Marcos, was not accorded the senior position he coveted and set himself up in opposition to Aquino, while Marcos used his financial reserves and the remnants of personal loyalty to urge the armed forces to overthrow Aquino. This resulted in a series of attempted coups in 1986, 1987 (which came close to success), 1988 and 1989. The attempted coups generally and the 1987 attempted coup in particular, made worse by mounting NPA activity, shook public confidence in Aquino's government (SarDesai 1997: 224–5). The 1989 coup attempt, which appeared to be otherwise succeeding, was quashed with the aid of US war planes from the Clarke Field air base. The main group behind the coup attempts was the Reform the Armed Forces Movement (RAM), which later became known as the Revolutionary Alliance Movement (RAM).

One of the leading figures of the RAM, Colonel Gregorio 'Gringo' Honasan, after orchestrating the 1987 attempted coup, was a Scarlet Pimpernel type of figure, on the run but thumbing his nose at the government, often through the media. Honasan was later pardoned and stood for the Philippines Senate, being elected as a senator. At the end of the 1990s, Honasan was still antagonistic towards the government, threatening the state with dire consequences should 13 RAM members charged with killing a union leader be convicted.[5]

The case of the Philippines well reflected the difficulties of political transitions from authoritarian rule. The 'transitions' paradigm, as initially articulated by O'Donnell and Schmitter (1986: 66), suggests structure over agency in the establishment of democratic forms. As O'Donnell and Schmitter make clear, such outcomes and the multiplicity of factors that lead to them are not linear, can usually not be known in advance, and are often not well understood until nearing their own completion. In so far as transitions are understood, they are frequently based on highly contingent and usually short-term calculations that cannot be predicted before the event. Political transition events are often unexpected and move quickly, requiring responses that are often ad hoc. Decisions makers thus appear from unanticipated places, elites quickly shift positions based on uncertainties and perceived trends, and the loyalty or even functionality of institutes becomes fluid or unreliable. In such circumstances, experiencing a political transition can be a wild ride. Such was the case in the Philippines under Aquino.

Aquino served the maximum two terms as President, being succeeded by former chief of the armed forces and Secretary for National Defence, Fidel Ramos. Ramos also served two terms as President, during which time challenges to civilian rule from within the army effectively ended through his personal military contacts. He also achieved a ceasefire agreement with the Moro National Liberation Front (MNLF) in 1996. As a result of Ramos' economic reforms, battered international confidence in the Philippine economy was restored and economic growth resumed (Nolan 1996: 7–23).

Ramos' presidency seemed relatively unremarkable at the time, Ramos being less charismatic than Aquino and more managerial in policy approach. But his presidency perhaps most ideally conformed to O'Donnell and Schmitter's paradigm that the political reformers most likely to be successful are those who come from within the ranks of the military (O'Donnell and Schmitter 1986: 39, 70).

Ramos was succeeded by his Vice-President and former movie actor Joseph Estrada, whose charismatic political style of politics manifested in a 'tough guy' approach to the, by this time, more powerful Moro Islamic Liberation Front (MILF). The initial attacks by the Armed Forces of the Philippines (AFP) were militarily relatively successful but exacerbated an already violent conflict in Mindanao, creating fewer options for a possible peace.

While this machismo approach to Islamic/ethnic insurgency was popular with many Filipinos, like many earlier Filipino politicians Estrada appeared to have a weakness for profiting from the status of office. Just two years into his term as President, Estrada was accused of having received a multi-million dollar pay-off for having officials turn a blind eye to a popular 'numbers' game. Within weeks, Estrada faced an impeachment hearing, brought by the House of Representatives and heard by an 'impeachment court' formed by the Senate. The hearing was broadcast live on radio and television, exposing Estrada's secret bank accounts and history of pay-offs. Transparency International later ranked Estrada as the world's tenth most corrupt political leader (with Ferdinand Marcos having achieved the number two ranking behind Indonesia's President Suharto (Transparency International 2004).

On 16 January 2001, the 'impeachment court' voted 11–10 not to open an envelope allegedly containing incriminating evidence, on the grounds that it was not included as part of the initial investigation. The minority voters on the court panel walked out in protest and the decision sparked mass protests. As a result of these protests, on 19 January, the AFP chief of staff Angelo Reyes withdrew his support for Estrada as President and shifted it to Vice-President Gloria Macagapal Arroyo. The following day the Supreme Court ruled that Estrada had 'constructively resigned' as President and swore in Arroyo as his replacement (for a detailed account of these events, see Supreme Court 2001).

Gloria Macagapal Arroyo's presidency started well enough, following the public disgrace of Estrada and the public rejection of high-level corruption. She came to office having been a professor in economics at Ateneo University, Manila, and, as the daughter of former President Diosdado Macagapal, had a steady rise through the Philippines' public service and politics. However, her pursuit of Estrada and then his son, Senator Jose Estrada, and others, on charges of 'plunder' – charges which continued to dog Estrada – led to a violent protest at the presidential office, Malacanang Palace. Because of the scale of the violence and some of the more prominent public figures associated with the event, Arroyo declared a 'state of rebellion', leading to numerous high profile arrests.

Arroyo's presidency appeared to settle, but discontent with her manner of taking office continued to rankle with some. In July 2003, more than 300 soldiers took over an apartment tower in Makati City, Manila, claiming to be protesting against what they said was Arroyo's corruption and a possible attempt to declare martial law. The so-called 'Oakwood Mutiny' had been, at least in part, organised by Senator Gregorio Honasan; Honasan had, as an army officer, previously led coup attempts against President Aquino. The Oakwood Mutiny was intended to be the start of a larger rebellion, but was discovered. A siege of the building ensued, there were negotiations and, eventually the rebel soldiers surrendered and returned to barracks. While the affair was ended well enough, it did show both continuing discontent within the AFP and a degree of preparedness to force political outcomes through military means.

As the situation settled, Arroyo went into the 2004 elections, winning by just under 3.5 per cent. It was the first time that both a President and a Vice-President, Noli de Castro, had been elected from the same party. However, in June the following year there was the public release of a recording of a phone conversation between President Arroyo and then election commissioner Virgilio Garcillano, allegedly talking about the rigging of the 2004 national election results. The House of Representatives then attempted to impeach Arroyo, being blocked by Arroyo's majority coalition the following September 2005. When called in for questioning, Garcillano disappeared, resurfacing in late 2005. In December 2006, Garcillano was cleared of perjury charges by the Department of Justice, although investigations continued and he was again charged with perjury in 2014. Some themes in the politics of the Philippines persisted, as though deeply ingrained as a part of (and in response to) oligarchic political culture.

It was the Garcillano affair that, in 2006, led Benigno Aquino III to quit his position as Deputy Speaker of the House of Representatives. As the fourth generation of a deeply embedded political family, Aquino III was in the middle of one of the coup attempts against his mother, President Cory Aquino. Three of his four body-guards were killed in the attack on Malacanang Palace, and he and another guard were wounded. Aquino III was elected to the House of Representatives in 1998, then as Deputy Speaker in 2004, and following the expiry of his terms limit he shifted to the Senate in 2007. As a member of the Liberal Party, he ran as part of the 'Genuine Opposition' coalition, opposing President Arroyo's attempt to change the constitution to a unicameral model with a higher degree of devolved power to the provinces. His main achievements in the Senate were to propose and have passed spending account-ability and anti-corruption bills.

The Liberal Party had, in 2008, endorsed Mar Roxas as its candidate for the 2010 elections, but the death of Aquino's mother Cory Aquino in 2009 shifted popular support behind Aquino III (ABS-CBN 2009). With the groundswell of support growing, in 2009 Roxas withdrew his candidacy in favour of Aquino III, choosing instead to be his running mate for the vice-presidency (he was defeated by former Makati City mayor Jejomar Binay). Aquino received just over 42 per cent of the vote compared to his leading opponent, Joseph Estrada (who was freed from house arrest following a presidential pardon in 2007), who received just over 26 per cent of the vote, with seven other candidates trailing behind.

Aquino's achievements as President included an average economic growth rate of just over 6 per cent and an increase in the country's competitive economic standing, although the Philippines' unemployment, poverty and income inequality were virtually unchanged. It was noted, however, that Aquino III's Priority Development Assistance Fund (PDAF), as well as the Disbursement Acceleration Program (DAP), designed to speed up public spending and alleviate poverty, were declared unconstitutional by the Supreme Court, leaving Congress reluctant to proceed with other public spending programs that might have alleviated poverty (Tupaz and Wagner 2015).

Mindanao

While the Philippines had for decades been wracked by a waxing and waning communist insurgency, its other main point of political instability emanated from its southern region, particularly the country's largest island of Mindanao. Political instability in Mindanao dated back to the origins of Spanish colonialism. It flared again, however, following the imposition of a poorly conceived (internal) transmigration program and a failure to adequately acknowledge and equitably incorporate the region's long restive Muslim population into the post-colonial state.

Following the Philippines' independence in 1946, the governments attempted to resolve problems with landless peasants that had been fuelling a communist rebellion by resettling some of them in Mindanao on what was claimed to be untitled land. Yet Mindanao's indigenous populations, only partially under the control of the central authority, had not developed a land titling system, relying instead on more traditional methods of recognition of land ownership. The displacement caused by this northern migration enhanced the sense of 'otherness' or opposition that many local inhabitants felt towards the new settlers (Kingsbury 2011).

Complicating this, even among Mindanao's new settlers there was a landed oligarchy embodying many of the worst features of the landed elites of the north but, with a greater sense of lawlessness across much of the island, employing more brutal and repressive measures against reluctant workers. The CPP was particularly successful in fomenting revolutionary activity in Mindanao. Between the formal military response to the communist insurgency, which further alienated many local inhabitants, deep levels of distrust between Muslims and Christians, and the military's own propensity towards corruption and brutality, often in league with local political and business leaders, much of the island quickly descended into even greater lawlessness and armed conflict.

As disputes over land ownership arose the Philippines government refused to recognise the Moros' traditional ownership, leading to deep-seated distrust of the government by the Moros. Already feeling discriminated against in areas of housing and education by the Catholic government, in 1968 a group of Muslim army trainees in Corregidor (as few as 28 by government accounts and as many as 200 by MNLF estimates) who were angry over their mission and pay began to rebel; they were murdered by their Christian colleagues. Mindanao Muslims deeply angered by this event decided to separate from the Philippines (George 1980; Anthony 2008).

The first Islamic independence group, under the leadership of academic Nur Misuari, was the Mindanao Independence Movement, which in the early 1970s morphed into the MNLF. At its height, the MNLF fielded around 30,000 armed combatants. In 1976 a peace agreement saw a ceasefire and agreement to establish an autonomous Muslim region including 13 provinces in the south. Despite the ceasefire, the Philippines government did not fulfil its agreement to establish an autonomous Muslim region, leading to internal disagreements within the MNLF and, in 1981, the establishment, under Salamat Hashim, of the more Islamic-hardline Moro Islamic Liberation Front.

In a peace agreement with the MNLF, in 1996 the government finally agreed to create the more limited Autonomous Region of Muslim Mindanao with Nur Misuari as Governor. While the MNLF accepted the agreement, the MILF did not. Following a failure of the Arroyo government to fully implement the 1996 agreement (citing Misuari's administrative incompetence), in 2001 Misuari led an unsuccessful rebellion and then fled the country. He was captured in Malaysia the following year and sent back to the Philippines, where he was placed under house arrest. He was allowed bail in 2008. The MNLF, however, fell into disrepair, with most of its members joining the MILF.

The MILF signed a ceasefire agreement with the government in 1997, which was abandoned by President Joseph Estrada in 2000 (Santos 2001; Rood 2005). Peace talks resumed in 2007 but a Memorandum of Agreement on the definition of Ancestral Domain (MOA-AD) that had been initialled by both the government and the MILF was rejected by the Philippines Supreme Court in 2008, leading to renewed fighting. The MOA-AD, which implied a comprehensive peace agreement on high levels of regional autonomy, was finally agreed to, as one of Aquino III's main political goals, in 2014, although it still had not received legislative endorsement at the time of writing.

Apart from the remnants of the MNLF and the still fully functional MILF, the Abu Sayyef Group (ASG) in the Sulu Archipelago also continued to engage in a more regionally specific, if somewhat notorious, separatist campaign. The ASG was established in 1991, also as an MNLF breakaway, formally seeking to establish an independent Islamic province in the Sulu area (the islands of Jolo and Basilan, and Zamoanga on Mindanao). While this area approximates to the pre-colonial Sulu sultanate, Basilan in particular is also one of the most impoverished parts of the Philippines. The ASG has since appeared to develop a wider Islamist orientation. The Philippines government considers the ASG to be a local branch of the regional Jemaah Islamiyah organisation, which in turn has links to Al Qaeda. Some of ASG's senior members had previous experience fighting with the mujahedeen in Afghanistan, from which it developed its extremist ideology.

The ASG is estimated to have had a maximum strength of about 1,000 fighters, reduced to 200–400 along with the loss of senior leaders by 2010, but with a large, active support base. While the ASG is regarded as an Islamist separatist organisation, in a number of ways it replicates the practices of previous inhabitants of the archipelago who engaged in piracy, kidnapping/ransom and extortion. Some observers believe the ASG has moved away from its original political aims and now functions largely as a criminal rather than an ideological organisation.

Aquino III's weaknesses

The 2014 peace agreement, though not formally ratified, could be considered an historic achievement of Aquino III's administration. Less positively, Aquino III's handling of the 'Rizal Park Hostage Crisis' of August 2010 was widely criticised. In this incident, a disgruntled police officer took hostage 20 Hong Kong tourists and a tour guide, and four Filipinos in a bus at Rizal Park, Manila. The arrest by police of the hostage-taker's brother, who had tried to (unofficially) ask his brother to surrender, inflamed the situation, leading to a bungled 90-minute gun battle which left eight tourists dead and several others injured. Aquino III's response after the event, saying 'Our problems now, in two or three years we can say that they are laughable when we recall that they were not that grave' (Chanco 2010), was heavily criticised in Hong Kong and widely regarded as an inept response.

Similarly, Aquino III's response to the handling of Typhoon Haiyan in 2013, in which at least 6,000 were killed and one and a half million families directly impacted, saw his popularity slump. Aid was often slow to be delivered and there was much criticism of aid money being siphoned off by corrupt officials, for which Aquino III bore some responsibility (Palatino 2014).

However, given the term limits imposed on Filipino presidents, there are structural restrictions on what they might be able to plan and implement while in office. There were also limits as to what an individual could achieve within an often semi-functional and corrupt political environment. The system of checks and balances as found in the Philippines means that vested interests and deep cultures of corruption and violence have numerous means to thwart presidential ambition, much less activity, even in the best of cases.

In May 2015, Rodrigo Duterte was elected as the Philippines' next President. While mayor of Davao City in southern Mindanao, Duterte had developed a notorious reputation as 'The Punisher' for his brutal, often extrajudicial approach to dealing with crime (and, some said, political opposition). Duterte had run his campaign based on a similarly harsh approach to 'law and order', saying he would fasten the fish of Manila Bay with the bodies of criminals, among other more frank comments. Duterte did, however, immediately commit to peacefully resolving the MILF insurgency, and took a more thoughtful approach to addressing the issue of the South China Sea, suggesting a possible revenue-sharing arrangement over resources found there.

While former human rights lawyer Leni Robredo was elected as Vice-President, she only just beat Senator Ferdinand 'Bongbong' Marcos, son of the former dictator, who campaigned on his father's record. Even though the vote count showed that Robredo had narrowly won the election, Marcos challenged the validity of the result. Not all, it seemed, were as committed to notions of democracy in the Philippines as they were to the idea of winning at almost any cost.

Conclusion

The Philippines appears to have come out of a long period of political and hence economic turbulence and perhaps shed its image as the 'sick man of Asia'. But the country does have its own distinctive and flawed political style that seems to be deeply embedded in how politics is done.

The Philippines has embraced electoral politics and it has a free-wheeling, sometimes inquiring and critical, and often shallow and superficial media. While the Philippines is not an absolute oligarchy, established families and vested interests wield very considerable political influence, while corruption remains a feature of both everyday life and political processes.

Warlordism prevails beyond the major metropolitan centres and even, to some extent, within them. Patron–client relationships play out in the Philippines, but sometimes in ways which allow less scope for volition on the part of the clients. The threat of violence hangs in the background, and sometimes the foreground, of local political thinking and the sometimes free-wheeling way in which politics is conducted can segue into lawlessness.

The Philippines began its post-colonial career as a client of its former colonial master, the US, and this has continued to influence and shape many elements of its political structure. If followed in the spirit with which it was originally intended, this might have allowed for a relatively liberal and potentially inclusive society. However, as a developing country that came into being as part of the battleground for the Cold War and has, moreover, carried the burden of Spanish colonial economic organisation and a winner-takes-all mentality, in the Philippines the more benign principles of US tutelage have been compromised by the excesses and abuses that are also available under political systems bequeathed by the US.

The Philippines has shed the worst excesses of its past and returned to electoral politics and some degree of political competition. But despite its electoral processes, its long-standing flaws have not fundamentally altered.

Notes

1 The term 'hybrid democracy' is not used, as the characteristics it encompasses are necessary but not sufficient to describe in a meaningful sense the political systems discussed here.

2 The author was previously engaged as a trainer in democratic processes at this level of government in 2008–10, and was exposed first-hand to these issues.

3 Following provincial elections in 2008, a large group of Filipino governors visited Australia for political training, including visiting the home of the author. On their return, one of the governors, who had won his governorship from a prior incumbent, was shot and wounded by the prior incumbent.

4 The National Citizens' Movement for Free Elections (NAMFREL) was founded in 1983. Its reporting of extensive fraud in the 1986 'snap' elections led to Marcos' ouster and the establishment of like organisations around the world.

5 The Philippines Senate account of Honasan has no mention of his activities between his military career in 1987 and his formally entering politics in 1995.

12 Indonesia

Democratisation has taken root in Indonesia, if of a particularly populist, often theatrical and money-influenced type, in which voters are as much clients and audience as they are participants. 'Money politics', which includes vote buying, local officials delivering a set quota of votes for payment, patron–client relations and corruption, is especially influential (Simandjuntak 2015), even if voter turnout remains relatively high.

The 'festivals of democracy' that had marked the Suharto era of Indonesian politics have been replaced by a more genuine sense of festival. Election days have become an opportunity for communities to come together in public places, celebrating both their vote (no matter how it is influenced) and especially the public count of the vote, which is somewhat similar to a public sporting contest, with more and less favoured contestants and related applause (again appealing to the idea of the traditional stage play).

Jokowi's Indonesia

Indonesia is a vast, sprawling, introspective and sometimes challenging country that, after decades of authoritarian rule, appeared to be established as one of the world's democracies. Yet, as with some of its neighbours and, indeed, its own history, it might be an error to assume that, because Indonesia has made a significant political transition, democracy is permanent or can only continue to head in the direction of liberalism. Even judging by the country's own recent democratic past, any assumption about the inevitability of democratic retention or progress would be quickly qualified.

Perhaps the principal defining feature of Indonesia is that, as a classic post-colonial state made up of formerly disparate polities and comprising some 17,000 inhabited islands, it has less territorial contiguity than any other state in the world. This physical fragmentation has meant that some of the country's distinct cultural groups have, from time to time, sought to separate themselves from the central government.

In turn, this lack of commitment to the idea of the state in some areas has produced an underlying sense of insecurity about the ideas of the state, of nationhood or of a common bonded political identity, and their viability. States that come together with a sense of confidence in their viability and correspondence with their peoples generally do so voluntarily. However, where there is reluctance, about either inclusion in the state or the orientation of the state, they tend to rely more on compulsion. Compulsion implies force and, sometimes, resistance to such force. This quality of compulsion and resistance has, as such helped inform how political relations within Indonesia are understood, with, despite a move towards decentralisation in 2001, a legacy of this form of understanding continuing to be reflected well into the post-New Order democratic era.

As with most societies, and in particular those that have undergone or are still under-going a political transition, Indonesia reflects a range of competing ideological and vested interests, broadly manifested as more and less reformist groups. Translated as electoral outcomes, this has produced a type of reform and reaction two-step, with first Presidents Habibie and Abdurrahman Wahid pursuing a reform agenda, then President Megawati Sukarnoputri replacing Wahid and running a more conservative and militar-ily reactionary agenda. Megawati was in turn replaced by the reformist Susilo Bambang Yudhoyono for two terms, although his second term was limited by both legislative reaction against continuing reform and his own natural caution about pushing too hard in the face of such resistance. In 2014, Yudhoyono was replaced by the reformist Joko Widodo ('Jokowi'), who promised much but got off to a doubtful start.

Indonesia's political system

Indonesia is a republic with an executive president and a bicameral legislature. The People's Representative Council (Dewan Perwakilan Rakyat, or DPR) and the Regional Representative Council (Dewan Perwakilan Daerah, or DPD) together comprise the People's Consultative Assembly (Majelis Permusyawaratan Rakyat, or MPR), which out-lines broad government policy and has the power to impeach the president. The DPR has been regularly criticised for its high level of corruption, in which political decisions have been regularly taken on the basis of payments.

During the New Order period the legislature, dominated by the then nominally apo-litical 'Functional Groups' (Golongan Karya, or Golkar) organisation, was effectively a rubber stamp for presidential decisions, although Suharto also ruled by decree in 1966, a status that underpinned his authority until 1993. Suharto again attempted to rule by decree just prior to his political fall in 1998. In response, Indonesia's constitution was amended in 1999, 2000, 2001 and 2002 to limit presidential authority and place greater authority in the hands of the legislature, to limit presidential terms to two, to establish the DPD, instituting direct presidential elections by voters (from 2004) instead of indirect elections by the MPR, and to establish a constitutional court.

The military was allocated seats in the DPR, 100 of 500 by 1982 but, reflecting a push from a reformist faction within the military, reduced to 75 again in 1997 and just 38 of 500 in 1998. All seats in the legislature were elected from 2004. The principal roles of the DPR are to pass legislation, consider the budget put forward by the president and provide oversight to the executive appointed by the president (Kingsbury 2005a: 279–83).

Indonesia was perhaps the Southeast Asian country that most vividly exposed the changing patterns of global influence as a consequence of the end of the Cold War. Despite being a reliable US anti-communist ally in the region, by the late 1980s that requirement had begun to recede, and the US was shifting towards more of a focus on human rights and promoting democracy as core foreign policy objectives (Dalpino 2000). The US (and its allies) tolerated the Suharto regime's worst excesses in human rights abuses and growing corruption while it suited their strategic interest but, during the 1990s, as disquiet grew amongst Indonesia's elite and especially within its military, and Suharto's rule became increasingly 'sultanistic' (Winters 2011a: 166), support both abroad and at home began to wane

When Indonesia's corruption-ridden economy was exposed to the full force of the Asian financial crisis of 1997, Suharto's rule became increasingly untenable. The US-dominated IMF stepped in, with lending conditions that destroyed the 'development contract' (Masuhara 2015: 10) that had allowed Suharto's rule to go more or less unchallenged for the previous three decades.

Indonesia's transition from authoritarianism was, predictably, not entirely smooth, as vested elites associated with the former regime baulked at some of the country's changes. In particular, when then Vice-President B.J. Habibie, who had replaced Suharto in 1998, agreed to a referendum on self-determination in Timor-Leste, the Indonesian military revolted against government policy. Rather than facilitate a free and fair vote, the Tentara Nasional Indonesia (TNI, the Indonesian National Military) and its proxy militias embarked on a campaign of violence, destruction and fear in order to derail the ballot. That attempt failed, with 78.5 per cent of East Timorese voting in favour of independence, and subsequent UN-sanctioned international intervention formalising the process.[1]

The move to allow Timor-Leste to 'escape' was deeply unpopular with Indonesia's elites and, facing humiliating defeat, Habibie chose to withdraw from the subsequent elections, which to the surprise of many saw Islamic cleric and reformer Abdurrahman Wahid elected by an Islamic-led coalition of parliamentarians (Kingsbury 2005a: 286–8). Wahid attempted to initiate a reform campaign, but quickly ran up against resistance in the TNI. Wahid's presidency was chaotic, in part as a result of Indonesia's continuing economic troubles, in part because of his own somewhat odd political style and in part because he was undermined by opponents wishing to slow the pace and orientation of reform, from within both Indonesia's legislature and the armed forces. This was especially so after Wahid sacked Coordinating Minister for Political and Security Affairs General (ret.) Wiranto in February 2000. There was considerable evidence that if the TNI did not actively foment violent conflict in a number of Indonesia's more fractious regions, it did facilitate or exacerbate such violence, in Ambon, Central Sulawesi, West Papua and Aceh. But Wahid himself was an idiosyncratic leader, while his first cabinet was dysfunctional and replaced within a year by another (Kingsbury 2005a: 93–4, 295–9).

Wahid's second cabinet was more functional and tightly coordinated, but it, too, quickly ran into trouble, as did Wahid's increasingly erratic personal political style. Wahid was charged with corruption and, although the charges were trumped up, by early 2001 his presidency was collapsing in the face of a legislative revolt and a military that treated the President with open contempt. Surrounding himself with relatives and close friends who were loyal but not especially effective, Wahid lashed out at what he saw as inaction. A series of bombings across Indonesia around Christmas 2000 and the improper use of some US$14 billion intended to bail out failing banks saw the DPR pass a censure motion against the President. In February 2001, the DPR began a process of impeachment which, from April, was voted to take place on 1 August. On 2 June, Wahid sacked five ministers and on 21 June, his impeachment was brought forward by the legislature.

In July Wahid attempted to declare a state of emergency and martial law, which failed to gain support or recognition from among his own ministers, the police or the army. On 22 July, around 2,000 military personnel from the armed forces' three services formed in Merdeka Square, opposite the presidential palace. They were supported by 35 tanks and 25 armoured personnel carriers with their guns aimed at the presidential palace. Wahid responded by again trying to declare a state of emergency. The following day, the legislature impeached Wahid and effectively sacked him as President, replacing him with Vice-President Megawati Sukarnoputri.

On one level, Wahid's ouster as President could be seen to have the hallmarks of a coup, but it was technically in line with constitutional processes. While Wahid's enemies ensured as chaotic a situation as possible to help bring about his downfall, Wahid also played into that process through his odd decisions as President and his assertion of authority when what was needed was conciliation. Wahid's sacking did not amount to a return to the Suharto era, but it did stop the reform process, and gave the country's elites an opportunity to reconsolidate (Kingsbury 2005a: 313–6). This was, in hindsight, conventional for a post-authoritarian environment.

Wahid's successor Megawati Sukarnoputri ran a more conservative administration, giving the TNI free rein in the restive provinces of Aceh and West Papua – in particular in Aceh, where a ceasefire signed with the Free Aceh Movement (Gerakan Aceh Merdeka, GAM) the year before was unilaterally ended on 19 May 2003.[2] The Indonesian government launched its largest military operation since the 1975 invasion of Timor-Leste, boosting existing troop numbers from around 20,000 to more than 50,000 (Suryakusuma 2003), and sending 12,000 police to the province, assisted by nine TNI-supported local militia organisations (Kingsbury 2006: 12). The renewal and escalation of the war signalled 'the symbolic death of reform and the de facto return of the military to the structures of national power' (Suryakusuma 2003).

It was otherwise 'business as usual', which in Indonesia meant 'perhaps one of the worst legislative institutions of any democratic society. It is marked by incompetence and corruption' (Gaffar 2002). As President, Megawati was seen as vision-less and ineffective, although with a reduction in the level of (sometimes orchestrated) chaos the economy improved a little. Going into the 2004 elections, however, Megawati and her PDI-P had no policies other than to begin to tackle those governance issues they had failed to address over the previous two years.

The SBY ascendancy

Having served as a cabinet minister under Wahid and then Megawati, former military reform leader[3] Lieutenant-General (ret.) Susilo Bambang Yudhoyono not only came to the presidential elections with a strong background in both effectiveness and reform, he also had policy visions for the future, including growing the economy, tackling corruption, furthering military reform and ending the conflicts in Aceh and West Papua. Each of these issues were linked.

That elections were held according to a schedule and, from 2004, power was transferred peacefully, indicated that while political processes in Indonesia might be stamped as peculiarly Indonesian, they had become regularised in ways that had been almost unthinkable in the last three decades of the twentieth century. When the election was held, after the initial round, Yudhoyono won with just under 61 per cent of the vote, with his Democratic Party (Partai Demokrat, PD) becoming established with around 10 per cent of the seats in the legislature, more than doubling this to over a quarter in the 2009 elections, which also saw Yudhoyono re-elected.

More than coincidentally, Yudhoyono was also the archetype of O'Donnell and Schmitter's (1986) most likely successful post-authoritarian leader; his cautious, military-backed reform agenda was an almost textbook example of successful post-authoritarian leadership, at least in his first term. But, despite attempting to address corruption and government inefficiency, even Yudhoyono discovered the limits of reform. Having overseen the successful resolution of the Aceh war in 2005, in which GAM gave up its military struggle in exchange for substantive autonomy (referred to as *pemerintah sendiri*, or 'self-government') and democratic elections, Yudhoyono had expended much of his political capital.[4]

Yudhoyono had started his second term as President with a massive popularity rating of 75 per cent in November 2009, yet his inaction as President saw that quickly decline, eventually coming as low as 38 per cent in September 2011 and 30 per cent in May 2013 (Mietzner 2014)). Yudhoyono's popularity became more positive from this very low point but, by that stage, attention was already focused on who would be his successor.

Yudhoyono's first term as President had seen some real gains (if not in achieving peace in West Papua), but his promise to achieve even more in his second term crashed upon the rocks of political resistance; while Yudhoyono had promised more reform in his second term, his political opponents wanted much less. As he came under an anti-reform backlash, especially in the sphere of attacking corruption, Yudhoyono became more cautious. For many, the reformer and great political communicator had been reduced to inaction and excuses. The second half of his second term in office was widely seen as one of marking time, even if underlying economic growth continued apace at over 6 per cent.

Despite reconfirming its democratic processes again in 2014, Indonesia remained marred by the presence of extralegal organisations that continued to exist unchecked (and indeed supported by some elite groups), while paramilitary security 'duty units' (*satuan tugas*, or *satgas*) continue to feature as an adjunct to conventional political life.

Indonesia was widely lauded as a democratic success story for rolling back the military, keeping radical Islam in check and institutionalising democratic freedoms. But these successes had costs in terms of democratic quality and elite resistance. Not everyone in Indonesia embraced reform, and very few did so with the same enthusiasm or intent as those who lauded Indonesia's new 'democracy'.

In July 2014, then, Indonesia was at a political and social crossroads. Its people had to choose whether they would revert to a 'strong', perhaps authoritarian, form of political leadership, to roll back at least some of the gains that had been made by the reform movement since the end of President Suharto's 32-year long tenure in 1998, or to resume the push for reform.

Indonesia's 2014 elections

While it has, as previously noted, been much lauded as a success story, Indonesian democracy was challenged in the 2014 elections by the triple threats of anti-reform actors, a high level of political malaise and popular disenchantment with the electoral process. One indicator of this potential threat was an increasing tendency by the TNI to reassert itself in the political debate.[5]

Indonesia headed into legislative elections in April and presidential elections in July, with lacklustre performance by the country's politicians turning off voters in droves. Against this backdrop, one of Indonesia's most senior army Generals raised the spectre of the army's return to politics. Army strategic command (Kostrad) head Lieutenant-General Gatot Nurmantyo criticised Indonesia's democracy as 'empty' and said that popular will expressed through elections was not always right (Kompas 2013). As a panacea, Nurmantyo called for a reassertion of the nationalist ideology of Pancasila (five principles), which underpinned Suharto's three decades as military-backed President.

Nurmantyo's comments to a Pancasila Youth (PP) rally in October reflected the confidence of TNI hardliners in challenging restrictions on the military flirting with politics. It was this hardline faction of the TNI that helped end Indonesia's military reform process around the time that President Yudhoyono began his second term as President.

In a political environment in which one of the two front-runners for the presidency was former military hardliner Lieutenant-General (ret.) Prabowo Subyanto, Nurmantyo's breaking of over a decade of military silence on domestic politics signalled a potential alternative to Indonesia's democratic path. Prabowo was then led in the presidential polls by Jakarta Governor Joko 'Jokowi' Widodo. However, Jokowi, himself a populist, did not then have the backing of a major political party, required for presidential nomination. Political support, when it came, was from former President Megawati Sukarnoputri's Indonesian Democratic Party of Struggle, which had also demonstrated pro-military leanings.

Set against growing voter apathy, generals such as Nurmantyo were well positioned to push Indonesia even further away from its recent path of reform. For Indonesia to further entrench its democratic credentials would have required a win by a convincingly reform-oriented presidential candidate. Scanning of Indonesia's political field ahead of the elections, however, offered little hope.

In June 2011, when comparing himself to other 'strong' leaders, Prabowo was quoted by journalist Alan Nairn as asking the rhetorical question: 'Do I have the guts, am I ready to be called a Fascist dictator?' That one of his supporters had recently made a music video wearing a Nazi-style uniform and that Prabowo paraded at political rallies on a horse in a style reminiscent of Italian fascist dictator Mussolini did not help calm those with concerns over his political orientation.[6]

Such a reversion, too, would have stamped Indonesia's political and economic elite as a true oligarchy, competing for the status of office but not letting office slip from their collective grasp. In the swings and roundabouts of political life and, in particular, of the uncertainty of transitions away from authoritarian rule, such an outcome would have been normatively disappointing but analytically unsurprising. The alternative was to opt for a form of political leadership that was more folksy, more reform-oriented, and originating outside the political, economic and social elite. Such leadership might have been more inwardly focused, as befitting traditional Javanese perspectives, but also focused, too, on the country's many pressing and growing needs and less inclined to come under the even greater influence of the outside world.

While one presidential candidate styled himself in military-cut shirt, jodhpurs and thigh-high boots on a horse in front his stadium full of admirers, the other wore an open-necked batik shirt and an equally open grin, walking among the people. Prabowo Subyanto, the former General and ex-son-in-law of President Suharto, brother of a rich businessman and son of a senior economic minister, had come from a relative lack of popularity – around 25 per cent at the outset of campaigning – to present a real challenge for the presidency. That he had a highly efficient and organised campaign team assisted a great deal, as did an average national age of 29, meaning that few had personal memory of his tainted past. That he also had the overwhelming majority of the country's major media on side also assisted him enormously in his task.

By contrast, Joko 'Jokowi' Widodo had come off the back of a huge wave of popularity in an initially large field, according to opinion polls, commanding up to 45 per cent of the polled vote ahead of his nearest rival, Prabowo, on 12 per cent. He easily overtook his own party's leader as preferred presidential candidate and seemed to have an unassailable lead. From such a commanding lead, however, he received little and mostly negative media coverage, as well as being seen to be too disorganised and too little of the decisive leader when it counted. As polling began in early July, Jokowi's team was still putting together its campaign strategy.

When the vote was counted, Jokowi's early popularity had been very significantly pared back. Backed by the country's elite, Prabowo had closed the gap, but could not prise away enough of Jokowi's support base to gain a majority. His appeal to the perceived 'certainties' of the past was always tinged with its human rights horrors, while Jokowi's appeal to the future recalled, if not so explicitly, the type of hope that accompanied his predecessor President Susilo Bambang Yudhoyono's first term in office from 2004 and, at least, the start of his second term from 2009.

The 2014 election result

When Indonesia's 180 million voters went to the polls, they were deciding whether Indonesia would continue, more or less, to further develop its democratic experiment, or whether it would turn away from the relatively open society which is necessary to allow democracy to flourish. As Mietzner has noted, Prabowo campaigned on a neo-authoritarian reform agenda while Jokowi proposed an inclusive, non-confrontational technocratic populism (Mietzner 2015).

Jokowi had started his presidential race with a massive lead, strongly bolstered by civil society activists, and had been seen as 'folksy' and shambolic. By contrast, the campaign of Prabowo, backed by the former party of Suharto, Golkar, had been slick and professionally run, aided by support from Indonesia's pro-Prabowo television media.

The single biggest concern expressed by voters – corruption – continued to haunt leading members of both candidates' parties, although Jokowi was personally seen to be a clean leader. Prabowo had also spoken out against corruption, but could not escape having been the son-in-law of President Suharto, who, with a family fortune of US$35 billion, was estimated to have been the most corrupt political leader in modern times.

There was little in policy substance to divide the candidates – both were nationalists intent on making Indonesia more self-sufficient. Domestically, both candidates favoured dropping politically sensitive fuel subsidies, introduced when Indonesia was a much poorer country but one that exported oil. Despite considerable oil reserves, Indonesia's lack of infrastructure maintenance and development had meant that it had become an oil importing country, and subsidies had become the government's single biggest economic cost. Moves to reduce the subsidies had, however, sparked widespread anger, and had always been prone to significant voter backlash. More importantly, while Jokowi was not aligned with outgoing President Susilo Bambang Yudhoyono, he was expected to have a more 'steady as she goes' style of leadership, as well as to tackle high-level corruption. However, Jokowi ran into significant resistance from his own party, as well as others in the legislature, like Yudhoyono before him.

There was a long-standing view that Prabowo was more favoured by Indonesia's still politically active military, and the last days of campaigning led to claims that both the army and the State Intelligence Service had actively supported his campaign. When this was added to smearing of the small business-oriented Jokowi as pro-communist, the widespread destruction of Jokowi election material and an increasing sense of intimidation, Prabowo's political style appeared to be showing through.

With a voter turnout of just a shade below 70 per cent, Jokowi's winning margin of almost 6 per cent – 53.15 per cent to Prabowo's 46.85 per cent – would have been seen in other electoral contests as a strong win. But it did indicate that more than 45 per cent – close to half – of the Indonesian population was in favour of a more conservative, 'strong-man' style of political leadership who fulfilled most of the technical criteria for being considered 'fascist' in style and, perhaps, intent. When considered in addition to support for 'democracy', or relatively free and fair electoral politics, running at only a little over 60 per cent, Indonesia was not as entirely committed to reform as many of its external supporters might have liked. Moreover, if Jokowi comfortably won the presidential election, he initially faced an overwhelmingly hostile legislature, a majority of whom formed what amounted to an anti-Jokowi bloc.

In Indonesia, this might have been seen as a balance against the former excesses of the office of the president. It might also have been seen as Indonesia's often venal politicians simply carving out an anti-reform position and, by so doing, perhaps protecting their own political and financial interests. But, in part, there was also a deep-seated ideological reluctance by many local representatives to embrace reform, which was one of the factors that had hobbled, if not crippled, the second term of Jokowi's predecessor.

In September 2014, the Prabowo-led majority (63 per cent) Koalisi Merah-Putih (Red and White, or 'nationalist') Coalition of the DPR scrapped direct elections for local officials (village heads, mayors, regents and governors), in opposition to Jokowi's own position. 'Taking away the people's right to choose their leader is a blatant betrayal of public trust and sidelines them from the democratic process altogether, rendering all the progress and costs of the last 10 years futile', the Jakarta Globe said in an editorial. 'Indonesia has returned to a system of elitist democracy controlled by a handful of corrupt politicians serving only their own interests' (*Jakarta Globe* 2014).

The second problem Jokowi encountered on assuming the presidency was in his appointment of his new cabinet of 34 ministers. The cabinet appointments needed to satisfy the often competing requirements of placating his own party and finding ministries to shore up support from other parties for his minority legislative coalition, along with some degree of technocratic competence and, not least, ministers willing to represent his reform platform. With so many competing and somewhat mutually exclusive requirements, it was not surprising that the announcement of Jokowi's cabinet was greeted with disappointment and, in some cases, dismay.

Jokowi's problems continued, with the head of his party, the PDI-P, former President Megawati Sukarnoputri telling him, in public, that although President, he was only a mere 'party official'. 'I made you [Jokowi] a presidential candidate. But you should remember that you are the party's official, with a function of implementing the party's programs and ideology', former president Megawati said during an event which was aired live by several television stations (*Jakarta Post* 2014). In April 2015, Megawati again humiliated Jokowi in public, at the PDI-P's national congress. Jokowi was not invited to address to congress, which he attended as an ordinary party member.

This followed Jokowi's nomination of Megawati-supported Budi Gunawan as police chief, even though he was being investigated by the Komisi Pemberantasan Korupsi (Corruption Eradication Commission, or KPK) for accepting bribes. Jokowi eventually dropped Gunawan, but only after much public criticism of his choice. Gunawan had been appointed at the behest of Megawati, to whom he was a former Adjutant. Jokowi's decision reportedly angered Megawati, who had increasingly personalised power within the PDI-P following the death of her husband, Taufik Keimas, in 2013, and strained relations between Jokowi and the party to which he belonged and relied upon for support (Wahyudi 2015).

Having promised to get tough on drug smuggling during his election campaign, Jokowi lifted the unofficial four-year moratorium on the death sentence, claiming 50 Indonesians died each day from drug-related causes. In January 2015 the move saw six drug offenders, five of whom were foreigners, executed by firing squad, and then a further eight, seven of whom were foreigners, were executed in April 2015. The executions led to widespread international condemnation, including the withdrawal of ambassadors by some countries and protest from the UN Secretary-General Ban Ki Moon. During the appeal process for the convicted drug smugglers, Jokowi admitted that he had signed off on their deaths without having read the documentation. Earlier that month he had said: 'I don't read what I sign.' He earned further domestic and international ridicule after having signed off on a regulation that entitled state officials, many of whom are already provided with work cars, to a 211-million rupiah ($21,000) down-payment on a car.

Having promised during his election campaign to focus on addressing the continuing problems of West Papua, in May 2015 Jokowi visited West Papua and pardoned five Papuans who had been jailed for between 12 and 20 years for sedition. He also promised to open West Papua to the international media, saying they could travel freely. No sooner had he made the comment than Coordinating Minister for Political, Legal and Security Affairs Tedjo Edhy Purdijatno said that journalists would still require permits to enter the troubled territory and that they would be 'screened' for suitability. He added that there remained 'forbidden areas' in West Papua, and also said that they should not report 'untrue data' provided by separatists, and should not defame Indonesia (Antara 2015). In December 2014, Indonesian police fired into a crowd of West Papuan protesters, killing five. Jokowi's intentions to resolve Papua's continuing problems appeared to be limited by ideological interests intent on not allowing any change to Papua's status quo on the one hand, and economic interests having the same intentions on the other.

Beyond these issues, close Megawati aide (and head of Jokowi's transition team) Rini Soemarno had been appointed as Minister of State Enterprises, which was known as a potential source of corrupt funds. Soemarno had been questioned by the KPK over involvement in the dispersal of almost US$13 billion to support failed banks in the Bank Indonesia Liquidity Assistance scandal. The new Home Affairs Minister, PDI-P secretary-general and all-round fixer Tjahjo Kumolo, had also been questioned by the KPK. Megawati's unpopular daughter, Puan Maharani, was appointed to a senior role, as Coordinating Minister for Human Development and Culture (overseeing eight ministries) but, perhaps most disturbingly, after an era of civilian defence ministers, Jokowi appointed former hardline General Ryamizard Ryacudu as Defence Minister, effectively overturning civilian oversight of the TNI. The rest of the cabinet comprised the usual mix of technocrats, party functionaries and a couple of reformers.

With such a cabinet, Megawati attempting to control the President via the PDI-P and a potentially hostile legislature, Jokowi quickly found his choices for reform limited. He was able to push through a cut to fuel subsidies and support for health care and education for the poorest Indonesians. More importantly, however, on his signature anti-corruption policy, Jokowi appeared largely trapped in the complex web of Indonesia's political context.

One area of reform that Jokowi has steered well away from was that of the TNI. This is not to say that the TNI has not reformed; it underwent a series of important reforms early in the post-New Order period, with the 2004 law on military business being a benchmark. But, beyond appointing a former hardline General as Defence Minister, and two other former generals to senior posts, Jokowi also presided over the TNI reinstituting a deputy-commander position, which had been abolished as part of the reform process. Moreover, Jokowi presided over allowing the TNI to engage directly with ministries and state-owned enterprises overseeing regional security, as well as allowing limited military budget oversight. This, then, had implications not just for accountability and corruption but also for civilian oversight of military functions, necessary to any functioning democracy.

It appeared that, in an environment in which he had many enemies and few real political friends, Jokowi was hesitant to tackle the TNI over further reform issues. As a result, the TNI remained under the nominal authority of the President, rather than the Defence Ministry, and the TNI's 'territorial' command structure, in which the TNI locates itself throughout the archipelago, remained in place, despite an earlier plan to end this arrangement. Having the territorial structure still in place meant that the TNI continued to be able to wield considerable political and business influence outside Jakarta. Coordinating Political and Security Affairs Minister and former hardline General Luhut Panjaitan denied that the TNI would reassert itself in Indonesia's political processes. Having said that, this came hard on the heels of Jokowi's announced opening of West Papua to foreigners being flatly contradicted by senior army officers and the closure of part of the Ubud Writers' Festival dealing with a re-examination of the military-initiated massacres of 1965–66. Panjaitan was outspoken in his opposition to there being any investigation into past human rights abuses by Indonesia's military.

The TNI also remained involved in 'off-line' sources of funding, including 'grey' and illegal business and legal business ventures (although it no longer directly owned or controlled such businesses). This off-line source of income meant there was a continuing lack of transparency in TNI finances, that the TNI was prone to being involved in corrupt or illegal activities, and that it was less accountable to civilian oversight. In October 2009, an inter-ministerial group was appointed to oversee the takeover of TNI enterprises by other government departments, with the military shedding its directly owned business activities but retaining private sources of income from renting property and through its cooperatives and 'foundations' owning 'arms-length' shareholdings in businesses. In 2009, the TNI's legal businesses were estimated to be worth around US$365 million, and previous estimates suggested that its illegal business activities, including running drugs and guns, smuggling, extortion, prostitution and gambling, were worth double that, or more. More positively, in 2014 the legislature put forward a bill for the external oversight of notoriously lax military judicial processes, although this was yet to be implemented at the time of writing. Jokowi did not appear eager to pursue this legislation, or other aspects of required TNI reform. In practice it would have been difficult for him to do so, but it did run counter to his promises for reform prior to being elected, and it continued to show him up as he was increasingly perceived – as a weak President.

All of this meant that while there were very high and perhaps unrealistic expectations of Jokowi when came to office, the reality was very much less than hoped for. A major survey across five broad sectors – the economy, justice and corruption eradication, security, education, and health – showed that only the last two received a public satisfaction rating of above 50 per cent, with health scoring 52.7 per cent and education scoring 51.4 per cent. Unsurprisingly, then, Jokowi's popularity as president slumped, from 74.6 per cent in October 2014 to 60 per cent in April 2015, but as low as 44 per cent in some polls and a solid 46 per cent a year after the election.

Reform or stability?

This trade-off between reform and stability came to define the leadership of Jokowi's predecessor, Susilo Bambang Yudhoyono. By the time it ended, the Yudhoyono decade was seen simultaneously as the period in which Indonesian democracy matured, and when its pathologies – corruption, money politics and sectarian discrimination – became entrenched. The commodities boom made it easier to obscure the serious structural deficiencies of Indonesia's economy. The politically thankless tasks of protecting human rights and cracking down on corruption were deferred.

This is how they remained. As Jokowi was an outsider to Jakarta's political elite, supporters hoped he would strive to preserve his autonomy from the establishment. This might have limited the influence of Indonesia's corrupt political parties over the executive branch. In reality, Jokowi seemed to have internalised the idea that his 'impostor' (outsider) status was a vulnerability. Jokowi has in fact maintained the accommodative stance seen in his formation of a cabinet dominated by party-linked patronage appointments.

What will be remembered as a, perhaps the, defining blunder of Jokowi's presidency came in February 2015 when he nominated a venal but politically connected officer as the new police chief after intense lobbying from party bosses. The ensuing public outrage saw the appointment cancelled but Jokowi's anti-corruption credentials have never recovered. Jokowi had signalled that he saw good governance as subordinate to quick policy implementation. As the powers of Indonesia's formidable Corruption Eradication Commission have come under renewed attack by politicians, Jokowi has expended little political capital in its defence. He seems to have endorsed instead the conservative trope that the Commission's anti-graft crackdown has 'slowed down development'. He has gone as far as to propose a decree protecting regional officials from prosecution for 'minor' infractions such as flouting procurement and budgeting rules.

Efforts by conservatives to tame the perceived excesses of Indonesian democratisation continue. These reactionary forces have been uninhibited by a President lacking Yudhoyono's concern for his international image, while the military has taken small but worrying steps towards restoring its position in civilian life. These include launching a 'defence of the nation' indoctrination program and pushing for regulations that allow it a greater role in domestic security. Censorship of public forums on the anniversary of the 1965 anti-communist massacres and sporadic anti-foreign outbursts by officials speak to the palpable return of a conservative nationalism under Jokowi.

Still, while advocates of good governance and human rights see little to praise in Jokowi, the gears of government still turn. Polls show that his popularity, which fell throughout 2015, has bottomed out as welfare programs inherited from Yudhoyono have been scaled up. Progress has been made on the centrepiece of his agenda: dealing with Indonesia's terrible infrastructure deficit. Opposition parties in parliament have largely laid down their political arms – some even defecting to the government coalition – in the knowledge that Jokowi represents business as usual.

Jokowi's renewed confidence in his political standing may prompt more risk-taking on economic policy, which had seen more misses than hits. A new courage was perhaps behind his announcement during a visit to Washington in October 2015 that Indonesia would seek to join the Trans-Pacific Partnership (TPP). This pledge was nothing if not ambitious. Indonesia's economy remains riddled with the protectionism and distorted domestic markets that the deal is supposed to inhibit. Joining the TPP is as good a pretext as any for pursuing overdue structural reforms.

But liberal proposals are politically toxic in Indonesia – and at odds with Jokowi's own track record. His ministers spent much of 2015 recapitalising state-owned enterprises with taxpayers' money, raising tariffs and promoting the misguided goal of 'food self-sufficiency'. A rhetorical lurch against foreign investors indicated that Jokowi had at least taken their criticisms seriously.

The reshuffle

Less than a year into his presidency, Jokowi undertook a major reshuffle of his cabinet. The reshuffle had been openly discussed for months prior to its implementation. Indeed, not only had the reshuffle been speculated upon but PDI-P executive board head Andreas Hugo Pareira had given Jokowi a deadline for it to occur (Jong 2015a). The reshuffle came as a significant shift in the orientation of the Jokowi cabinet, perhaps instilling a degree of rigour but also further asserting the control of the PDI-P and, in so doing, illustrating again the seeming weakness of Jokowi's presidency. The reshuffle also followed the above-noted string of public disasters for Jokowi (Halim 2015).

The appointment of former central bank Governor Darmin Nasution, replacing Sofyan Djalil, as Coordinating Minister for Economic Affairs was regarded as an important step given the country's lacklustre economic performance. Djalil had been close to Vice-president and Golkar Party representative Jusuf Kalla, and his replacement was seen as weakening Kalla's sometimes competing influence in the cabinet. The appointment, as Trade Minister, of Tom Lembong, who helped restructure Indonesia's banking system, was widely viewed as encouraging foreign investment (Parameswaran 2015b).

More overtly political appointments were Luhut Panjaitan as Coordinating Minister of Political, Legal and Security Affairs, in effect foreign relations, defence, law and human rights, making him the second most powerful politician in Indonesia alongside the Vice-President. Panjaitan, who was close to PDI-P head Megawati Sukarnoputri, had been Jokowi's chief of staff and was said to introduce more discipline, coordination and organisation into the previously semi-functional cabinet. Panjaitan replaced Tedjo Edhy Purdijatno who, among other things, had been widely criticised after deriding the KPK (Halim 2015). Panjaitan, a retired senior General, had a strong military career and was widely viewed as 'hawkish' on security matters.

The cabinet reshuffle bolstered Indonesia's business investment and its security focus. Jokowi also appointed former Jakarta Governor Lieutenant-General (ret.) Sutiyoso as the new chief of the Indonesian Intelligence Agency (Badan Intelijen Negara, or BIN), giving that organisation a sharper intelligence focus. Sutiyoso was controversial in some quarters given his past as an army Captain in charge of a notorious special forces (Kopassus) unit, Tim Susi, and being Jakarta Governor during the political turbulence of 1997–98.

In all, while Jokowi attempted to bolster the performance of his cabinet while appeasing his political controllers, his public stocks continued to decline. From a high of 75 per cent approval rating when he entered office, promising reform and to clean up corruption, in just a few months his *disapproval* rating had increased to just under 75 per cent (Jong 2015b).

Indicating just how pervasive corruption was in Indonesia, and how bold some officials were about their corrupt activities, the Speaker of the House of Representatives, Setya Novanto, and businessman Muhammad Reza Chaild were investigated over seeking 20 per cent of the shareholding of the giant $16 billion Freeport Indonesia company, which operates the world's largest gold mine and third largest copper mine at its Grasberg site in West Papua. The pair claimed to be representing Indonesia's most powerful minister, Coordinating Politics, Security and Justice Minister Luhut Panjaitan, in their discussions with the new Freeport chief executive officer Maroef Sjamsoeddin about the renewal of Freeport's mining contract. Maroef was a former Air Vice-Marshall and deputy head of the BIN (*Jakarta Post* 2015a, 2015b, 2016). There was a boldness to this attempted corruption that, even in Indonesia, almost inspired admiration for its audacity.

Conclusion

Both within Indonesia and beyond, the country is widely hailed as an established democracy and it does have regular and largely free and fair elections. If Indonesia had declining faith in its political leaders, this is an increasingly common global phenomenon in electoral politics, but does not go to the question of democratic process as such. That Indonesia also feels the heavy hand of elite interest is also not its exclusive privilege, even if it is more overt than in some other places. Similarly, the compliance of voters with patron–client interests is common enough, if to varying degrees, across Southeast Asia and much of the rest of the world.

But what all this does add up to is that while Indonesia has regular and fairly clean and efficient elections and probably passes the 'democracy' test, it does so in its own distinctive way. As with other democratic states, one cannot take Indonesia's political system for granted, or assume that it will remain a permanent feature of the political landscape. But it does appear to have embedded itself in the Indonesian popular psyche and it would appear to require a major shift in circumstances to change it. While Indonesia's 'democracy' continues to serve elite interests so well, there is little incentive for it to be significantly altered.

Notes

1 The author was an UN accredited observer to the Timor-Leste ballot in 1999, as coordinator of the Australia East Timor International Volunteer Observer Project, the largest international observer group accredited to the ballot.

2 At a meeting in Tokyo between the two sides, GAM was offered the option of accepting the existing status of 'special autonomy', which meant surrender, or a return to fighting. Half of the GAM negotiating team, in Banda Aceh as part of the ceasefire agreement, was arrested on their way to the meeting, implying a lack of faith by Indonesia in the negotiation process from the outset.

3 Yudhoyono was the author of the *Paradim Baru* (New Paradigm) document that was designed to remove the military from its political role.

4 The author was adviser to the Free Aceh Movement in the Helsinki peace talks, and drafted or negotiated substantive parts of the agreement.

5 This section was previously published by the author, in revised form, under the heading 'Anti-reform actors hover over Indonesia's coming elections' (Kingsbury 2014a).

6 This section was initially published by the author, in revised form, as 'Indonesian democracy may rest on election' (see Kingsbury 2014b).

13 Timor-Leste

Timor-Leste is the most recently independent state of Southeast Asia, having only formally gained independence in 2002. Its independence from Indonesia, as an occupying power, closely reflected the contours of the Cold War, with the invasion of Timor-Leste based on the strong anti-communist orientation of Indonesia's Suharto-led New Order government and the leftist-oriented Fretilin movement of 1975, at a time when Vietnam, Cambodia and Laos had each undergone communist revolutions.

Similarly, Timor-Leste's independence followed Indonesia's own move towards democratisation following Suharto's political demise, which in turn reflected a lack of support from Indonesia's erstwhile Cold War ally, the US. Notably, too, then US President Bill Clinton actively encouraged the Australian-led international mission to restore order following the violence and destruction surrounding Timor-Leste's ballot for independence in August 1999. This marked the end of Indonesian rule and began a post-occupation transition process overseen by the United Nations.

Between 2002 and the time of writing, Timor-Leste has had three rounds of major elections, all of which have been widely regarded as meeting international criteria for being free and fair. There has also been one change of government on the basis of these elections. On these grounds, some observers have suggested that Timor-Leste has met the benchmark for having consolidated its democracy, having passed the 'turnover test' (Linz and Stepan 1986). Indeed, it could be argued that Timor-Leste was, or was equal to, the most democratic state in Southeast Asia, with the fairest and least tainted elections.

However, Timor-Leste continues to face future economic challenges which can be expected to impact upon its political environment, given that states with high levels of poverty, unemployment and food shortages are more prone to political instability. Given that Timor-Leste's political party system relies heavily on charismatic individuals and, apart from Fretilin, has poor party structures, loss of established political leaders could have a further destabilising effect. Expected economic problems are likely to manifest around the same time that the current generation of political leaders becomes no longer active.

Timor-Leste's political system

Timor-Leste's political system, and its constitution, is closely based on the 1976 version used by Portugal, its former colonial power. Timor-Leste is a parliamentary republic, in which legislative authority is vested in the parliament, elected on the basis of party list proportional representation, with executive authority held by the prime minister and his cabinet. Cabinet ministers are usually chosen from within the parliament but may also be selected from outside the parliament.

If a minister is chosen from among parliamentarians, his or her place is removed from parliamentary representation until such time as they leave the ministry, and that place is filled by the next person on the party list. Reflecting the influence of the UN on incorporating women more actively into public life, at least one in three candidates on each party list must be a woman. This has given Timor-Leste 38 per cent representation of women in parliament, the highest proportion in the Asia-Pacific region and among the highest in the world.

Timor-Leste also has an elected president who may serve a maximum of two consecutive terms. The presidency is a largely ceremonial position, although the president does have emergency and reserve powers, if employed in consultation with the prime minister and/or Council of State (RDTL 2002: 2.86). Because Timor-Leste's first two presidents, Xanana Gusmao and Jose Ramos-Horta, were politically active and occasionally exceeded their constitutional authority, and because of the derivation of Timor-Leste's constitution from an earlier Portuguese version which itself devolves considerable powers to the president (such powers being reduced in 1982), Timor-Leste has regularly, if incorrectly, been identified as a semi-presidential political system.

According to Duverger, who coined the term to describe the then French model, a semi-presidential system devolves considerable executive authority to the president, including usually foreign affairs and often defence (Duverger 1980). Timor-Leste's political system allocates relatively few powers to the president (RDTL 2002: 2.85, 2.86, 2.87) but, because the Portuguese political system was referred to as being semi-presidential, there has sometimes been a conflation of the two in the way that the current system is identified.

Contextualising the democratic experiment

After a faltering start, Timor-Leste's young democracy has stabilised and solidified. In particular, its people have fully embraced the electoral process, regarding (and celebrating) elections as a genuine process of participatory politics. The country started to transition away from the 'resistance era' leadership from 2015, with the stepping down as Prime Minister of Xanana Gusmao. Gusmao had been considering stepping down as Prime Minister to make way for a younger generation of Timor-Leste leadership since 2013, a year after his coalition government was re-elected.

Timor-Leste has generally met the benchmark for being considered a 'democracy', against a matrix of theoretical criteria (Collier and Levitsky 1996) and, employing further theoretical criteria (Schedler 1998; O'Donnell 1996), has made remarkable political gains over a relatively short period. This is all the more notable given a distinct fracturing of its political processes in and around 2006. While Timor-Leste has institutionalised key democratic criteria, those political gains being based on vulnerable economic and institutional foundations means they remain susceptible to reversal (see O'Donnell 1996 on democratic vulnerability).

Timor-Leste had been an international experiment in democracy, along with state building, following its destruction by and separation from Indonesia in 1999. This followed 24 years of Indonesian occupation in which up to a quarter of its population was killed or otherwise died as a result of that occupation (CAVR 2005). The United Nations Transitional Administration in East Timor (UNTAET) oversaw elections for a constitutional commission in 2001, which was transformed into the country's first parliament upon independence in 2002. The Fretilin (Frente Revolucionaria de Timor-Leste Independente; Revolutionary Front for an Independent East Timor) party took two-thirds of the parliamentary seats and formed the country's first elected government. Resistance leader Jose Alexandre 'Kay Rala Xanana' Gusmao was elected President. In part as a result of the international community's eagerness to leave the fledgling state to its own devices in 2003 (Russell 2008), and a strongly stated desire by the country's elites for the international community to leave as soon as possible, without international supervision Timor-Leste quickly descended into chaos.

Within months of the UN's departure, Timor-Leste's capital, Dili, was wracked by protests, which quickly turned into riots in which protesters were shot and a number of buildings destroyed (Kingsbury 2009a: 112–14, 131). These riots recurred again in 2004 and, by 2005, the expatriate-led Fretilin government was widely viewed as inflexible, unresponsive and combative. It was on the defensive against an influential and increasingly hostile church, there were growing tensions between the police and the army, and divisions within the army itself were beginning to surface. The divisions that were opening up in Timor-Leste reflected a complex of factors, including most of Fretilin's leadership having been in exile since 1975 and hence being disconnected from the experiences of the subsequent 24 years.

This alien political leadership was compounded by the destruction of 1999, Indonesia's departure causing a decline in living standards, and UNTAET's qualified record on institution building (Chopra 2002). In part, UNTAET's qualified institution building can be attributed to it initially being established under the auspices of the UN's Department of Peace-Keeping Operations rather than its Department of Political Affairs, to the change of its primary objective from state-building to local empowerment (Lemay-Hebert 2012), and in part to the low capacity of some UNTAET staff and in particular a failure to adequately impart necessary skills. This was further compounded by a lack of language skills on the part of most UN staff, which meant that East Timorese counterparts were often selected for their knowledge of English or Portuguese rather than other formal capacities, while UNTAET translators were usually not skilled in other technical fields (see also Shurke 2001: 11).

Perhaps most critical for the young country's cohesion, however, was a serious split between resistance leader Xanana Gusmao and Fretilin, which in turn divided domestic loyalties. The split initially arose in 1988 when Gusmao took Fretilin's guerrilla force Forcas Armadas da Libertacao Nacional de Timor-Leste (Falintil, Armed Forces for the National Liberation of East Timor) out of the party and made it a national army, initially under the umbrella organisation the National Council for Maubere Resistance (CNRM), which evolved into National Council for Timorese Resistance (CNRT). It was the CNRT which was formally identified with the pro-independence vote in 1999. However, in 1988 there had been some resistance to Gusmao's move to 'de-ideologise' Falintil, one consequence of which was that some otherwise loyal local commanders were killed, and another of which was Fretilin's alienation from Gusmao. This alienation only deepened after 1999 as Gusmao promoted reconciliation with former pro-Indonesia Timorese, including forming political alliances with some of them.

This complex of factors all spiralled out of control in 2006, starting with a strike and protest by a section of the army that was considered by some as a mutiny. The 'strike' arose over disputes between former guerrilla fighters who had been incorporated into the reformed Falintil-Forcas de Defesa de Timor Leste (F-FDTL, Falintil-Timor-Leste

Defence Force) and 159 new recruits, often from the west of the country, who were accused by some of being less loyal to the independence struggle and who in turn complained of discrimination on that basis.

The striking soldiers, joined by almost 300 other soldiers with grievances, protested outside the government offices in Dili, resulting in a heavy-handed government response and a rapid descent into widespread gang-led violence and destruction which left dozens dead, thousands of homes destroyed and 15 per cent of the population displaced. The country was divided into camps that were pro- and anti-Fretilin in approximate east and west geographic orientation. After a promising democratic start to independence, by 2006 Timor-Leste appeared to be heading for civil war. In response to enormous internal and external pressure, the Prime Minister, Mari Alkatiri, resigned. He was replaced by non-Fretilin Foreign Minister Jose Ramos-Horta at the head of a Fretilin government. International military and police forces were requested by the Timor-Leste government to return to the country a stable situation, with the UN returning to help rebuild the country's shattered institutional base (Kingsbury 2009a: 135, 138–53).

Against this background, the three rounds of Timor-Leste's 2007 elections – two for the presidency and one for the parliament – were seen as an opportunity to channel discontent through a regulated framework to produce a political outcome that better reflected the changed, if deeply held, convictions of the population. The 2007 elections themselves were marked by some violence, although relatively little compared to the events of 2006, and produced an outcome that was widely regarded as having met international criteria for being free and fair (VLGA Observer Mission 2007).[1]

Fretilin had won a plurality of votes but not enough to command a majority, and was unable to form a majority coalition. The formation of the post-election majority coalition government headed by the CNRT saw a fresh outbreak of rioting and destruction, with a number of people being killed. Subsequent analysis referred to the period of political violence as not just being over a couple of months in 2006 but extending, if sometimes sporadically, from early 2006 until the near fatal shooting of President Jose Ramos-Horta in February 2008, which was characterised, if incorrectly, by some observers as an 'attempted coup' (Kingsbury 2009a: 2, 8).

While by 2007 it was much too early to say that Timor-Leste's democracy had been consolidated, over the period following Ramos-Horta's shooting, however, a widespread sense of shock at that event and the removal of a key destabilising factor appeared to settle the political environment. Arguably the key destabilising actor of the post-2007 election period, rebel leader Major Alfredo Reinado, was killed in the events of February 2008, and his death allowed the government clear space to begin resolving its most pressing problems (Kingsbury 2009b).

Added to a windfall profit from a coincidental spike in oil prices, the government was able to return around 150,000 'internally displaced persons' to their homes, with cash grants of US$5,000 to build new homes if they had been destroyed, and to make payments of $8,000 to the 'striking' (and since sacked) soldiers whose grievances had triggered the events of 2006. Other disgruntled elements of the community, not least of whom were the 'veterans' of the struggle against Indonesian occupation, were also given financial settlements. Despite still having international peace-keepers and a large international aid presence, Timor-Leste went into the 2012 elections appearing to be a country at peace with itself. The 2012 elections were run by the East Timorese with very little international assistance and were, by any standard, remarkably successful (Kingsbury and Maley 2012). Upon the announcement of a new coalition government there was some relatively limited and quite brief violence, but it appeared that democracy had been embedded in Timor-Leste.

Three of the parties that helped comprise the 2007 government – the Conselho Nacional de Reconstrucao de Timor (CNRT, Timorese Council for National Reconstruction), the Partido Democratico (PD, Democratic Party) and the Frente Mudanca (Change Front) (da Silva 2007) – returned to office in 2012 in a new coalition.

Timor-Leste generally meets the criteria for being a democracy based on Collier and Levitsky's 'expanded procedural minimal' requirements (1996). Timor-Leste's elections have been held according to an established timetable and have been highly competitive for the major parties. There has been no detectable fraud, according to election monitor reports, and there is a universal suffrage for all citizens above 17 years of age (RDTL 2002: 1: 7). To the extent that Timor-Leste's citizens enjoy basic civil liberties, they do so in a generally accepted fashion, but one in which the line between tolerance and violence has sometimes been crossed. In particular, Timor-Leste's police force, the Policia Nacional de Timor-Leste (PNTL), is known for its excessive use of force (ETLJB 2013), including its responses to political protest (La'o Hamutuk 2007). This could be considered a minor qualification to the enjoyment of basic civil liberties by Timor-Leste's citizens. There have also been periodic attempts by Timor-Leste's government to limit the media's ability to report freely (IFJ 2014), particularly on issues of corruption (IFJ 2006: 9), through threats of the use of defamation laws and through restrictions on government advertising. Despite these efforts, the media has remained relatively unconstrained.

Beyond this, Timor-Leste continues to face a number of structural challenges, not least its low levels of institutional capacity, which is captured in Collier and Levitisky's 'expanded procedural minimum' democratic criterion of having an 'effective power to govern'. Despite receiving high levels of international assistance over more than a decade, as noted by an EU assessment, 'Though the government has made great strides, institutional capacity remains weak in Timor-Leste' (Tsilogiannis 2010). The weaknesses that continue to need to be addressed, as noted by the EU, include 'skills and knowledge, systems and processes, and attitudes and behaviours' (Tsilogiannis 2010: 63).

Parliament and in particular its committees regularly fail to meet a quorum and the legislative process is backlogged, not assisted by legislation being drafted in Portuguese while the language of Parliament being Tetum, with most parliamentarians being illiterate in Portuguese. Government jobs are commonly seen by employees as a sinecure rather than a service, and there is a high level of reluctance to make decisions even on matters well within the authority of individual officers, up to and including ministers. In all, it is widely regarded as safer to do nothing and not make mistakes than to actually do things but risk errors. Where there is some effort at implementing state authority, by the police and the courts, the former continues to prove to often be corrupt, brutal and inefficient, while the judicial system is slow, under-prepared, overwhelmed, linguistically challenged and swamped by the task of dispensing justice.

If state institutional capacity is a key criterion for democratic performance, then Timor-Leste performs relatively poorly and probably fails in this area. However, while poor institutional performance can hamper the delivery of government programs, illustrated not least by various ministries' year-on-year failure to expend their budgets (La'o Hamutuk 2011), institutional capacity probably does not speak to democratic intent or principle, but rather more to the delivery of some of its intended benefits. This is, of course, to adopt a state-centric view of 'institutions'. There could be said to be greater institutional depth than that allowed by a formal or modernist understanding of the term 'institution' if it included traditional institutions such as *lian nain* (traditional knowledge keepers), who often act as arbiters in the case of local disputes, and the quasi-traditional role of the *xefe de suco* (village chief) who sometimes also acts in such a capacity (Nixon 2012; Hohe 2002).

Further, desirable but not necessary democratic qualities, according to Collier and Levitsky's matrix, could include political, economic and social features associated with industrial democracy (e.g. trade unions, strong civil society/non-government sector), and socio-economic equality and/or high levels of popular participation in economic, social and political institutions. In these respects, Timor-Leste clearly lags behind regarding trade unions, socio-economic equality and high levels of popular participation in key institutions, although its civil society/NGO sector is relatively strong. In particular, organisations such as the Judicial Systems Monitoring Program, which scrutinises both legal and parliamentary processes, is well regarded both within Timor-Leste and by donor agencies, while La'o Hamutuk has a robust program examining government policies, in particular its economic policies and budgets.

Yet Timor-Leste does enjoy a democratic form of government and that form appears to be increasingly embedded in political practice and participation. While Timor-Leste's national identity was challenged by the events of 2006, there are a number of key commonalities across Timor-Leste, which define a coherent national identity and an increasingly common, if not universal, national language (Kingsbury 2010), it enjoys effectively uncontested territory, and there is wide acceptance of regulated conflict resolution. Timor-Leste's military is not formally involved in internal affairs, although it had been involved in 'policing' matters prior to 2006. Timor-Leste's per capita GDI is in the lower-middle band, although this gives the lie to its actual rate of income distribution, the median of which remains closer to the absolute poverty line (UN Data 2011), with half the population living below the poverty line of US$2 per day (World Bank 2012b). However, when last measured Timor-Leste's Gini Coefficient (measuring the gap between rich and poor) was just below the middle of the international rankings band and relatively low for a least developed country (World Bank 2009).[2] Timor-Leste's literacy rate for younger people has improved, but that overall literacy remains at around 58 per cent (UNICEF 2011).

As noted, Timor-Leste's legal system functions relatively well in a rudimentary sense, but faces a number of serious problems. As a result of too few trained judges, there is a backlog of cases, with limited access to justice for more remote communities (Marriott 2008). Further complicating the legal process is the use of multiple languages, with Timor-Leste's laws written and judges trained in the official language of Portuguese (spoken by a relatively small percentage of the population), most lawyers being trained in Indonesian, and most plaintiffs or defendants speaking either the non-technical national language of Tetum or a 'home' language (Marriott 2008: 24), and with court translators having varying levels of competence and often interpreting questions and answers beyond their brief. This complex translation environment means, in practical terms, that even when citizens go to court, their ability to communicate in a common language and hence have meaningful access to the judicial system is limited. According to Timor-Leste's Judicial Systems Monitoring Program: 'The justice sector in Timor-Leste has come a long way since independence but there remains a continuing need for further assistance to develop local capacity and to ensure the independence and efficacy of the justice sector' (JSMP 2013).

More positively, Timor-Leste's electoral institutions, the Technical Secretariat for Electoral Administration (STAE) which runs the election process, and the National Electoral Commission (*Comissao Nacional Das Eleicoes* – CNE) which oversees it, are well established and functioning as key state institutions. The STAE and CNE were established in 2001, had significant responsibility in the running of the 2007 elections, and ran the country's 2012 elections with very little external assistance. The STAE and CNE's running of the three rounds of the 2012 elections was widely regarded as having demonstrated competence in this regard. Timor-Leste passed the 'government turnover test' in 2007, although accompanied by sporadic violence, considerable destruction and some deaths. However, the country's political environment calmed relatively quickly and by mid-2008 was stable. The elections of 2012 were almost entirely incident free.

While Timor-Leste does not have Huntington's ideal of a long history of democratic participation, it does have a short history of a close embrace of such a process. Voter turnout in Timor-Leste has been high (Kingsbury and Maley 2012). What this means is that, despite having to travel in often difficult circumstances, including trekking several kilometres across mountainous terrain, Timor-Leste's citizens continue to enthusiastically embrace the voting process. In both 2007 and 2012, there were celebrations prior to voting along with early attendance at polling stations, voters wore their best clothes, and they celebrated again after voting. This all implies more than just the drudgery of feeling compelled to vote, but rather a deep acceptance of the process that, in traditional Timorese belief systems, has begun to look as though it has become *lulik* (sacred).

It is this commitment to and internalisation of the value of the electoral process that stands as a powerful indicator of the extent to which at least the electoral element of democracy has become institutionalised as 'the only game in town' (Di Palma 1991: 13; see also Linz and Stepan 1996: 5). The question is, however, whether this institutionalisation is contingent on other factors.

While all of Timor-Leste's political leaders had previously been civilians, both its prime minister and its president following the 2012 elections were former guerrilla chiefs, with President Taur Matan Ruak (proper name Jose Maria Vasconcelos) also having been commander of the F-FDTL. That Ruak was a former military commander would be less notable except for the fact that, as President, he initially promoted compulsory universal military conscription as a policy to be adopted by the Timor-Leste government (Office of the President of the Democratic Republic of Timor-Leste 2013). Apart from exceeding his 'competencies' under Timor-Leste's constitution by actively promoting a particular policy, this also tended to reflect Ruak's sense of engagement with civilian affairs in a military manner. Ruak's successor, Major-General Lere Anan Timor, was also not shy about commenting on matters beyond defence, including questioning whether people associated with former pro-Indonesia militias should return to Timor-Leste, despite the government's policy of reconciliation (*Timor Post* 2013). Ruak opposed Lere's reappointment as military chief in early 2016, sparking a parliamentary backlash against him and threats to have him impeached.

Notably, too, although many Fretilin members were deeply unhappy with the events of 2006 and the resignation of its leader, Mari Alkatiri, as Prime Minister, it vigorously contested the following year's elections. Fretilin accepted the election result, if less so the constitutional interpretation on the formation of government.[3] In a very practical sense, there was explicit agreement that elections and a democratic form of government were 'the only game in town', and the practice of the parties in their public campaigning for office confirmed this as the preferred and most viable form of achieving political power.

Timor-Leste's underlying material fragility

Timor-Leste continues to be challenged by very low levels of material development which, along with a residue of widespread post-traumatic stress disorder, have helped to create a fragile social environment. Should there be an economic crisis, continuing tensions borne of high levels of poverty and widespread and numerically rising unemployment could either spill over or be easily manipulated by political leaders with a limited commitment to electoral processes.

Regardless of the will of Timor-Leste's political leadership or the overwhelming public acceptance of its electoral process, the economic and material problems faced by its people since independence have been improved only in some areas, while remaining problematic in others. Although privileging material factors over agency, there has continued to be a flow of evidence supporting the proposition that as material conditions worsen, the chances of democracy surviving reduce (e.g. see Pzeworski and Limongi 1994; Cheibub, Przeworski, Limongi and Alvarez 1996; Huntington 1991). In Timor-Leste, since independence, after a significant fall, there has been only a marginal improvement in material living conditions for most people. High levels of cash flowing through the economy have impacted on prices, with the mid-2012 inflation rate running at just under 11 per cent, if down from 15 per cent in mid-2011. Areas outside Dili were less affected by inflation, reflecting more limited business opportunities and the more restricted flow of money beyond the capital.

Broad human development indicators have also improved in Timor-Leste, if unevenly, with per capita GDP rising to over US$3,000, but with mean incomes being closer to $730, with poverty remaining high, if declining very slightly to 37 per cent of the population (UNDP 2012). A report by the UN Special Rapporteur on Human Rights also highlighted the continuing extent of extreme poverty in Timor-Leste (Carmon 2012). Many in Timor-Leste's rural areas have seen only modest improvement in their lives since 2002. The UN special rapporteur on extreme poverty estimated that a majority of the 75 per cent of Timorese living in rural areas were 'entrenched in inter-generational cycles of poverty' (UN News Centre 2011), and that some 58 per cent of children suffered from chronic malnutrition, with almost half of all children under five underweight for their age (a problem that had historically afflicted Timorese children). The same report claimed that income inequality had 'risen significantly', with particularly stark gaps between people living in Dili and those in rural areas.

Easing the burden on households, Timor-Leste's fertility rate declined from a high of 7.1 live births per thousand women (some estimates had it as high as 7.8) in 2000 to around 5.45 live births in 2011, and appears to be continuing to reduce (World Bank 2012b). Countering this improvement, even with longevity increasing to an average of 62 years, 70 per cent of Timor-Leste's population remains under 30 years of age, while unemployment, notoriously difficult to determine in a country that has never had much formal employment, is disturbingly high. One view that has been widely discussed, although rarely formally articulated, is that Timor-Leste's rapidly growing population and its limited opportunities for employment represent a demographic time bomb for the country.

Despite a growing annual budget, only four per cent of the 2016 budget was dedicated to health, with 9 per cent on education, representing a decline in both areas (La'o Hamutuk 2016). The school enrolment rate is around 70 per cent; UNDP 2012). Literacy remains problematic, with the literacy rate being at around half for those aged 15 and above, and declining with increased age (reflecting exclusion under both the Portuguese and Indonesian administrations). On balance, human development indicators in Timor-Leste have improved, especially in the areas of infant and maternal mortality, which were cut by half over the decade to 2016. However, after a quick improvement after 2007 (probably due to increased government handouts in 2008–09), the rate of improvement dramatically slowed.

Timor-Leste has underpinned its overall economy with receipts from the country's Petroleum Fund, based on the Norwegian sovereign wealth model. The Petroleum Fund was established to provide for government expenditure based on withdrawals from the interest only, but has increasingly been used by the IV and V Constitutional Gusmao-led governments for major projects and recurrent expenditure. Oil and gas receipts provided 95 per cent of Timor-Leste's state revenues and 81 per cent of its GDP based on 2011 figures (La'o Hamutuk 2013). The Timor-Leste government's dispute with Woodside Petroleum over the location for the processing plant for the development of the Greater Sunrise natural gas field in the Timor Sea stalled, possibly ending the generation of a further US$11 billion to the Petroleum Fund's $14 billion base. Timor-Leste's argument that the liquid natural gas (LNG) should be processed on-shore to purportedly kick-start a petro-chemical industry was countered by Woodside's preference to process from a floating platform. Timor-Leste's government said, claiming the gas rightly belonged to it under the UN Convention of the Law of the Sea, that it should benefit from its processing. Woodside's preference for a floating platform reflected a move away from being tied to the constraints of national governments more generally and deep reservation about the costs, viability and sovereign risk involved in building such a plant on Timor-Leste's south coast.[4]

Further, there was a sense of unease expressed by another major oil development partner, Conoco-Philips, which raised questions about rule of law in Timor-Leste impeding future economic development (*Journal Independente* 2013). Beyond this, the Gusmao-led government intended to proceed with investing in its own US$5 billion infrastructure development for a LNG processing facility as the basis for a future petro-chemical industry on the island's south coast. Gusmao's logic, outlined during the 2007 election campaign, was that Timor-Leste needed to spend funds now to secure the survival of its people while investing in its non–oil/gas future. Given that there was no LNG upstream supplier in place in Timor-Leste, the country's low skills base and other low levels of capacity, and that a local petro-chemical industry would have to compete with a number of other regional industries, such as that in Singapore, the country's economic future and its ability to provide growing employment was, at best, looking hazardous.

This sense of hazard was pronounced when one considers that levels of government expenditure were proposed at US$1.562 billion in 2016 (similar to the 2015 figure), almost half of which was to be withdrawn in excess of the sustainable withdrawal rate (La'o Hamutuk 2016). If this spending approach were to continue, Timor-Leste's Petroleum Fund would be depleted by 2024. With better planning and more reserves than currently known, the fund would be depleted by 2027, and with a lot of luck around finding new reserves and a great deal of skill in managing its income, the fund would be depleted by 2036. However, if large infrastructure projects currently being discussed by the government were to proceed, Timor-Leste could deplete its Petroleum Fund well before 2024, possibly as early as 2020 (Schiener 2013).

The loss of the funds provided by its Petroleum Fund, and of viable significant industry at the level provided for by the fund, then, created the spectre of significantly reduced government spending, and hence reduced overall economic activity and fewer jobs in an already deeply constrained employment market, and reduced government support for social groups receiving benefits (veterans, pensioners) and for broadly available subsidised rice. In short, based on this economic approach, Timor-Leste looked to be headed towards an economic crisis. Coming from an already low and fragile development base, the social consequences of this reduction in government spending would be significant and would be likely to play out in the political field. La'o Hamutuk's Charlie Schiener described the forecast as a 'wake-up call', but acknowledged that, without significant policy change, Timor-Leste's economic future looked bleak.

Xanana resigns

Xanana Gusmao had been the towering figure in Timor-Leste's politics, and a great stabilising influence, especially after the chaos of 2006–07, combining what Weber (1948, p. 245) referred to as charismatic authority, elements of traditional authority and rational-legal authority. There was some doubt about whether, when he was no longer the national leader, the state would descend into chaos. Yet he chose the timing of his standing down, and the method of his succession, so as to avoid that outcome.

Since 2008, Gusmao had been the key stabiliser of Timor-Leste's politics and a centralising force in political decision making. He attracted criticism for personalising power, yet Timor-Leste's ministers have often been inept and, without central decision making, little would have been achieved. As it is, Timor-Leste's development record has been mixed, improving off a low base, especially after the destruction of 1999, but with major projects running over time and over budget. There was also extensive criticism of blossoming official corruption under Gusmao's prime ministership. This was directed primarily at the awarding of government contracts to family members of cabinet ministers. But Gusmao showed that charismatic, dominant leaders can choose the timing of their political departure, and can better manage the departure to support transition from a position of continuing authority rather than its sudden loss.

His resignation as Prime Minister in February 2015 and the appointment of a new cabinet marked a fundamental change in the young country's political landscape. Gusmao's successor was the former Fretilin Deputy Prime Minister under Jose Ramos-Horta's prime ministership and Fretilin Health Minister, Rui Araujo. At 50, Araujo was considered to be one of the 'young generation', and was widely liked and respected. Araujo's appointment indicated that a long-discussed 'government of national unity' has come to fruition.

Araujo was known for being methodical and having a strong grasp of the country's finances. As a former independent, before formally joining with Fretilin, he was seen as a moderate who was able to maintain good relations with major donor countries, notably Australia and the US. This 'government of national unity' would, by bringing East Timor's major political groupings into the same government, very likely provide a much more stable political environment than one in which there continued to be a high level of political division. The disadvantage of such an arrangement is, however, that it leaves the government without a viable opposition, which reduces political accountability. If such an arrangement is in place until the next elections, scheduled for 2017, this might be seen as an adequate post-Gusmao period of transition. If it goes beyond those elections, however, Timor-Leste might start to look more like some other 'dominant party' states, such as Malaysia, where coalitions rule effectively unchallenged. As for Gusmao himself, he remains in a senior ministerial role and continues to exercise a considerable influence over major state affairs, particularly around the Timor Sea dispute and the Petroleum Fund. The President, Taur Matan Ruak, is also keeping a close watch on the post-Gusmao environment; it is no coincidence that his name, a *nom de guerre*, translates as 'Two Eyes Watching'.

Timor-Leste pushed ahead with its desire to see a permanent maritime boundary established between it and Australia. As Gusmao was resigning, Timor-Leste's parliament passed a law establishing a Maritime Council which has oversight of settling permanent boundaries with Australia. If successful, this would mean overturning the current 50-year arrangement in which the resources of the Timor Gap are shared between the two countries, based on an earlier Indonesian agreement that favoured Australia. There is also hope that the Greater Sunrise LNG field dispute, worth tens of billions of dollars and critical to Timor-Leste's economic future, may be resolved under the new government. However, there is no particular indication this will be the case.

The 2016 Government Budget was passed by parliament on 18 December 2016 and sent to the President for final approval. On 29 December, the President vetoed the budget. The main points of concern involved the unsustainability of the proposed budget, the size of the veteran's take from the budget (*c.* $100 million), too much being spent on major infrastructure projects of questionable economic value (Oecusse Special Economic Zone, the Suai Supply Base, airport and port developments and so on) and there being too little spending on areas such as education, health and agriculture.

With an orderly transition from the leadership of the country's dominant political actor, it may be that Timor-Leste is moving towards a phase in its development when it can concentrate on planning its future rather than be distracted by its present. It will need to, if it is to survive the challenges of improving the livelihoods of its people, and to sustainably manage the all-important petroleum fund that underpins the country's economy.

Six months after the transition had taken place, with Rui de Araujo as Prime Minister overseeing a CNRT-Fretilin coalition government, Timor-Leste was continuing along a path of stability. Araujo seemed increasingly aware of the country's future challenges and had begun to lay the groundwork for diversification, even if primarily only into more efficient and sustainable agriculture, but with very limited practical input into tourism (Siswo 2015). With Ramos-Horta already departed from Timor-Leste's domestic politics in 2012, it was also likely that there would be a wider transitioning from the 'Generation of '75' over the period ahead of the scheduled 2017 elections, potentially including the current leadership of Fretilin.

This transition, then, exposes potential for political fragmentation, exacerbated by Timor-Leste's large number of parties relative to its small population, and acts as a potential complication to the projected depletion of Timor-Leste's revenues. In particular, low material indicators are already testing Timor-Leste's democratisation and a further economic decline would place the country in a statistically dire category in relation to a possible return to political violence (Collier 2004; Collier and Sambanis 2005). The implications of this for the country's fragile democracy are unknown other than, based on such probability indicators, it is likely the resilience of its commitment to, and ability to sustain, a democracy would be tested. This would be especially so should there again be widespread social disturbance and the consequent political intervention of the army.

Conclusion

By conventional criteria, Timor-Leste fulfils most of the requirements for having established a democracy according to an expanded procedural minimum requirement and is arguably the most democratic state in Southeast Asia. It has also gone a considerable way towards consolidating that democracy, if with a few aspects that qualify its success. But consolidation implies not just the completeness and depth of democratic process, but also its prospects for survival, and raises the question, posed by O'Donnell (1996), of whether the teleological idea of 'consolidation' is an appropriate benchmark for democratic success. The real issue is, then, not whether Timor-Leste has 'consolidated' its generally healthy democracy, but whether that democracy can be sustained in good health over the longer term.

The still young state has made remarkable political gains over a relatively short period, which are all the more notable given a distinct fracturing of its political processes in and around 2006. While Timor-Leste has institutionalised key democratic criteria, those political gains have been based on vulnerable economic and institutional foundations, meaning they remain susceptible to reversal.

There is, of course, no way to accurately predict Timor-Leste's political future, but which way it goes would seem to be largely shaped by one of two competing sets of criteria. Despite what looks to be Timor-Leste's coming economic crisis, it might still be possible to save its democracy (and avoid political chaos) if there remains a strong sense of popular democratic ownership allied with a clean, accountable and wise government. However, Timor-Leste's prospects of retaining its democracy look very much more fragile if there is a lack of democratic ownership or a retreat to a sense of 'democratic fatalism' or democratic inevitability, and the government becomes less accountable and continues to make what might come to be seen as unwise economic decisions.

At the time of writing, Timor-Leste's people and its political leaders appeared deeply committed to democratic processes and attempting to achieve relatively high levels of transparency and accountability. The wisdom of the government's economic planning, however, was at best open to doubt and was likely to increase negative structural pressure on otherwise positive democratic intentions.

Timor-Leste is still finding its way along a difficult post-independence path. This is a period in which many other countries stumble or fall. Gusmao choosing his own timing to step down smoothed the transition process. But the many problems of this young and still fragile nation remained to confront his successor.

Notes

1 The author was coordinator of the principle Australian observer mission to the 2007 Timor-Leste elections; see Kingsbury 2007b.
2 More recent data on Timor-Leste's Gini Coefficient has not been compiled, although anecdotal evidence suggests there are significantly greater disparities in wealth.
3 The Constitution Section 106 says that the government should be formed by the 'most voted' party or a coalition of a majority of parties. Fretilin argued that, receiving the greatest single vote, it was the 'most voted' party and therefore should have been given an opportunity to form a minority government. However, CNRT was able to assemble a majority coalition, with President Jose Ramos-Horta regarded as also meeting the constitutional requirement for government as well as being a more workable parliamentary proposition. Fretilin members continued to argue against this latter interpretation for some months after the appointment of the new government, initially boycotting parliament but eventually agreeing to become an active opposition.
4 Based on confidential commercial discussions.

14 Southeast Asian regionalism

This chapter considers how the sometimes disparate states of Southeast Asia function collectively, notably through the Association of Southeast Asian Nations (ASEAN) with its evolving membership. Within this, the character of individual states and their leaders and proposed regional agreements, such as the free trade agreement, influence the character of the region as a bloc (or otherwise) in other international forums and in relation to external challenges. This has particular importance in relation to China's encroachment in the South China Sea and reassertion of regional power, the 'pivot' of the United States back towards the Asia-Pacific region, and the role of other major powers such as Russia and India; and in response to domestic challenges such as Islamist terrorism, unregulated population flows and other regional security issues.

Commonalities

There has long been a view that the Association of Southeast Asian Nations (ASEAN) had little meaning after initially being formed in 1967 as a type of peace offering by Indonesia towards its more politically conservative neighbours. The organisation's membership has since expanded in number, to include its communist or formerly communist neighbours as well as Myanmar, and has started to take on a stronger strategic role as the centrepiece of the development of the ASEAN Regional Forum (ARF).

At one level, the ASEAN group of states are disparate, with populations varying from that of Indonesia, at more than 250 million, to Brunei, with less than half a million. GDP, too, varies from just a little under one trillion US dollars for Indonesia to the impoverished Laos with a GDP of $12 billion. Per capita GDP is also enormously varied, from Singapore at over $55,000 to Cambodia at just over $1,000. International trade is similarly skewed, with Singapore trading around three-quarters of a trillion dollars a year while Laos is at about six billion dollars (World Bank 2016).

Similarly, while there have been a number of changes, the ASEAN region also comprises a range of political models, including Vietnam and Laos' authoritarian one party state status; Thailand's on-again/off-again constitutional monarchy and democracy/military junta; the dominant party states of Cambodia, Singapore and Malaysia; Indonesia and the Philippines' chaotic democracies; Brunei's monarchy; and, most recently, Myanmar's evolving participatory politics.

Perhaps ASEAN's greatest achievement has been the incorporation of all Southeast Asian states, with Timor-Leste still under consideration. Added to this, long discussed but still awaiting implementation, has been the 'ballast'[1] in the ASEAN relationship through a Free Trade Area. With ASEAN states having a high degree of commonality in economic output, trade between them has been relatively limited. More sophisticated manufacturing states such as Thailand and, to a lesser extent, Malaysia have engaged in some export to other ASEAN states but, beyond that, intra-ASEAN trade has been limited and exports are primarily destined for developed or Organisation of Economic Cooperation and Development (OECD)[2] economies.

One answer to this relative lack of intra-ASEAN trade has been the policy of forming an ASEAN free trade zone. The development of an ASEAN Free Trade Area (AFTA) in the 1990s saw some tariffs decline, but little increase in intra-ASEAN trade. After many years of discussion about the AFTA and its relative failure to stimulate intra-ASEAN trade, the ASEAN states agreed to a more close-knit ASEAN Economic Community (AEC) as a single market, brought forward from its original implementation date of 2020 to, in theory, come into effect by the end of 2015. While the issue of economic overlap was likely to remain, there was more scope for intra-ASEAN investment, as well as the ability to present a more coherent economic front to international forums such as the World Trade Organization (WTO), especially when negotiating free trade agreements with other countries or economic blocs (Das 2015).

While a free trade zone had long been discussed – as an AEC since 2003 – and there had been some movement towards it, the final push towards an AEC, 2007, was the impact of the global financial crisis (GFC) on global economies, in particular how it impacted upon exports from developing economies to OECD members which were in a number of cases severely impacted by the GFC.

While the AEC had begun to be implemented in 2015, despite the formal timeline for completion it was unlikely to have been fully implemented by the end of that year. Dismantling and rearranging economic regulations, taxes and duties can be a slow process for any country, but presented an extra challenge to the bureaucracies and other state institutions of some of the less administratively organised or efficient regional economies. Observers of the AEC process were less than convinced it would come to fruition according to the proposed timeline, or perhaps even in the ways initially envisaged. 'The reality on the ground does indicate that 2015 *will be another signpost* in ASEAN's quest for regional integration' (Thuzar 2015; my emphasis). However, Thuzar also noted that, despite it not being immediately obvious, there did seem to be a 'nascent sense of community developing among the younger generation' (Thuzar 2015).

The AEC's intention is to promote free regional trade to enhance equitable economic development, to reduce poverty and to increase the dynamism of regional economies. This relies heavily on a neo-liberal understanding of economics development, which has been proven successful in only some circumstances and usually as a consequence of local factors such as skills base, proximity or social organisation rather than its universal truth.

As ASEAN members progress with the deepening of their economic integration, an ASEAN customs union (CU) may become a possibility. With Singapore already not having tariffs on trade in goods, either all ASEAN members will need to move towards also having no tariffs on goods or they will retain a standard tariff but not include Singapore, which would imply a partial customs union. Either way, the benefits from such a CU could be limited, with some members states gaining little or nothing from such an arrangement (Das, Sen and Srivastava 2015).

Overall, the combined ASEAN economy was expected to have grown by 5.6 per cent in 2016, having charting a slight upward trend over the preceding three years, although representing a slight drop from 5.7 per cent in 2012. This compares to 6.3 per cent projected growth for China, down from its preceding highs of 7.8 per cent and marking a shift in the Chinese economy from construction to consumption. The economic performance of each of the ASEAN states has remained fairly steady, with a low of 3 per cent projected growth off a high base for Singapore to 8.5 per cent projected growth off a very low base for Myanmar (IMF 2015).

One potential problem with the ASEAN Free Trade Zone could be the competition that would come from the Trans-Pacific Partnership (TPP), a Pacific Basin free trade agreement that includes in its ranks Singapore, Brunei, Vietnam and Malaysia. This acts as direct competition for the ASEAN group generally and for non-signatories to the TPP in particular. The strength of the TPP comes from its partnership with a range of other economies, including the US, Japan, Canada and Australia, among others. Thailand, Indonesia, the Philippines and Laos are also considering joining the TPP, as is South Korea, but had not yet done so at the time of writing.

The TPP is also expected to have some impact on aspects of ASEAN trade, with the US, Japan and Australia accounting for just over 20 per cent of all ASEAN trade in 2014 and almost a quarter of all foreign direct investment (Masykur 2016).

The ASEAN way

ASEAN has long touted what it has referred to as the 'ASEAN Way', which has essentially boiled down to non-interference in the internal affairs of member states. This model held up well when ASEAN was restricted to explicitly pro-Western states, prior to the end of the Cold War. However, since the conclusion of the Cold War and the inclusion of Cambodia, Laos, Vietnam and Myanmar in ASEAN, that model of non-interference has begun to fragment. Thailand has had, at times, testing relations with Laos, Cambodia and Myanmar, particularly over issues of disputed territory and in particular with Cambodia allowing deposed Thai Prime Minister Thaksin Shinawatra to use Phnom Penh as a base from which to launch verbal attacks against his ousters.

ASEAN unity has, in the face of this non-interference requirement, been tested from time to time. The greatest division occurred when Cambodia was ASEAN chair in 2012, which resulted in ASEAN developing a formula that allowed a group of ASEAN states to proceed with a particular motion while leaving a member state out of the count, for example in expressions of concern over China's expansion into the South China Sea. According to Thayer, it remains too soon for there to be a simple majority binding vote by ASEAN members. ASEAN has greatest solidarity over its pursuit of economic arrangements and its expression of socio-cultural values, but is less united over politico-security issues due to members' different relations with China, particularly in the case of Cambodia but also Myanmar, and with the US. Given these differing relations, and each state's specific interests, e.g. Cambodia–Vietnam or Thailand–Cambodia border issues, ASEAN is unlikely to play a meaningful role in local dispute resolution (Thayer 2015a).

The ASEAN member states have renewed a formal commitment to closer cooperation around regional political and security issues, based on an agreement reached in 2003. However, the 2016–2026 *ASEAN Political-Security Committee Blueprint*, adopted from a document of the same title published in 2009, does not break any new ground or propose any meaningful changes to the status quo. The latest iteration of the plan is, according to at least one analyst, 'unexciting' (Chalermpalanupap 2016). As with the previous document, the key ASEAN focus is to more closely integrate economic relations, with a 'steady as she goes' approach to managing the South China Sea dispute despite China's advances in the area; for ASEAN to be a 'rules-based' organisation; a reiteration of commitment to fighting the drug trade and regional corruption; and, at least rhetorically, a recommitment to respecting human rights.

There have also been criticisms between states over human rights records, claims to natural resources (notably between the Philippines and Malaysia) and the treatment of guest workers (primarily of Indonesians and Filipinas in Singapore), and Malaysian and Singaporean criticism of Indonesia over smoke haze from 'illegal'[3] burning and clearing of forests. Recognising that there had been disputes between ASEAN neighbours, in 2010 the organisation instituted a dispute resolution process in which, according to ASEAN Deputy-Secretary Mochtan, 'the rule of law is strengthened and disputes are resolved through peaceful means with legal certainty and predictability' (ASEAN 2014). 'This Protocol to the ASEAN Charter, together with the existing Treaty of Amity and Cooperation in Southeast Asia and the Protocol on Enhanced Dispute Settlement Mechanism (EDSM), is a significant achievement in establishing reliable and trustworthy dispute settlement mechanisms' (ASEAN 2014).

Relations with China

There is no doubt that China has had a significant impact upon Southeast Asia, both historically and more contemporarily. Historically, when China was strong, it asserted its authority throughout much of the region, claiming and often being able to impose suzerain status, if resisted with varying degrees of success from time to time. In the past, the state most influenced by China has been Vietnam, which adopted many of its traditions and which can still be considered the most Chinese-influenced of the Southeast Asian states, if also the most resistant to China's direct involvement. Throughout much of Southeast Asia, it is said that when China is weak it retreats into itself, but when it is strong its power is felt widely.

China had been a weak state during much of its modern association with Europe and, hence, Westerners have long regarded China as a weak and disorganised state. Its communist revolution did little to alter that perception, other than to put it firmly in an anti-Western ideological camp, and, in that some Southeast Asian state were aligned with the US, this constructed an antithetical relationship during the Cold War period.

However, Cold War alignments were never as simple as often thought during that time. Few outside Vietnam, for example, appreciated that Vietnam was wary of China's influence and preferred the friendship of allies further afield, such as the Soviet Union; more than most, Vietnam had a long memory of China's historical embrace. However, since the late 1980s and China's own return to growth, it has again reached out to its regional neighbours, through trade and what is sometimes referred to as 'soft power' diplomacy, such as development assistance (which usually involves imported Chinese goods and labour), cheap development loans, trade agreements and supply of military equipment.

China's closest Southeast Asian partner is Cambodia. Cambodia, or rather Kampuchea as it was then known, was closely allied with China throughout the period of 1975–78, and China continued to support the ousted Khmer Rouge between 1979 and their dissolution in the late 1990s. Similarly, China also provided support and sanctuary for Cambodia's royalty during times of crisis. Yet despite the Cambodian People's Party initially having come to and retaining power with the support of Vietnam and hence the Soviet Union, since Vietnam's withdrawal between 1989 and 1991 Cambodia has increasingly moved back towards China, becoming, by 2015, overwhelmingly China's closest friend in the region. In part this reflects a deep mistrust within Cambodia of

Vietnam, and the opportunity to construct a counter to its near and sometimes intrusive neighbour (Cambodian memory of the loss of 'Kampuchea Krom', or what is now the southernmost quarter of Vietnam, remains alive).

China has become a major investor in Cambodia, particularly in its low-cost garment manufacturing industry, and a major arms and military training supplier. For its part, Cambodia has been loyal to China, particularly over the South China Sea dispute, which has united other regional states in opposition to China's expansion into those territorially disputed waters.

Myanmar has also been close to China, and the beneficiary of investments and the supply of weapons. However, while this suited the Myanmar government when it was widely regarded as an international pariah and blocked from much international investment, it has been argued that China's sometimes heavy-handed desire to influence was one of the factors that encouraged the government of Myanmar to consider moderating its international image in the (now successful) hope of attracting new international friends.

China remained a significant source of investment for Myanmar, but that country's opening after 2011–12 allowed it to push back against Chinese influence, most notably through its decision not to proceed with the US$3.6 million Chinese-funded Myitsone Dam project – the world's fifteenth largest – in Kachin State. Construction of the dam displaced thousands of villagers and proved to be deeply unpopular in Kachin State, home of a large and long-standing separatist movement. In an early act of his 'reformist' presidency, Thein Sein halted the project indefinitely (Eleven 2011).

China's relations with the other Southeast Asian states are generally positive, but for the South China Sea dispute. China has significant trade and investment in Laos and views it, with Vietnam, as its most influential external partner. It has a high profile in Timor-Leste, where it has constructed a number of major public buildings and assisted by providing naval patrol boats. Following a break in diplomatic relations between 1967 and 1990, China has increasingly developed diplomatic relations with Indonesia, and since the early twenty-first century this relationship has been a growing source of trade.

Relations between China and Malaysia have historically been strong, with links going back over a millennium. They continue to be very positive on both the diplomatic and economic fronts, with Malaysia's large minority ethnic Chinese population facilitating trade and investment. Strategic relations between Malaysia and China are also warm – if not to the same extent of closeness as with Cambodia, at least more so than with some other ASEAN states. Malaysia has protested about Chinese shipping in its territorial waters, but has otherwise been more relaxed than some other states regarding China's expansion in the South China Sea. It has, by way of moderating some concerns, pushed for a 'Code of Conduct' in the South China Sea, which China has, to the time of writing, wholly ignored.

One important aspect of the relationship between the ASEAN states and China was the ASEAN–China Free Trade Agreement (ACFTA) signed in 2002, which came into effect in 2010. The volume of trade within the ACFTA is the third largest in the world, behind the European Union and the North American Free Trade Area and with a combined gross domestic product of six trillion dollars. The agreement removed tariffs on 90 per cent of goods traded between the countries (ASEAN 2002). However, protests in Indonesia over what was claimed to be excessive access by Chinese companies led to the reimposition of some restrictions (Asmoro 2009). As with Malaysia, much of the trade has been facilitated by ethnic Chinese living in Southeast Asia, often for many generations (Cheung and Gomez 2012).

While economic links with China have grown, China's rise as an economic and a military power, and its push into the South China Sea, has created a sense of strategic uncertainty in Southeast Asia. The United States had refocused its international attention away from Southeast Asia after retreating from the Indochina conflict in 1975 and militarily it had withdrawn from its last bases, in the Philippines, by 1992. The US instead focused its attention on the Middle East, notably with the First Gulf War in 1990–91, with its interest in regional Southeast Asian allies waning. Its focus on the Middle East sharpened again following the events of 11 September 2001. But, after difficult military engagements in Afghanistan and Iraq following the events of 2001, Southeast Asia again became a focus of US attention, with its pivot away from the Middle East back towards Asia from 2011.

While some US officials have argued that the US never lost interest in the East Asia region and that, with a Pacific coastline, it had always been a 'Pacific power', there is little doubt that China's economic rise and strategic reach has also encouraged the US to shift its strategic priorities. As a result, the states of Southeast Asia are caught, to a greater or lesser degree, in an economic, diplomatic and strategic competition between these two global powers.

Largely, ASEAN leaders have chosen a path of careful diplomacy, noting that friendship with one did not preclude friendship with the other. However, the US is widely seen to be a power that has weakened since its heyday, particularly in economic terms, while its global commitments have continued to divide its international attention. Set against China's economic rise and assertion of strategic reach, this has created what has been referred to as an era, and a region, of 'strategic uncertainty' (Thayer 2014b).

Thayer has suggested that, broadly, Southeast Asia's maritime states have encouraged the US to retain a strategic presence in the region to balance and perhaps limit further assertions of China's power. However, mainland states, in particular Cambodia, Myanmar and Laos, have generally had a closer relationship with China, seeking to benefit from China's developing economic prosperity and to avoid unnecessary political (or other) conflict (Thayer 2014b: 129). There has also been concern that the US pivot back towards the region could heighten tensions with China, creating an unstable strategic environment. There has been related concern over the perception that the US commitment to the pivot, while manifested in increased naval operations and base agreements, is over-stating and under-delivering on its robustness.

> China's concentration of its SSBN [Ship Submersible Nuclear Ballistic] fleet and patrols in the South China Sea is turning the sea into a major arena for the strategic rivalry between the United States and China. The importance of SSBNs to China in this rivalry will likely mean that China's interests in gaining greater sea control over the South China Sea and the assertion of Chinese sovereignty in its disputed waters will not be deterred by diplomatic pressure from ASEAN or unfavorable international arbitration rulings.
>
> (Cook 2015: 3)

On balance, it would appear that China's assertion on questionable sovereignty, literally made more concrete by the construction of an air base and other defence facilities on artificial islands, will not be deterred and that, while its legal claim to the region is at best doubtful, it will continue to assert through force its control and effective ownership of the area. The only question will be whether the US will continue to assert its own right of freedom of navigation and overflight of the region, the extent to which China responds, and what role the ASEAN states might or might not play in such a scenario.

Southeast Asian regionalism?

Southeast Asia exists, as a region, primarily because of the proximity of its respective countries, because there have been some common cultural influences (notably from India), and because there has been a largely shared experience of colonialism. The period of decolonisation saw the region divided into two approximate camps, reflecting the main themes of the Cold War. Yet that period has now passed and, while remnant political organisations continue to exist and indeed flourish, the rationale for previous political typologies has similarly passed. What exists is a continuation of, in many cases, or a reversion to, previous political themes.

In part, Southeast Asia is the sum total of what it is not; it is not part of China or India, its large and powerful neighbours, both of which have historically influenced much of the region, and it has a tenuous connection with its southern, predominantly European neighbour, Australia. Between these three land masses and the Indian and Pacific Oceans, it is a region that necessarily shares some of the attributes of neighbourliness, as well as competition, if historically often in shifting and unreliable ways.

But as modern states with bounded borders and a generally high regard for international rule of law in matters of territorial sovereignty, the state of Southeast Asia are – at least for the time being – fixed entities. The brief moment of Indonesia's millennial fragility has passed, with the legal and colonial anomaly of Timor-Leste now being a state in its own right. Myanmar in particular still faces challenges to its conception of the state as unitary and it may eventually devolve to a different state model (e.g. federal), but it seems unlikely to change its external boundaries. So, too, while Thailand and Cambodia, from time to time, have minor spats about ancient temple sites and access to them, the borders between those two countries, for so long vulnerable to changing fortunes, now seem settled, as with Laos.

Vietnam, Malaysia, Brunei and the Philippines each have a claim to the South China Sea, although not to the extent that they conflict with each other over such claims. Such tension that arises is due to China's territorial (over) reach, the implausible rationale for its claims but the strength with which it is backing them. Indeed, as the world's second largest economy and an increasingly powerful strategic actor, China may again come to dominate parts of Southeast Asia as it has historically done when its empires have been strong. The rules of international engagement have changed, but China has been adept at finding ways to exercise influence within, and sometimes beyond, such rules.

The United States, too, remains a major global actor and a continuing economic and strategic force in the region, if less so than it once was. It remains, however, a convenient alternative when smaller states seek a balance of power, as those of Southeast Asia do collectively and individually. But none of the states of Southeast Asia define themselves by their relationship with the United States, even if, some decades before, they had.

Perhaps what defines Southeast Asia, as a region, is its ability to increasingly cohere around common interests and the value of its bond in relation to external pressures. There are some commonalities between the states and there are many differences. But, like nations themselves, sometimes what acts as the bonding agent is less what they have, pre-existing, in common than what they what in common they fear or oppose. That they share proximity and some measure of comfort in unity in the face of a challenging world continues to provide sufficient rationale for them to remain coherent, if only up to a certain point. In this respect, and perhaps not uncommonly, the states of Southeast Asia are, together and separately, the sum of what they are as well as the sum of what they are not.

Notes

1 The term 'ballast' was originally used by Australian Foreign Minister Gareth Evans to describe the importance of economic relations between Australia and Indonesia when other aspects of the relationship might be tested.

2 That is, the advanced industrial economies.

3 It is illegal to clear and burn forests without a permit in Indonesia. However, the practice is widespread, primarily due to extensive official corruption, especially in Sumatra, and causes thick smoke to flow across peninsular Malaysia and Singapore.

Bibliography

Abas, A. and Aziz, F. 2016. 'AG's Chambers Clears Najib of Wrongdoing in Donation, SRC International Cases', *New Straits Times* 26 January 2016.

ABC 2013. 'Burma Gave Rice to N. Korea for Weapons: WikiLeaks Cable', Australian Broadcasting Corporation, 5 September 2011. www.radioaustralia.net.au/international/2011-09-05/burma-gave-rice-to-n-korea-for-weapons-wikileaks-cable/202612 (accessed 10 July 2013).

ABS-CBN 2009. '"Noynoy for President" Signature Drive Launched', ABS-CBN News, 27 August 2009. http://news.abs-cbn.com/nation/08/27/09/noynoy-president-signature-drive-launched (accessed 10 March 2016).

Acemoglu, D. and Robinson, J. 2006. *Economic Origins of Dictatorship and Democracy* Cambridge University Press, Cambridge.

Adams, B. 2013. 'Myanmar Army Continues to Live in Denial over Abuses', *Bangkok Post* 9 May 2013.

ADB 2011. 'Governance', *Sectors and Themes*, Asian Development Bank, 12 August 2011.

ADB 2012. 'Poverty Analysis (Summary)', Interim Country Partnership Strategy: Myanmar, 2012–2014, Asian Development Bank, Manila.

Ahlberg, K. 2013. *Foreign Relations of the United States, 1977–1980, Volume II, Human Rights and Humanitarian Affairs* US State Department, Washington, DC.

Ahmad, R. 2014. 'Malaysian Opposition Split Over Move to Impose Hudud', *New Straits Times* 7 May 2014.

AI 2009. 'Brunei Darussalam Submission to the UN Universal Periodic Review', Amnesty International, 13 April 2009.

Akamatsu, K. 1962. 'A Historical Pattern of Economic Growth in Developing Countries', *Journal of Developing Economies* Vol. 1, No. 1, pp. 3–25.

Alim, G. 2014. 'Peacetalk: Challenges (and Hopes) in the Post CAB Bangsamoro: From the Third Eye', *Minda News* 29 June 2014. www.mindanews.com/mindaviews/2014/06/29/peacetalk-challenges-and-hopes-in-the-post-cab-bangsamoro-from-the-third-eye/ (accessed 18 September 2015).

Alvarez, M., Cheibub, J.A., Limongi, F. and Przeworski, A. 1996. 'Classifying Political Regimes', *Studies in Comparative International Development Summer* Vol. 31, No. 2, pp. 3–36.

An, S. 2002. Opening address, Workshop on Doctrine of Precedents, Separation of Power, Checks and Balances, Ministry of Justice, Phnom Penh, 10–11 June, 2002.

Anderson, B. 1991. *Imagined Communities* 2nd ed., Versa, London.

Ang, P. 2013. 'Open Letter to PM Lee – Residents' Committee', *The Online Citizen*. www.theonlinecitizen.com/2013/03/open-letter-pm-lee-residents-committee/ (accessed 7 January 2016).

Anon 2014. 'Mystery Surrounds Death of Key Laos Officials', Crikey.com, 10 June 2014.

Antara 2015. 'Foreign Media Should Obtain Permits to Cover Papua: Chief Minister', 11 May 2015.

Anthony, T. 2008. *Rebels of Mindanao* Beaufort Books, New York.

AOW 2011. 'Burma's Resource Curse', Arakan Oil Watch, March 2011. www.burmacampaign. org.uk/images/uploads/Burmas-Resource-Curse.pdf (accessed 10 July 2013).

AOW 2012. 'Burma's Resource Curse: The Case for Revenue Transparency in the Oil and Gas Sector'. Arakan Oil Watch. www.burmacampaign.org.uk/images/uploads/Burmas-Resource-Curse.pdf (accessed 25 August 2015).

AP 2016. 'Vietnam's Prime Minister Nguyen Tan Dung Withdraws from Contest for Communist Party Chief', Associated Press/*South China Morning Post* 25 January 2016.

ASC, TI, CSS, PRC 2003. *Failed and Collapsed States in the International System* The African Studies Center; The Transnational Institute, Leiden; The Center for Social Studies, Amsterdam; The Peace Research Center-CIP-FUHEM, Coimbra University, December 2003.

ASEAN 2002. *Framework Agreement on Comprehensive Economic Co-Operation Between ASEAN and the People's Republic of China*, 4 November 2002.

ASEAN 2014. 'ASEAN Builds Strong Dispute Settlement Mechanisms', ASEAN Secretariat News, 31 October 2014.

Asia Steel Construction 2013. 'Myanmar Steel Industry and Trade'. www.asiasteelmyanmar.com/ index.php/84-industry-info/82-myanmar-steel-industry-and-trade (accessed 8 July 2013).

Asmoro, A. 2009. 'ASEAN–China Free Trade Deal: Let's Face the Music', *Jakarta Post* 23 December 2009.

Attachai, U. 2012. 'Analysing National Elections on Thailand in 2005, 2007 and 2011 – Graphical Approach', *International Journal of Business and Social Science* Vol. 3, No. 109, pp. 69–79.

Aung San Yamin. 2013. 'Suu Kyi Calls for Collaboration With Military at NLD Anniversary', *The Irrawaddy* 27 September 2013.

Badgley, J. 2004. 'Strategic Interests in Myanmar', NBR Analysis Vol. 15, No. 1, pp. 13–27.

Bandial, Q. 2015. 'HM Censures Police for Corrupt Practices', *The Brunei Times* 1 April 2015.

Bangkok Declaration 1993. 'Final Declaration of the Regional Meeting for Asia of the World Conference on Human Rights', Bangkok, 2 April 1993.

Barr, M. 2014. *The Ruling Elite of Singapore: Networks of Power and Influence* I.B. Taurus, London.

Barr, M. 2015a. 'Lee's Legacy', *East Asia Forum* 30 March 2015. www.eastasiaforum. org/2015/03/30/lees-legacy/ (accessed 14 January 2016).

Barr, M. 2015b. 'Singapore: Flight to Safety Trumps Performance Legitimacy', *Asian Currents* 19 September 2015.

Barr, M. 2015c. 'Singapore's Election May Hurt the PM, but the Government is Safe', *East Asia Forum* 6 September 2015. http://asaablog.tumblr.com/post/129458418836/singapore-flight-to-safety-trumps-performance (accessed 26 May 2016).

Bartholomew, J. 1990. *The Richest Man in the World*, 2nd ed., Penguin Books, Harmondsworth, UK.

Basic Principles of the Union 2003. ('Seven Point Roadmap'), Government of the Union of Myanmar.

BBC 2004. 'Sultan of Brunei Reopens Parliament', BBC World News, 25 April 2004.

BBC 2006. 'China Gives Cambodia $600m in Aid', BBC World News, 8 April 2006. http://news. bbc.co.uk/2/hi/asia-pacific/4890400.stm (accessed 31 August 2015).

BBC 2012. 'Vietnam Prime Minister Nguyen Tan Dung Urged to Resign', 12 November 2012.

BBC 2013. 'Brunei Profile – Media', 13 June 2013. www.bbc.com/news/world-asia-pacific-12990064 (accessed 23 September 2015).

BBC 2015a. 'Malaysia Profile – Media', BBC Asia-Pacific, 28 October 2015. www.bbc.com/ news/world-asia-pacific-15384221 (accessed 9 December 2015).

BBC 2015b. 'Malaysia Pumps $4.6bn into Stock Market', BBC Business, 14 September 2015.

BDPMO 2012. 'Jabatan Perdana Menteri' (First Ministerial Position), Prime Minister's Office, Bandar Seri Begawan, Brunei Darussalam.

Beech, H. 2013. 'The Face of Buddhist Terror', *Time* 1 July 2013.

Belkin, A. and Schofer, E. 2003. 'Toward a Structural Understanding of Coup Risk', *The Journal of Conflict Resolution* Vol. 47, No. 5, pp. 594–620.

Benda, H. 1960. 'Non-Western Intelligensias as Political Elites', *Australian Journal of Politics and History* Vol. 6, No. 2, pp. 205–18.

Bercovitch, J. and De Rouen, K. 2005. 'Managing Ethnic Civil Wars: Assessing the Determinants of Successful Mediation', *Civil Wars* Vol. 7, No. 1, pp. 98–116.

Blancas, L., Isbell, J., Isbell, M., Hua J.T. and Tao, W. 2014. *Efficient Logistics: A Key to Vietnam's Competitiveness* World Bank, Washington, DC.

BMI Research 2015. 'Political Risk – Stable Politics Owing To LPRP's Tight Grip On Power, Risk Summary – Laos – APR 2015', *South East Asia* Vol. 1, March 2015/Laos/Political Risk.

Boehler, P. 2012. 'Vietnam's Blogosphere: The Battleground for Rival Factions of the Ruling Communists', *Time* 27 December 2012.

Bogais, J. 2015. 'Cambodia on the Brink', *Asian Currents* 4 December 2015. http://asaa.asn.au/cambodia-on-the-brink/ (accessed 4 December 2015).

Boudreau, J. and Diem, P. 2014. 'Vietnam Falling Short in Tackling Corruption, Says Party Chief', *Bloomberg Business* 6 May 2014.

Boulos, N. 2014. 'Brunei: A Kingdom of Gold and Green', *The Independent* 18 January 2014.

BSP 2015a. 'History of Oil and Gas', in *About Brunei Shell Petroleum* Brunei Shell Petroleum, Seria.

BSP 2015b. 'Overview of our Business', in *About Brunei Shell Petroleum* Brunei Shell Petroleum, Seria.

Buchanan, J. 2013. 'Translating Thailand's Protests: An Analysis of Red Shirt Rhetoric', *Australian Journal of South-East Asian Studies* Vol. 6, No. 1, pp. 60–80.

Bunte, M. 2011. 'Burma's Transition to "Disciplined Democracy"', Working Paper No. 177, German Institute of Global and Area Studies, August 2011.

Burton, M., Gunther, R. and Higley, J. (eds) 1992. *Elites and Democratic Consolidation in Latin America and Southern Europe* Cambridge University Press, Cambridge.

Bush, K. and Saltarelli, D. (eds) 2000. *The Two Faces of Education in Ethnic Conflict: Towards a Peacebuilding Education for Children* UNICEF, Florence, Italy.

Callahan, M. 2012. 'The Generals Loosen Their Grip', *Journal of Democracy* Vol. 23, No. 4, pp. 120–31.

Canada Gazette 2010. 'Regulations Amending the Special Economic Measures (Burma) Regulations', Vol. 146, No. 10, 9 May 2010.

Carl-Yoder, S. 2009. 'Burma: State-Owned Enterprise Demonstrates Military's Hold on Economy', 6 February 2009. https://wikileaks.org/plusd/cables/09RANGOON83_a.html (accessed 24 May 2016).

Carmon, M. 2012. 'Report of the Special Rapporteur on Extreme Poverty and Human Rights', Mission to Timor-Leste, Human Rights Council, United Nations General Assembly, New York, 24 May 2012.

Carothers, T. 2010. 'The End of the Transitions Paradigm', in L. Diamond, M. Plattner and P. Costopoulos (eds), *Debates on Democratisation* Johns Hopkins University Press, Baltimore, MD.

CAVR 2005. *Conflict-Related Deaths in Timor-Leste 1974–1999: The Findings of the CAVR Report Chega* Commisao de Acolhimento, Verdade, e Reconciliacao de Timor-Leste (Timor-Leste Commission for Reception, Truth and Reconciliation), Dili. www.cavr-timorleste.org/en/chegaReport.htm (accessed 2 September 2013).

CBD 1959. *Constitution of Brunei Darussalam*, amended 1984, Brunei Sarussalam.

Chachavalpongpun, P. 2014. 'Thai Junta Beset By Corruption Scandals', *The Diplomat* 12 October 2014.

Chalermpalanupap, T. 2016. 'More of the Same: Political-Security Cooperation in ASEAN Over the Next Decade?', in *ASEAN 2025: Forging Ahead Together, ASEAN Focus* Institute for Southeast Asian Studies/Yusof Ishak Institute, Singapore, January 2016.

Chamberlain, P., Helmersson, H., Poza, F., Spindler, A. and Bergstein, N. 2014. 'Letter to Deputy Prime Minister, Keat Chon', signed on behalf of Philip Chamberlain, C+A; Helena Helmersson, H&M; Felix Poza, CSR; Angela Spindler, Tchibo GmbH; Nanda Bergstein, Next Retail Ltd; Chris Grayer, Next Retail Ltd; Katharine Stewart, Primark; and Roger Wightman, New Look, 18 September 2014.

Chan Dung Quyen Luc 2015. 'Results Confidence Vote Politburo', Secretariat of the Central Conference 10, Portraits of Power. http://chandungquyenluc.blogspot.com.au/2015/01/ket-qua-bo-phieu-tin-nhiem-bo-chinh-tri.html (accessed 19 January 2015).

Chanco, B. 2010. 'P-Noy: Be Careful What You Say!', *The Philippines Star* 10 September 2010.

Chanda, N. 1986. *Brother Enemy: The War After the War* Collier Books, New York.

Chandler, D. 1992. *A History of Cambodia* Westview Press, Boulder, CO.

Chandler, D. 2010. *International Statebuilding: The Rise of Post-Liberal Governance* Routledge, London.

Chandler, D. and Kiernan, B. (eds) 1983. *Revolution and its Aftermath in Kampuchea: Eight Essays* Yale University Southeast Asian Studies Monograph Series No. 25, Yale Center for International Area Studies, New Haven, CT.

Chee, C.H. 1993. 'Democracy: Its Evolution and Implementation', paper presented at conference on Asian and American Perspectives on Democracy, Singapore.

Chee, S.J. 1998. *To Be Free: Stories from Asia's Struggle Against Oppression* Monash Asia Institute, Melbourne.

Cheibub, J., Przeworski, A., Limongi, F. and Alvarez, M. 1996. 'What Makes Democracies Endure?' *Journal of Democracy* Vol. 7, No. 1, pp. 39–55.

Cheung, G. and Gomez, E. 2012. 'Hong Kong's Diaspora, Networks, and Family Business in the United Kingdom: A History of the Chinese "Food Chain" and the Case of W. Wing Yip Group', *China Review* Vol. 12, No. 1, pp. 45–71.

Chong, T. 2015. 'Upcoming Election a Tipping Point for Singapore's Ruling PAP', Institute for Southeast Asian Studies/Yusof Ishak Institute, East Asia Forum, Singapore, 6 September 2015.

Chong, T. 2016. 'Economic and Social Challenges Ahead for Singapore', *Perspective* No. 4, Institute for Southeast Asian Studies/Yusof Ishak Institute, Singapore, 25 January 2016.

Chopra, J. 2002. 'Building State Failure in East Timor', *Development and Change* Vol. 33, No. 5, pp. 27–29.

Chow, S. and Dao, T.N. 2013. 'Bribes for Enrolment in Desired Schools in Vietnam', in Transparency International (ed.), *Global Corruption Report* Earthscan, London.

Cœdes, G. 1968. *The Indianized States of Southeast Asia*, trans. S. Cowing, University of Hawaii Press, Honolulu.

Cohen, D., Hyde, M. and van Tuyl, P. 2015. *A Well-Reasoned Opinion? Critical Analysis of the First Case Against the Alleged Senior Leaders of the Khmer Rouge (Case 002/01)*, East–West Center, Honolulu, HA.

Collier, P. 1998. 'The Political Economy of Ethnicity', paper to the Annual World Bank Conference on Development Economics, Washington, DC, 20–21 April 1998.

Collier, P. 2004. 'Development and Conflict', Centre for the Study of African Economies, Department of Economics, Oxford University, 1 October 2004.

Collier, P. 2009. *Wars, Guns and Votes: Democracy in Dangerous Places* Harper Collins, New York.

Collier, D. and Adcock, D. 1999. 'Democracy and Dichotomies: A Pragmatic Approach to Choices about Concepts', *Annual Review of Political Science* Vol. 2, June 1999, pp. 537–65.

Collier, R. and Collier, D. 1991. *Shaping the Political Arena: Critical Junctures, the Labor Movement, and Regime Dynamics in Latin America* Princeton University Press, Princeton, NJ.

Collier, P. and Collier, R. 2002. *Shaping The Political Arena* University of Notre Dame Press, Notre Dame, IN.

Collier, D. and Levitsky, S. 1996. 'Democracy "With Adjectives": Conceptual Innovation in Comparative Research', Working Paper #230, The Helen Kellog Institute for International Studies, August 1996.

Collier, D. and Levitsky, S. 1997. 'Democracy with Adjectives: Conceptual Innovation in Comparative Research', *World Politics*, Vol. 49, No. 3, pp. 430–51.

Collier, P. and Sambanis, N. 2005. *Understanding Civil War: Evidence and Analysis Vols 1, 2, 3* The World Bank, Washington, DC.

Commission on Global Governance 1995. *Our Global Neighborhood: The Report of the Commission on Global Governance* World Bank, Washington, DC.

Constitution of the Republic of the Union of Myanmar 2008.

Constitution of Vietnam 2013. *Constitution of the Socialist Republic of Vietnam* International Institute for Democracy and Electoral Assistance, Stockholm.

Cook, M. 2015. 'Littoral Southeast Asia', *ASEAN Focus* No. 1, Institute of Southeast Asian Studies/ Yusof Ishak Institute, Singapore.

CPJ 2015. 'Singapore Blogger Convicted of Contempt of Court', Committee to Protect Journalists, 23 January 2015. https://cpj.org/2015/01/singapore-blogger-convicted-of-contempt-of-court. php (accessed 11 January 2016).

Crouch, H. 1996. *Government and Society in Malaysia* Allen & Unwin, Sydney.

da Silva, S. 2007. 'The Law on Political Parties (No.3/2004) and the Decision of the Timor Leste Court of Appeal in the Case of Vitor da Costa and Others v FRETILIN (12 August 2006)', Legal analysis – 2 January 2007, TimorTruth.com, www.timortruth.com/articles/Article_in_ relation_to_the_secret_ballot_for_website_020107.pdf (accessed 24 May 2016).

Daalder, I. and Stares, P. 2008. 'The UN's Responsibility to Protect', *The New York Times* 13 May 2008.

Dahl, R. 1970. *After the Revolution: Authority in Good Society* Yale University Press, New Haven, CT.

Dahl, R. 1971. *Polyarchy and Opposition: Participation and Opposition* Yale University Press, New Haven, CT.

Dahl, R. 2000. *On Democracy* Yale University Press, New Haven, CT.

Daily Mail 2014. 'Sultan of Brunei Hits Back at Foreign Criticism of Looming Implementation of Sharia Law that Will Introduce Amputations and Stonings as Punishments', 6 March 2014.

Dains, R. 2004. *Lasswell's Garrison State Reconsidered: Exploring a Paradigm Shift in US Civil–Military Relations*, PhD thesis, University of Alabama, Tuscaloosa.

Dalpino, C. 2000. *Promoting Democracy and Human Rights: Lessons of the 1990s* Brookings Institute, Washington, DC.

Das, S. 2015. 'The ASEAN Economic Community: An Economic and Strategic Project', *Perspective* No. 4, Institute for Southeast Asian Studies, Singapore.

Das, S., Sen, R. and Srivastava, S. 2015. 'The Feasibility of an ASEAN Customs Union Post-2015', Working Paper No. 1, Institute for Southeast Asian Studies, Singapore.

David, R. 2014. 'Ninoy Aquino's Assassination', *Philippine Daily Inquirer* 21 August 2014.

Davies, N. 2015. 'Vietnam 40 Years On: How a Communist Victory Gave Way to Capitalist Corruption', *The Guardian* 22 April 2015.

Dawai Project Watch 2012. 'UMEHL to Establish Oil Refinery Near Dawei Deep Sea Port Project', 26 August 2012. http://daweiprojectwatch.blogspot.com.au/2012_08_26_archive. html (accessed 9 July 2013).

De Bary, W. 1998. *Asian Values and Human Rights: A Confucian Communitarian Perspective* Harvard University Press, Cambridge, MA.

Decalo, S. 1976. *Coups and Army Rule in Africa* Yale University Press, New Haven, CT.

Desch, M. 1999. *Civilian Control of the Military: The Changing Security Environment* Johns Hopkins University Press, Baltimore, MD.

DFAT 2013. 'Myanmar Country Brief', Department of Foreign Affairs and Trade, Government of Australia. www.dfat.gov.au/geo/myanmar/myanmar_brief.html (accessed 28 November 2013).

Di Palma, G. 1991. *To Craft Democracies: An Essay on Democratic Transition* University of California Press, Berkeley.

Diamond, L., Linz, J.J. and Lipset, S.M. 1989. *Democracy in Developing Countries: Comparing Experiences with Democracy* Lynne Rienner, Boulder, CO.

Dommen, A. 1985. *Laos: Keystone of Indochina* Westview Press, Boulder, CO.

Duverger, M. 1980. 'A New Political System Model: Semi-Presidential Government', *European Journal of Political Research* Vol. 8, No. 2, pp. 165–87.

DVB 2013. 'Ethnic Alliance, Government Aim to Hold Talks in July as Clashes Continue', Democratic Voice of Burma, 24 July 2013. www.dvb.no/news/ethnic-alliance-govt-aim-to- hold-talks-in-july-as-clashes-continue/28941 (accessed 10 July 2013).

ECM 2013. '2013 Election Data', Electoral Commission of Malaysia.

The Economist 2006. 'Old Soldiers, Old Habits', 21 September 2006.

The Economist 2010. 'As Father Fades, His Children Fight', 18 March 2010.

The Economist 2013. 'Waiting for the Dividend', 5 October 2013.

The Editors 2015. 'What's Wrong With Thailand's New Constitution', Bloomberg View, 20 April 2015. www.bloombergview.com/articles/2015-04-20/thailand-needs-elected-leaders-not-a-new-constitution (accessed 17 July 2015).

EIU 2014. *The Democracy Index*, Economist Intelligence Unit.

Eleven 2011. 'President Thein Sein Sent a Letter to Parliament for Cancellation of Myitsone Dam Project', Eleven Media Group, 31 August 2011. www.news-eleven.com/index.php?option=com_content&view=article&id=10335:2011-09-30-04-38-33&catid=42:2009-11-10-07-36-59&Itemid=112 (accessed 31 August 2015).

Eleven 2013. 'Renewed Clashes between Myanmar Army and SSA', Eleven Media Group, 26 June 2013. http://elevenmyanmar.com/national/2597-renewed-clashes-between-myanmar-army-and-ssa (accessed 10 July 2013).

Elleman, B. 2001. *Modern Chinese Warfare, 1795–1989* Routledge, New York.

Eriksen, T. 2002 *Ethnicity and Nationalism*, 2nd ed., Pluto Press, London.

ETLJB 2013. 'Fundasaun Mahein (FM): PNTL Police Brutality Continues', *East Timor Law and Justice Bulletin* 21 June 2012. http://easttimorlegal.blogspot.com.au/2012/06/fundasaun-mahein-fm-pntl-olice.html#sthash.dfQFRZUg.dpuf (accessed 12 August 2013).

EU 2013. 'Council Conclusions on Myanmar/Burma', 3236th Foreign Affairs Council Meeting, Council of the European Union, Luxembourg, 22 April 2013.

Evans, G. 1998. *The Politics of Ritual and Remembrance: Laos since 1975* University of Hawaii Press, Honolulu.

Fagen, R. 1986. 'The Politics of Transition' in R. Fagen, C. Deere and J. Coraggio (eds), Transition and Development: Problems of Third World Socialism Monthly Review Press, New York.

Fan Yew Teng 1999. *Anwar Saga: Malaysia On Trial* Genting Raya Sdn Bhd, Seri Kembangan, Malaysia.

Ferrara, F. 2015. *The Political Development of Modern Thailand* Cambridge University Press, Cambridge.

Fineman, D. 1997. *A Special Relationship: The United States and Military Government in Thailand* University of Hawaii Press, Honalulu.

Forbes 2008. 'The Top 15 Wealthiest Royals', *Forbes*. www.forbes.com/global/2008/0901/038.html (accessed 7 September 2015).

Frankum, R. 2007. *Operation Passage To Freedom: The United States Navy in Vietnam, 1954–1955* Texas Tech University Press, Lubbock.

Frater, P. 2015. 'Malaysia Censors Get Tough On Government Critics And Women', *Variety* 10 July 2015.

Freedom House 2014a. 'Brunei'. https://freedomhouse.org/report/freedom-world/2012/brunei#.VGliQcmGf0U (accessed 17 November 2014).

Freedom House 2014b. 'Hong Kong'. www.freedomhouse.org/report/freedom-world/2014/hong-kong-0#.VEcHbcmGf0U (accessed 22 October 2014).

Fukuyama, F. 1992. *The End of History and the Last Man* The Free Press, New York.

Fukuyama, F. 2004. 'The Imperative of State Building', *Journal of Democracy* Vol. 15, No. 2, pp. 17–31.

Fukuyama, F. 2007. 'The History at the End of History', *The Guardian* 3 April 2007.

Fuller, T. 2013. 'A Myanmar in Transition Says Little of Past Abuses', *The New York Times* 14 June 2013.

Fuller, T. 2014a. 'Cambodia Steps Up Crackdown on Dissent With Ban on Assembly', *The New York Times* 5 January 2014.

Fuller, T. 2014b. 'Myanmar's Leader Backs Change To Constitution', *The New York Times* 2 January 2014.

Fuller, T. 2015. 'Conservatives in Myanmar Force Out Leader of Ruling Party', *The New York Times* 13 August 2015.

Funston, J. 2001. *Government and Politics in Southeast Asia* Institute of Southeast Asian Studies, Singapore.

Gaffar, A. 2002. 'A Question of Leadership', *Van Zorge Report on Indonesia* Vol. IV, No. 20, 13 December 2002.

Gainsborough, M. 2010. *Vietnam: Rethinking the State* Zed Books, London.

Galache, C. 2013. 'Democracy, Suu Kyi and Ethnic Rights in Burma', Democratic Voice of Burma. www.dvb.no/analysis/democracy-suu-kyi-and-ethnic-rights-in-burma/26044

GAN 2014. 'Business Corruption in Vietnam', GAN Integrity Solutions, June 2014.

Gellner, E. 1983. *Nations and Nationalism* Cornell University Press, Ithaca, NY.

George, T. 1980. *Revolt in Mindanao: Rise of Islam in Philippine Politics* Oxford University Press, Kuala Lumpur.

Gernet, J. 1962. *Daily Life in China on the Eve of the Mongol Invasion, 1250–1276*, trans. H. Wright, Stanford University Press, Stanford, CA.

Goldsworthy, D. (ed.) 1991, *Development and Social Change in Asia* Radio Australia/Monash Development Studies Centre, Melbourne.

Goodman, A. 1973. *Politics in War: The Bases of Political Community in South Vietnam* Harvard University Press, Cambridge, MA.

Grawert, E. 2009. *Departures From Postcolonial Authoritarianism* Peter Lang, Frankfurt am Main.

Gregorian, D. 2010. 'Judge Bans Prince Porn', *New York Post* 10 November 2010.

Gromping, M. 2015. 'Southeast Asian Elections Worst in the World', New Mandala. http://asia pacific.anu.edu.au/newmandala/2015/02/19/southeast-asian-elections-worst-in-the-world/ (accessed 27 February 2015).

Grugel, J. 2002. *Democratisation: A Critical Introduction*. Palgrave Macmillan, Houndsmills, UK.

The Guardian 2015. 'Thai Crown Prince's Poodle, Air Chief Marshal Foo Foo, Has Been Cremated', 6 February 2015.

Habermas, J. 2001a 'A Constitution for Europe?', *New Left Review* Vol. 11, pp. 5–26.

Habermas, J. 2001b. *A Postnational Constellation* MIT Press, Cambridge, MA.

Halim, H. 2015. 'Public Outraged by Minister Tedjo's Derogatory Remarks', *Jakarta Post* 26 January 2015.

Hamilton-Merritt, J. 1999. *Tragic Mountains: The Hmong, the Americans, and the Secret Wars for Laos, 1942–1992* Indiana University Press, Bloomington.

Hamin, Z. and Mangsor, M. 2013. 'Media Ownership Regulation in Malaysia: Lessons from the United Kingdom', 5th International Conference on Financial Criminology, Shah Alam, Malaysia, 28–29 May 2013.

Han, F., Fernandez, W. and Tan, S. 1998. *Lee Kuan Kuan Yew: The Man and His Ideas* Times Editions, Singapore.

Han, K. 2012. 'The Sorry State of Unions in Singapore', *Waging NonViolence* 8 June 2012. http:// wagingnonviolence.org/feature/the-sorry-state-of-unions-in-singapore/ (accessed 6 January 2016).

Harding, T. and Petras, J. 1988. 'Introduction: Democratisation and Class Struggle', *Latin American Perspectives* Vol. 15, No. 3, pp. 3–4.

Harnecker, M. 1994. 'Democracy and Revolutionary Movement', in S. Jonas and E. McCaughan (eds), Latin America Faces the Twenty-First Century: Reconstructing a Social Justice Agenda Westview, Boulder, CO.

Hasani, E. 2003. 'Uti Possidetus Juris: From Rome To Kosovo', *Fletcher Forum of World Affairs* Summer/Fall 2003.

Hayton, B. 2011. *Vietnam: Rising Dragon* Yale University Press, New Haven, CT.

Hewison, K. 2010. 'Thailand's Conservative Democratisation', in Y. Chu and S. Wong (eds), *East Asia's New Democracies Deepening, Reversal, Non-liberal Alternatives* Taylor and Francis, London.

Hlaing, K. 2012. 'Understanding Recent Political Changes in Myanmar', *Contemporary Southeast Asia* Vol. 34, No. 2, pp. 197–216.

Hobsbawm, E. 2004. *Nations and Nationalism since 1870: Programme, Myth, Reality* Cambridge University Press, Cambridge.

Hohe, T. 2002. 'Totem Poles: Indigenous Concepts and "Free and Fair" Elections in East Timor', *International Peacekeeping* Vol. 9, No. 4, pp. 69–88.

Holden, W. 2015. 'Deep Roots of Revolution: the New People's Army in the Bicol Region of the Philippines', *Canadian Journal of Tropical Geography* Vol. 2, No. 2, pp. 1–14.

Holliday, I. 2010. 'Voting and Violence in Myanmar: Nation Building for a Transition to Democracy. In L. Dittmer (ed.), *Burma or Myanmar? The Struggle for National Identity* World Scientific, Singapore.

Hope, B. and Wright, T. 2016. '1MDB Scandal: Deposits in Malaysian Leader Najib's Accounts Said to Top $1 Billion', *The Wall Street Journal* 1 March 2016.

Hoppe, H. 2001. *Democracy: The God That Failed* Transaction Publishers, Rutgers, NJ.

Horowitz, D. 1985. *Ethnic Groups in Conflict* University of California Press, Berkeley.

Howard, R. 1983. 'The Full Bellies Thesis: Should Economic Rights Take Precedence Over Civil and Political Rights: Evidence from sub-Saharan Africa', *Human Rights Quarterly* Vol. 5, No. 4, pp. 467–90.

HRW 2015. 'Rights Groups Urge ASEAN to Break Silence on Enforced Disappearance of Sombath Somphone', Human Rights Watch, 15 December 2015.

Huang, R. 2013. 'Re-thinking Myanmar's Political Regime: Military Rule in Myanmar and Implications for Current Reforms', *Contemporary Politics* Vol. 19, No. 3, pp. 247–61.

Huntington, S. 1957. *The Soldier and the State: The Theory and Politics of Civil–Military Relations* Belknap Press, Cambridge, MA.

Huntington, S. 1968. *Political Order in Changing Societies* Yale University Press, New Haven, CT.

Huntington, S. 1991. 'Democracy's Third Wave', *Journal of Democracy* Vol. 2, No. 2, pp. 12–34.

Huntington, S. 1993. *The Third Wave: Democratisation in the Late Twentieth Century* University of Oklahoma Press, Oklahoma.

Hutchcroft, P. 1998. *Booty Capitalism: The Politics of Banking in the Philippines* Cornell University Press, Ithaca, NY.

IANS 2014. 'Technical Error Behind Laos Plane Crash', *New Indian Express* 20 May 2014.

IBAHRI 2015a. 'IBAHRI Report Highlights Extent of Corruption in the Cambodian Judiciary', International Bar Association Human Rights Institute, 17 September 2015. www.ibanet.org/Article/Detail.aspx?ArticleUid=fb11e885-5f1d-4c03-9c55-86ff42157ae1 (accessed 5 December 2015).

IBAHRI 2015b. *Justice Versus Corruption Challenges to the Independence of the Judiciary in Cambodia* International Bar Association Human Rights Institute, September 2015.

IBP 2008. *Brunei Sultan Haji Hassanal Bolkiah Muizzaddin Waddaulah Handbook*, 4th ed., International Business Publications, Washington, DC.

IBP 2009. *Laos Diplomatic Handbook*, 6th ed., International Business Publications, Washington, DC.

Ibrahim, I. 2013. *Brunei and Malaysia: Why Sultan Omar Ali Saifuddin Refused to Join the Federation* I.B. Taurus, London.

ICG 1998. 'Cambodia's Elections Turn Sour', Asia Report No. 3, International Crisis Group, Phnom Penh, 10 September 1998.

ICG 2010. 'Stalemate in Southern Thailand', Asia Report No. 113, International Crisis Group, 3 November 2010.

ICG 2013. 'The Dark Side of Transition: Violence Against Muslims in Myanmar', Asia Report No. 251, International Crisis Group, 1 October 2013.

ICG 2014. 'A Coup Ordained? Thailand's Prospects for Stability', Asia Report No. 263, International Crisis Group, 3 December 2014.

ICJ 1986. 'Frontier Dispute; Judgment', Reports, International Court of Justice, The Hague.

IFJ 2006. 'Timor Leste: Newspaper Editor Faces Criminal Defamation Charges in Timor Leste', media release, International Federation of Journalists, 21 January 2009.

IFJ 2014. 'East Timorese Journalists Express Concern on Proposed Media Laws', International Federation of Journalists, 18 February 2014. http://asiapacific.ifj.org/en/articles/east-timorese-journalists-express-concern-on-proposed-media-laws (accessed 18 February 2014).

IMF 2015. *World Economic Outlook Database* International Monetary Fund, Washington, DC, April 2015.

The Irrawaddy 2011. 'Military Firms Excluded from Tax Evasion Law', 7 January 2011.

The Irrawaddy 2013a. 'No Plan to Repeal Two Repressive Junta-Era Laws: Minister', 11 July 2013.

The Irrawaddy 2013b. 'Weekend Clashes Reported Near IDP Shelters in Kachin State', 24 June 2013.

ISEAS 2015a. 'Cambodia', Yusof Ishak Institute paper No. 5, Institute for Southeast Asian Studies, Singapore.

ISEAS 2015b, 'Findings from Latest Surveys on the Thai Prime Minister and the Media and the Draft of Constitution (2015)', *Perspective* No. 26, Institute for Southeast Asian Studies, Singapore, 3 June 2015.

Izzuddin, M. 2015. 'The Pakatan Rakyat Collapse: Implications for Party Politics in Malaysia', *Perspective* No. 41, Institute for Southeast Asian Studies/Yusof Ishak Institute, Singapore, 5 August 2015.

Jackson, R. 2008. *The Malayan Emergency and Indonesian Confrontation: The Commonwealth's Wars 1948–1966* Pen and Sword Aviation, Barnsley, UK.

Jacob, M. 2015. 'Free and Fair? As Myanmar Goes to the Polls, Questions Swirl over "Dirty Tricks" and Voters Who Are Being Left Out', *Mizzima* Vol. 4, No. 45, 5 November 2015.

Jakarta Globe 2014. 'Editorial: Shame on SBY and His Non-Democrats', 26 September 2014.

Jakarta Post 2014. 'Jokowi Only a "Party Official" Abiding by PDI-P: Megawati', 16 May 2014.

Jakarta Post 2015a. 'Freeport Threatened Legal Action Against RI: Setya', *Jakarta Post* 19 November 2015.

Jakarta Post 2015b. 'Jokowi Condemns Freeport Fiasco', *Jakarta Post* 7 December 2015.

Jakarta Post 2016. 'AGO Summons Setya in Freeport Case', *Jakarta Post* 11 January 2016.

Jefferess, D. 2008. *Post-Colonial Resistance: Culture, Liberation and Transformation* University of Toronto Press, Toronto.

Jenkins, N. 2015. 'A Thai Man Faces Nearly 40 Years in Jail for Insulting the King's Dog', *Time* 16 December 2015.

Jomo, K. 2003. *M Way: Mahatir's Economic Legacy* Forum, Kuala Lumpur.

Jonas, S. 1989. 'Elections and Transitions: The Guatamalan and Nicaraguan Cases', in J. Booth and M. Seligson (eds), *Elections and Democracy in Central America* University of North Carolina Press, Chapel Hill.

Jones, L. 2014. 'The Political Economy of Myanmar's Transition', *Journal of Contemporary Asia* Vol. 44, No. 1, pp. 144–70.

Jong, H. 2015a. 'PDI-P Gives Jokowi Reshuffle Deadline', *Jakarta Post* 9 August 2015.

Jong, H. 2015b. 'People Starting to Lose Faith in Jokowi, Says Survey', *Jakarta Post* 22 January 2015.

Jory, P. 2015. 'Thailand Has Entered the Interregnum', *Perspective* No. 21, Institute for South East Asian Studies, Singapore, 21 October 2014.

Josey, A. 1970. *Democracy in Singapore: The 1970 By-Elections* Asia Pacific Press, Singapore.

Journal Independente 2013. 'Future Investment Sits on Policy Changes, Conoco Phillips', Dili, 1 August 2013.

JSMP 2013. '"Outcomes", Fair Trial and the Right to Appeal', Judicial Systems Monitoring Program National Seminar, Delta Nova, Dili, 28 June 2013.

Kalathil, S. 2006. 'Timor-Leste Media Assessment', USAID, February 2006.

Kaplan, B. 2005. 'From Friedman to Whitman: The Transition of Chicago Political Economy', *Econ Journal Watch* Vol. 2, No. 1, April, pp. 1–21.

Kenyon, A. and Marjoribanks, T. 2007. 'Transforming Media Markets: The Cases of Malaysia and Singapore', *Australian Journal of Emerging Technologies and Society* Vol. 5, No. 2, pp. 103–18.

Kevin, T. 1999. 'Cambodia and Southeast Asia', lecture to the Cambodian Institute for Cooperation and Peace, Phnom Penh, 22 July 1999.

Keyes, J. 2015. 'Democracy Thwarted: The Crisis of Political Authority in Thailand' Trends in Southeast Asia No. 11, Institute of Southeast Asian Studies, Singapore.

Karl, T. 1991. 'Dilemmas of Democratisation in Latin America', *Comparative Politics* Vol. 23, No. 1, pp. 1–21.

Karl, T. 2005. 'From Democracy to Democratisation and Back: Before Transitions from Authoritarian Rule', Center on Democracy, Development and Rule of Law Working Papers, Stanford Institute on International Studies, CA.

Kasahara, S. 2004. 'The Flying Geese Paradigm: A Critical Study of Its Application to East Asian Regional Development', United Nations Conference on Trade and Development, Discussion Paper No. 169, April 2004.

Kha, K. 2015. 'Ethnic Leaders Call on Thein Sein to Recontest the Presidency', *The Irrawaddy* 4 August 2015.

Khine, C. 2013. 'Affordable Mobile in Burma Gets Off to Shaky Start', *Asian Correspondent* 26 April 2013. http://asiancorrespondent.com/106509/affordable-mobile-in-burma-get-off-to-shaky-start/ (accessed 11 July 2013).

Kiernan, B. 1985. *How Pol Pot Came To Power* Verso, London.

Kiernan, B. 1993. *Genocide and Democracy in Cambodia* Yale Southeast Asia Monograph Series No. 41, Yale Center for International Area Studies, New Haven, CT.

Kiernan, B. 1996. *The Pol Pot Regime* Yale University Press, New Haven, CT.

Kingsbury, D. 2005a. *The Politics of Indonesia*, 3rd ed., Oxford University Press, Melbourne.

Kingsbury, D. 2005b. *Southeast Asia: A Political Profile* Oxford University Press, Melbourne.

Kingsbury, D. 2006. *Peace in Aceh: A Personal Account of the Helsinki Peace Process* Equinox, Jakarta.

Kingsbury, D. 2007. *Political Development* Routledge, London.

Kingsbury, D. 2007b. *Preliminary Report on Round One of the Timor-Leste Presidential Election, 9 April 2007*, Victorian Local Governance Association, Melbourne, 21 April 2007.

Kingsbury, D. 2009a. *East Timor: The Price of Liberty* Palgrave Macmillan, New York.

Kingsbury, D. 2009b. 'Timor-Leste in 2008: Year of Reconstruction', in D. Singh (ed.) *Southeast Asian Affairs 2009* Institute of Southeast Asian Studies, Singapore.

Kingsbury, D. 2010. 'National Identity in Timor-Leste: Challenges and Opportunities', *South-East Asia Research* Vol. 18, No. 1, pp. 133–59.

Kingsbury, D. 2011. 'Separatism in Mindanao', in A. Pavkovic and P. Radan (eds), *Ashgate Research Companion on Secession* Ashgate, Farnham.

Kingsbury, D. 2014a. 'Anti-Reform Actors Hover over Indonesia's Coming Elections', Crikey.com, 17 January 2014.

Kingsbury, D. 2014b. 'Indonesian Democracy May Rest on Election', The Drum, 8 July 2014. www.abc.net.au/news/2014-07-08/kingsbury-indonesian-democracy-may-rest-on-election/5581354 (accessed on 21 May 2016).

Kingsbury, D. 2014. 'Thailand's "Roadmap to Democracy" Filled with Detours and Potholes', Crikey.com, 2 June 2014.

Kingsbury, D. 2015. 'Union Aid Abroad-APHEDA, Myanmar Election Report Summary: Myanmar's Elections Largely Free but Lacks Constitutional Fairness', Yangon, 9 November 2015.

Kingsbury, D. and Maley, M. 2012. *Observer Missions by AusTimorFN for Timor-Leste Elections 2012: Formal Report: Presidential Election 17 March 2012, 21 March 2012.* www.idea.int/vt/country view.cfm?id=222 (accessed 2 August 2013).

Kirk, D. 2013. 'Freedom Comes at a Price in Pyongyang', *Asia Times* 15 August 2009. www.atimes.com/atimes/Korea/KH15Dg01.html (accessed 10 July 2013).

Kirkpatrick, J. 1981. 'Democratic Elections, Democratic Government, and Democratic Theory', in D. Butler, H.R. Penniman and A. Ranney (eds), *Democracy at the Polls: A Comparative Study of Competitive National Elections* American Enterprise Institute, Washington, DC.

Kompas 2013. 'TNI Ragu Demokrasi' (TNI [on] Free Democracy), 28 October 2013.

Krader, L. 1976. *Dialectic of Civil Society* Prometheus Books, New York.

Kremmer, C. 1997. *Stalking the Elephant Kings* Allen and Unwin, Sydney.

Kyaw-Zaw, T. 2009. 'Burma's Gem Mines Face Closure', BBC Burmese Service, 17 March 2009. http://news.bbc.co.uk/2/hi/7947914.stm (accessed 17 July 2013).

Lansdale, E. 'Practical Jokes', in *US Department of the Army Psychological Operations*, DA Pamphlet, US Department of the Army, 525-7-1, April 1976.

Lao PDR 2003. *Constitution of the Lao People's Democratic Republic*, amended as decreed by the President, Khamtay Siphandone, Vientiane, 28 May 2003.

La'o Hamutuk 2007. 'Screening PNTL Back into Service', *La'o Hamutuk Bulletin* Vol. 8 No. 2, June 2007.

La'o Hamutuk 2011. 'Understanding the 2011 State Budget', 25 February 2011. www.laohamutuk.org/econ/OGE11/exec/11BudgetExecutionEn.htm (accessed 13 August 2013).

La'o Hamutuk 2013. '2013 General State Budget', 26 June 2013. www.laohamutuk.org/econ/OGE13/12OGE13.htm (accessed 7 August 2013).

La'o Hamutuk 2016. '2016 General State Budget', 7 March 2016.

Larkin, S. 2015. 'Myanmar's Tycoons: Vested Interests Resisting Reform or Agents of Change?' *Perspective* No. 39. Institute of Southeast Asian Studies, Singapore.

Lasswell, H. 1941. *The Garrison State* University of Chicago Press, Chicago.

Lauren, J. 2010. *Some Girls: My Life in a Harem* Plume, New York.

Le, H.H. 2015. 'Power Shifts in Vietnam's Political System', *East Asia Forum* 5 March 2015.

Lee, H.L. 2015. 'English Speech by Secretary General Lee Hsien Loong', Singapore, 9 September 2015. www.dailymotion.com/video/x35x9pk (accessed 15 January 2015).

Lee, K.Y. 1998. *The Singapore Story: Memoirs of Lee Kwan Yew* The Straits Times Press, Singapore.

Lee, L. 2014. 'As Thai King Bhumibol Is Ailing, Elites Worry About Crown Prince's Ties To Former Prime Minister Thaksin', *International Business Times* 9 December 2014. www.ibtimes.com/thai-king-bhumibol-ailing-elites-worry-about-crown-princes-ties-former-prime-minister-1743572 (accessed 3 August 2014).

Lee, N. 2003. 'The "Legacy Problems" and Democratic Consolidation in South Korea and the Philippines', *Journal of East Asian Studies* Vol. 3, No. 1, pp. 43–73.

Lemay-Hebert, N. 2012. 'Coerced Transitions in Timor-Leste and Kosovo: Managing Competing Objectives of Institution Building and Local Empowerment', *Democratisation* Vol. 19, No. 3, pp. 465–85.

Lev, D. 2005. 'Conceptual Filters and Obfuscation in the Study of Indonesian Politics', *Asian Studies Review* Vol. 4, No. 9, pp. 345–56.

Lijphart, A. 1999. *Patterns of Democracy: Government Forms and Performance in Thirty-Six Countries* Yale University Press, New Haven, CT.

Liljas, P. 2014. 'Is Brunei's Harsh New Form of Sharia a Godly Move or a Cunning Political Ploy?', *Time* 27 May 2014.

Linantud, J. 1998. 'Whither Guns, Goons, and Gold? The Decline of Factional Election Violence in the Philippines', *Contemporary Southeast Asia* Vol. 20, No. 3., pp. 298–318.

Lingle, C. 1996. *Singapore's Authoritarian Capitalism: Asian Values, Free Market Illusions and Political Dependency* Locke Institute, Fairfax, VA.

Linz, J. 1978. *The Breakdown of Democratic Regimes* Johns Hopkins University Press, Baltimore, MD.

Linz, J. 1990. 'Transitions to Democracy', *Washington Quarterly* Vol. 13, No. 3, pp. 143–64.

Linz, J. and Stepan, A. 1996. *Problems of Democratic Transition and Consolidation: Southern Europe, South America, and Post-Communist Europe* Johns Hopkins University Press, Baltimore, MD.

Locke, J. 2010 (1689). *Two Treatises of Government and a Letter Concerning Toleration*, ed. I. Shapiro, Yale University Press, New Haven, CT.

Lopez, G. 2015. 'The Plot to Topple Malaysia's Prime Minister', *Asian Currents* 27 November 2015. http://asaa.asn.au/the-plot-to-topple-malaysias-prime-minister/ (accessed 1 December 2015).

Loveman, B. 1994. 'Protected Democracies and Military Guardianship: Political Transition in Latin America 1978-1993', *Journal of Inter-American Studies and World Affairs* No. 36, pp. 105–89.

Low, L. and Quan, E. 1992. *Public Policies in Singapore* Times Academic Press, Singapore.

Mahmud, T. 2011. 'Colonial Cartographies, Post-Colonial Border and Enduring Failures of International Law: The Unending Wars Along the Afghanistan–Pakistan Border', *Brooklyn Journal of International Law* Vol. 36, No. 1, pp. 1–74.

Mainwaring, S. 1992. 'Transitions to Democracy and Democratic Consolidation: Theoretical and Comparative Issues' in S. Mainwaring, G. O'Donnell and J.S. Valenzuela (eds), *Issues in Democratic Consolidation* Notre Dame University Press, Notre Dame, IN.

Majid, H.A. 2007. *Rebellion in Brunei: The 1962 Revolt, Imperialism, Confrontation and Oil* I.B. Taurus, London.

Malaysiakini 2015. 'Najib's Support Sees Divide between Warlords and Members', 31 October 2015. www2.malaysiakini.com/news/317905 (accessed 7 December 2015).

Mao, Z. 1938. 'Problems of War and Strategy', in *Selected Works*, Vol. II, Foreign Languages Press, Peking (Beijing).

Maremont, M. 2009. 'Royal Dispute Over Billions in Brunei Nears a Resolution', *The Wall Street Journal* 25 September 2009.

Marriott, A. 2008. 'Justice In The Community, Justice In The Courts: Bridging East Timor's Legal Divide', in D. Mearns (ed.), *Democratic Governance in Timor-Leste: Reconciling the Local and the National* Charles Darwin University Press, Darwin.

Marshall, A. and Szep, J. 2012. 'Special Report: Myanmar Military's Next Campaign: Shoring Up Power', Reuters, 15 November 2012.

Masykur, S. 2016. 'How TPP Can Disrupt ASEAN Economic Integration', *Jakarta Post*, 6 January 2016.

McCargo, D. 2005. 'Network Monarchy and Legitimacy Crises in Thailand', *Pacific Review* Vol. 18, No. 4, pp. 499–519.

McNamara, R. 1995. *In Retrospect* Time Books, New York.

Masli, U. 2009. 'Brunei drops all claims to Limbang', *The Brunei Times* 17 March 2009.

Masuhara, A. 2015. *The End of Personal Rule in Indonesia*, Vol. 24, Center for Southeast Asian Studies, Kyoto University Press, Kyoto.

Matsui, M. 2015. 'Military Makes Clear Who Is in Charge in Myanmar', *Nikkei Asian Review* 27 August 2015.

Mazower, M. 2012. *Governing the World: The History of an Idea* Penguin, Harmondsworth, UK.

Meehan, P. 2011. 'Drugs, Insurgency and State-building in Burma: Why the Drugs Trade is Central to Burma's Changing Political Order', *Journal of Southeast Asian Studies* Vol. 42, No. 3, pp. 376–404.

Meisburger, T. 2014. *Electoral Reform and the Consolidation of Democracy in Cambodia* Asia Foundation, Bangkok. www.asiafoundation.org/publications/pdf/1386 (26 May 2016).

Mendoza, R. 2015. 'Senator Nancy Binay, You Got It Wrong', *Rappler* 18 June 2015 www.rappler.com/thought-leaders/96460-nancy-binay-meritocracy-risk (accessed 18 September 2015).

Mietzner, M. 2014. 'Jokowi: Rise of a Polite Populist', *Inside Indonesia* No. 116, April–June 2014. www.insideindonesia.org/jokowi-rise-of-a-polite-populist (accessed 28 September 2015).

Meitzner, M. 2015. 'Reinventing Asian Populism: Jokowi's Rise, Democracy, and Political Contestation in Indonesia', *Policy Studies* No. 72, East–West Center, Honolulu, HA.

Miliband, R. 1992. 'The Socialist Alternative', *Journal of Democracy* Vol. 3 No. 33, pp. 118–24.

Miller, D. 1993. 'In Defence of Nationality', *Journal of Applied Philosophy* Vol. 10, No. 1, pp. 3–16.

Miller, D. 1995. *On Nationality* Oxford University Press, Oxford.

MoF 2015. 'Income Growth, Inequality and Mobility Trends in Singapore', Ministry of Finance Occasional Paper, Ministry of Finance, Singapore, August 2015.

Mokhtar, I. 2012. 'PSC Report on Electoral Reforms Passed in Parliament', *New Straits Times* 3 April 2012.

MoM 2015. 'Foreign Workforce Numbers', Ministry of Manpower, Government of the Republic of Singapore. www.mom.gov.sg/documents-and-publications/foreign-workforce-numbers (accessed 6 January 2016).

Mon, Y. 2015. 'Anger as Advance Votes Push USDP to Lead in Lashio', *Myanmar Times* 10 November 2015.

Monitor 2015. 'Malaysia', Monitor No. 6, Institute of Southeast Asian Studies/Yusof Ishak Institute, Singapore.

Monk, P. 1990. 'Truth and Power: Robert S. Hardie and Land Reform Debates in the Philippines, 1950–87', Monash Papers on Southeast Asia No. 20, Monash University, Melbourne.

Moore, C. 2010. 'Political and Military Coups', in J. Ishiyama and M. Breuning (eds), *21st Century Political Science: A Reference Handbook* Sage, London.

Morris-Jung, J. 2015. 'Online Petitions: Promoting a Public Voice in Vietnamese Politics', *Perspective* No. 38, Institute of Southeast Asian Studies, Singapore.

Muller, E. 1985. 'Income Inequality, Regime Repressiveness, and Political Violence', *American Sociological Review* Vol. 50, No. 1, pp. 47–61.

Murphy, D. 2009. 'Philippines Massacre: The Story Behind the Accused Ampatuan Clan', *Christian Science Monitor* 24 November 2009.

Myo Thant. 2012. 'Shwe Mann Delivers Reformist-Style Speech', *Mizzima* 9 February 2012.

Nasution, A. 2013. 'Remarkable Indonesia Rising? Only God Knows', *Jakarta Post* 27 December 2013.

New Straits Times 2015. 'What You Need to Know about Malaysia's Bersih Movement', 27 August 2015.

Nixon, R. 2012. *Justice and Governance in East Timor: Indigenous Approaches and the 'New Subsistence State'* Routledge, Abingdon, UK.

Niyomyat, A. 2015. 'Draft Thai Constitution Complete, but Strife Seen Ahead', Reuters, 17 April 2015. www.reuters.com/article/2015/04/17/us-thailand-politics-constitution-idUSK BN0N81RP20150417 (accessed 17 July 2015).

Nolan, J. 1996. *Philippines Business: The Portable Encyclopedia for Doing Business with the Philippines* World Trade Press, San Rafael, CA.

OAV 2011. 'Current Situation of Business Sectors in Myanmar (as of 25 January 2011)', OAV German Asia-Pacific Business Association, p 9. www.oav.de/uploads/tx_ttnews/Business_Sector_Myanmar_01.pdf (accessed 9 July 2013).

O'Donnell, G. 1996. 'Illusions About Consolidation', *Journal of Democracy* Vol. 7, No. 2, pp. 34–51.

O'Donnell, G. and Schmitter, P. 1986. *Transitions from Authoritarian Rule: Tentative Conclusions about Uncertain Democracies* Johns Hopkins University Press, Baltimore, MD.

O'Donnell, G., Schmitter, P. and Whitehead, L. (eds) 1986. *Transitions from Authoritarian Rule: Comparative Perspectives* Johns Hopkins University Press, Baltimore, MD.

Office of the President of the Democratic Republic of Timor-Leste 2013. 'Presidency of the Republic Hosts Seminar on Military Conscription', media release, 28 May 2013.

Ouyyanont, P. 2014. 'Thailand: A New Polity in the Making?' *Perspective* No. 59, Institute of Southeast Asian Studies, Singapore, 7 November 2014.

Ouyyanont, P. 2015. 'Crown Property Bureau in Thailand and its Role in Political Economy', Trends in Southeast Asia No. 13, Institute of Southeast Asian Studies, Singapore.

Palatino, M. 2014. 'Philippines Struggles to Recover a Year After Typhoon Haiyan Tragedy', *The Diplomat* 10 November 2014.

Palatino, M. 2015. 'Laos' Economic Agenda', *The Diplomat* 12 May 2015.

Parameswaran, P. 2015a. 'Thailand Completes Troubling New Constitution', *The Diplomat* 18 April 2015.

Parameswaran, P. 2015b. 'What Does Indonesia's Cabinet Reshuffle Mean?' *The Diplomat* 13 August 2015.

Pasuk, P. and Baker, C. 2002. *Thailand: Economy and Politics* Oxford University Press, New York.

Pawakapan, P. 2015b. 'Thai Junta Militarizes the Management of Natural Resources', Trends in Southeast Asia No. 18, Institute for Southeast Asian Studies/Yusof Ishak Institute, Singapore, 3 September 2015.

Pawakapan, P. 2015c. 'Will Thailand's New Constitution Be a Return to Authoritarianism?', *Perspective* No. 3, Institute for Southeast Asian Studies, Singapore, 27 January 2015.

People's Daily Online 2010. 'New Steel Plant Expedites State Infrastructure Building in Myanmar: State Media', 23 March 2010, http://english.people.com.cn/90001/90778/90858/90863/692 8010.html (accessed 10 July 2013).

Pereira, A. 2008. 'Whither the Developmental State: Explaining Singapore's Continued Developmentalism', *Third World Quarterly* Vol. 29, No. 6, pp. 1189–203.

PhilStar 2014. 'Who's Who: the Ninoy Aquino Assassination', *The Philippine Star* 21 August 2014. www.philstar.com/news-feature/2014/08/21/1359746/whos-who-ninoy-aquino-assassination (accessed 29 January 2016).

Phnom Penh Post 1997. 'Cambodia: July 1997: Shock and Aftermath', 27 July 1997.

Poling, G., Nguyen, P. and Weatherby, C. 2014. 'Myanmar's Constitutional Review Committee Shies Away from Needed Changes', cogitASIA, Center for Strategic and International Studies, Washington, DC, 5 February 2014.

Prashanth, P. 2015. 'Thailand Completes Troubling New Constitution', *The Diplomat* 19 April 2015.

Przeworski, A. 1986. *Capitalism and Social Democracy* Cambridge University Press, Cambridge.

Pzeworski, A. and Limongi, F. 1994. 'Modernization: Theories and Facts', Working Paper No. 4, Chicago Centre for Democracy, University of Chicago, November 1994.

PYO 2011a. 'Myanmar Ready to Sweeten Terms for Foreign Brewers', PYO Action Group. http://burmacampaign.org.uk/images/uploads/PoisonClouds.pdf (accessed 10 July 2013).

PYO 2011b. 'Poison Clouds: Lessons from Burma's Largest Coal Project at Tigyit', PYO Action Group. http://burmacampaign.org.uk/images/uploads/PoisonClouds.pdf (accessed 10 July 2013).

Querubin, P. 2012. 'Political Reform and Elite Persistence: Term Limits and Political Dynasties in the Philippines', paper to the American Political Science Association 2012 Annual Meeting, New Orleans.

Radio Australia 2013. 'Aung San Suu Kyi Attends Myanmar Military Parade', 28 March 2013.

Radio Free Asia 2009. 'Lao Officials Slam Corruption', 11 February 2009.

Radio Free Asia 2012a. 'Suu Kyi "Not Hostile" Toward Military', 6 June 2012.

Radio Free Asia 2012b. 'Suu Kyi Warns of "Mirage of Success"', 19 November 2012.

Radio Free Asia 2013. 'Hun Sen Says He Will Stay in Power Until He's 74', 6 May 2013.

Radio Free Asia 2015. 'Lao Officials Use State Funds to Build Roads to Their Homes', 20 May 2015.

Rajak, W. 2014. 'MIB is a System, Not Just a Slogan', *The Brunei Times* 17 April 2014.

Ramo, J. 2004. *The Beijing Consensus* The Foreign Policy Centre, London.

Rasul, J. 2003. *Agonies and Dreams: The Filipino Muslims and Other Minorities* CARE Minorities, Quezon City, Philippines.

RDTL 2002. *Constitution of the Democratic Republic of Timor-Leste*.

Remmell, P. 2013. 'Sultan of Brunei and His 5,000 Car Collection', du Pont Registry, 27 April 2013.

Reuters 2013. 'Foreign Investment Jumps Fivefold in Burma', *The Irrawaddy* 13 May 2013.

Rocamora, G. and Wilson, R. 1994. 'Low Intensity Democracy', in S. Jonas and E. McCaughan (eds), *Latin America Faces the Twenty-First Century: Reconstructing a Social Justice Agenda* Westview, Boulder, CO.

Rood, S. 2005. *Forging Sustainable Peace in Mindanao: The Role of Civil Society* East–West Center, Washington, DC.

Rueschemeyer, D., Stephens, E. and Stephens, J. 1992. *Capitalist Development and Democracy* University Chicago Press, Chicago.

Runciman, S. 1960. *The White Rajahs: A History of Sarawak from 1841 to 1946* Cambridge University Press, London.

Russell, T. 2008. *Institution Building Problems in East Timor, 1999–2002*, PhD thesis, Deakin University, Melbourne.

Rustow, D. 1970. 'Transitions to Democracy: Toward a Dynamic Model', *Comparative Politics* Vol. 2, No. 3, pp. 337–63.

RWP 2015. 'World Press Freedom Index', Reporters Without Borders. https://index.rsf.org/#!/ (accessed 23 September 2015).

Saat, N. 2015. 'UMNO General Assembly 2015: Najib's Call for Unity and Loyalty is Hardly Enough', *Perspective* No. 72, Institute for Southeast Asian Studies/Yusof Ishak Institute, Singapore, 29 December.

Samuelson, P. and Nordhaus, W. 2001. *Microeconomics*, 17th ed., McGraw-Hill, New York.

Santos, S. 2001. *The Moro Islamic Challenge: Constitutional Rethinking for the Mindanao Peace Process* University of the Philippines Press, Quezon City.

SarDesai, D. 1997. *Southeast Asia: Past and Present* Westview Press, Boulder, CO.

Sartori, G. 1965. *Democratic Theory* Praeger, New York.

Sartori, G. 1987. *The Theory of Democracy Revisisted* Chatham House, Chatham, NJ.

Schanberg, S. 1997. 'Return to the Killing Fields', *Vanity Fair* October 1997, pp. 110–21.

Schedler, A. 1998. 'What is Democratic Consolidation?', *Journal of Democracy* Vol. 9, No. 2, pp. 91–107.

Schiener, C. 2013. 'How Long Will The Petroleum Fund Carry Timor-Leste?' La'o Hamutuk, Dili, 15 July 2013.

Schmitter, P. and Karl, T. 1991. 'What Democracy Is . . . and Is Not', *Journal of Democracy* Vol. 2, No. 3, pp. 3–16.

Schuler, P. and Ostwald, K. 2016. 'Delayed Transition: The End of Consensus Leadership in Vietnam', *Perspective* No. 2, Yusof Ishak Institute/Institute for Southeast Asian Studies, Singapore, 14 January 2016.

Schumpeter, J. 1976. *Capitalism, Socialism and Democracy* Allen and Unwin, London.

Seagrave, S. 1988, *The Marcos Dynasty* Fawcett Columbine, New York.

Sen, A. 1999. *Development as Freedom*, Random House, New York.

Sein, T. 2013. 'Myanmar's Complex Transformation: Prospects and Challenges', speech to Chatham House, London, 15 July 2013.

Seymour, M. 2000. 'On Redefining the Nation', in N. Miscevic (ed.), *Nationalism and Ethnic Conflict. Philosophical Perspectives* Open Court, Chicago.

Shamsul, A. 1999. 'The "New Politics" in Malaysia: A Viewpoint', unpublished paper delivered to the Centre for Malaysian Studies, Monash University, Melbourne, 14 April.

Shanghai Daily 2014. 'Almost 150 Million USD Lost to Corruption in Laos', 22 July 2014. www.shanghaidaily.com/article/article_xinhua.aspx?id=231097 (accessed 29 May 2014).

Shevtsova, L. 1996. 'Russia's Fragmented Armed Forces' in L. Diamond and M. Plattner (eds), *Civil–Military Relations and Democracy* Johns Hopkins University Press, Baltimore, MD.

Shurke, A. 2001. 'Peace-Keepers as Nation Builders: Dilemmas of the UN in East Timor', *International Peacekeeping* Vol. 8, No. 4, p. 11.

Simandjuntak, D. 2015. 'Persistent Patronage: Explaining the Popularity of Former Corruption Convicts as Candidates in Indonesia's Regional Elections', *Perspective* No. 55, Institute for Southeast Asian Studies, Singapore, 6 October 2015.

Siswo, S. 2015. 'Timor Leste Plans Major Reforms as Country Forges Peaceful Future', interview with Rui de Araujo, Channel News Asia, 25 June 2014.

Skehan, C. 1998. 'Mahatir Defiant on Sacking', *The Age* 5 September: 19.

Smith, A. 1986. *Nationalism and Modernism* Routledge, London.

Smith, B. 2010. 'A Tree Falls in Laos', *Asia Times* 5 October 2010. www.atimes.com/atimes/Southeast_Asia/LJ05Ae01.html (accessed 22 October 2015).

Smith, R. 1958. *Philippine Freedom 1946–58* Columbia University Press, New York.

Son, B. and Nicholson, P. 2015. 'Vietnam Moves Cautiously on Constitutional Reform', *Asian Currents* 15 June 2015. http://asaablog.tumblr.com/post/121628118436/vietnam-moves-cautiously-on-constitutional-reform (accessed 16 September 2015).

Souksavanh, O. 2015. 'High-Ranking Provincial Official Involved in Land Grab in Northern Laos', Radio Free Asia, 11 May 2015.

Stepan, A. 1986. 'Paths toward Redemocratisation: Theoretical and Comparative Considerations', in G. O'Donnell, P. Schmitter and L. Whitehead (eds), *Transitions from Authoritarian Rule: Comparative Perspectives Pt III* Johns Hopkins University Press, Baltimore, MD.

Stuart-Fox, M. 1997. *A History of Laos* Cambridge University Press, Cambridge.

Stuart-Fox, M. 2007. 'Laos: Politics in a Single Party State', *Southeast Asian Affairs* pp. 159–180.

Stuart-Fox, M. 2011. 'Family Problems', *Inside Story*. http://insidestory.org.au/family-problems (accessed 5 November 2014).

Sturtevant, D. 1969. *Agrarian Unrest in the Philippines: Guardia de Honor – Revitalization within the Revolution, and Rizalistas – Contemporary Revitalization Movements in the Philippines* Ohio University, Center for International Studies, Athens, OH.

Sturtevant, D. 1976, *Popular Uprisings in the Philippines: 1840–1940* Cornell University Press, Ithaca, NY.

Supreme Court 2001. 'G.R. No. 146710-15, Joseph E. Estrada, Petitioner, *vs.* Aniano Desierto, in His Capacity as Ombudsman, Ramon Gonzales, Volunteers Against Crime and Corruption, Graft Free Philippines Foundation, Inc., Leonard De Vera, Deniis Funa, Romeo Capulong and Ernesto B. Francisco, Jr., Respondent', 2 March 2001, Manila.

Suryakusuma, J. 2003. 'Aceh Pays the Price: A Little War to Bolster the Ratings', *The New York Times* 29 August 2003.

Suttner, R. 2006. 'Party Dominance "Theory": Of What Value?' *Politikon* Vol. 33, No. 3, pp. 277–97.

Swaine, J. 2010. 'WikiLeaks: Doubts over Suitability of Thailand's Playboy Prince', *The Telegraph* 15 December 2010.

Tan, J. 2015. 'Water Privatization, Ethnicity and Rent-Seeking: Preliminary Evidence from Malaysia', Working Paper No. 3, Institute of Southeast Asian Studies/Yusof Ishak Institute, Singapore.

Tarmizi Mohd Jam 2014. 'Hudud: Mursyidul Am PAS minta Umno Cermin Diri', *Harakah* No. 26, 9 May 2014, p. 2.

Taylor, R. 2012. 'Myanmar: From Army To Constitutional Rule', *Asian Affairs* Vol. 52, No. 3, pp. 221–36.

Thayer, C. 1994. *The Vietnam People's Army Under Doi Moi* ISEAS Strategic Papers, Institute of Southeast Asian Studies, Singapore.

Thayer, N. 1998. 'Dying Breath', *Far Eastern Economic Review* 30 April 1998, pp. 18–21.

Thayer, N. 2011. 'What Happened to the Khmer Rouge? They Are Back in Power', *Sympathy for the Devil: A Journalist's Memoir from Inside Pol Pot's Khmer Rouge.* Unpublished manuscript.

Thayer, C. 2014a. 'Background Briefing: Cambodia: Factionalism in the Cambodian People's Party', Thayer Consultancy, October 2014.

Thayer, C. 2014b. 'New Strategic Uncertainty and Security Order in Southeast Asia', in E. Atanassova-Cornelis and F.-P.van der Putten (eds), *Changing Security Dynamics of East Asia* Palgrave Macmillan, Houndsmills, UK.

Thayer, C. 2015a. 'Background Briefing: ASEAN: Looking Back Forty-Eight Years'. Thayer Consultancy, Canberra, 5 August 2015.

Thayer, C. 2015b. 'Background Briefing: Cambodia: Hun Sen's Three Decades as Prime Minister', Thayer Consultancy, Canberra, 13 January 2015.

Thayer, C. 2015c. 'Background Briefing: Cambodia: Who Do the Lower Ranks of the Military Support?', Thayer Consultancy, Canberra, 21 January 2015.

Thayer, C. 2015d. 'Background Briefing: Vietnam: An Analysis of Politburo and Secretariat Vote of Confidence', 19 January 2015. Thayer Consultancy, Canberra.

Thayer, C. 2015e. 'Background Briefing: Vietnam's 12th Party Congress: What to Expect, Why Is it Important?', Thayer Consultancy, Canberra, 27 December 2015.

Thayer, C. 2015f. 'Vietnam's China Factor', *Policy Forum* 9 September 2015. www.policyforum.net/vietnams-china-factor/ (accessed 11 September 2015).

Thayer, C and Amer, R. 1999. 'Introduction', in C. Thayer and R. Amer (eds), *Vietnamese Foreign Policy in Transition* Institute of Southeast Asian Studies, Singapore.

Thuzar, M. 2015. 'ASEAN Community 2015: What's in it for the Region?', *Perspective* No. 9, Institute of Southeast Asian Studies, Singapore.

Timor Post 2013. 'Lere Does Not Agree with Former Militia Returning to Timor-Leste', 8 January 2013.

Toft, M., Philpott, D. and Shah, T. 2011. *God's Century: Resurgent Religion and Global Politics* W.W. Norton and Co., New York.

Trading Economics 2015. 'Malaysia Government Debt to GDP', www.tradingeconomics.com/malaysia/government-debt-to-gdp (accessed 10 December 2015).

Transparency International 2004.'World's Ten Most Corrupt Leaders', *Transparency International Global Corruption Report 2004*. Transparency International, Berlin.

Transparency International 2013. 'Corruption Perception Index 2013', Transparency International, Berlin.

Transparency International 2015a. 'Government Defence Anti Corruption Index', Transparency International, Kuala Lumpur.

Transparency International 2015b. 'Singapore', Transparency International. www.transparency.org/country/#SGP (accessed 18 January 2015).

Tsilogiannis, C. 2010. *Minister-Counselor/Head of Operations, Delegation of European Union – Timor Leste, Country Strategy Paper and National Indicative Program for the Period 2008–2013*, briefing paper, 30 April 2010, pp. 63–64.

Tupaz, E. and Wagner, D. 2015. 'Aquino's Legacy in the Philippines', *The World Post* 3 August 2015. www.huffingtonpost.com/edsel-tupaz/aquinos-legacy-in-the-phi_b_7922082.html (accessed 7 February 2016).

UN 2005. *Lao People's Democratic Republic. Public Administration: Country Profile* Department of Economic and Social Affairs, United Nations, January 2005.

UN Data 2011. 'Timor-Leste Country Profile', United Nations Statistics Division, New York.

UN News Centre 2011. 'Not All Timorese Benefiting from Economic Gains, UN Human Rights Expert Says', 18 November 2011. www.un.org/apps/news/story.asp?NewsID=40437&Cr=timor&Cr1= (accessed 6 August 2013).

UNDP 2012. 'Human Development Indicators, Country Profile: Timor-Leste', United Nations Development Program, New York.

UNDP 2013a. 'Cambodia', in *The Rise of the South: Human Progress in a Diverse World, Human Development Report 2013* United Nations Development Program, New York.

UNDP 2013b. 'International Human Development Indicators', United Nations Development Program, New York. http://hdr.undp.org/en/statistics/ (accessed 8 October 2013).

UNDP 2013c. 'Vietnam', in *The Rise of the South: Human Progress in a Diverse World, Human Development Report 2013* United Nations Development Program, New York.

UNESCAP (United Nations Economic and Social Commission for Asia and the Pacific) 2011. *What Is Good Governance?* United Nations Economic and Social Commission for Asia and the Pacific, New York.

UNHCR 2009. 'Deportation of Lao Hmong Must Stop: UN High Commissioner for Refugees', United Nations High Commissioner for Refugees, 28 December 2009.

UNICEF 2011. 'At A Glance: Timor-Leste', Dili.

UNODC 2014. 'Opium Production in the Golden Triangle Continues at High Levels, Threatening Regional Integration', United Nations Office on Drugs and Crime, 8 December 2014.

US Embassy 2007. 'Viewing cable 07RANGOON283, BIOGRAPHY: SHWE MANN, BURMA'S DICTATOR-IN-WAITING (07RANGOON283)', cable, 16 March 2007.

US Embassy 2009. 'CONTRACT FARMING IN BURMA (C-AL8-02135)', cable, 12 January 2009.

US State Department 2005. *Singapore: Country Report on Human Rights Practices 2004* Bureau of Democracy, Human Rights, and Labor, Washington, DC.

US State Department 2013. 'Burma: Termination of Presidential Proclamation 6925', Media Note, Office of the Spokesperson, Washington, DC, 2 May 2013.

Valenzuela, J.S. 1990. 'Democratic Consolidation in Post-Transitional Settings: Notion, Process and Facilitating Conditions', Kellogg Institute Working Paper No. 150, Kellogg Institute for International Studies, University of Notre Dame, Notre Dame, IN.

Vanderklippe, N., 2015. 'Brunei's Oil-Fuelled Economy Running on Empty', *The Globe and Mail* 2 February 2015.

Vanhanen, T. 1990. *The Process of Democratisation* Taylor and Francis, New York.

Vientiane Times 2014a. 'Laos–Russia to Deepen Ties, Cooperation', 22 September 2014.

Vientiane Times 2014b. 'Surge in Energy Generation, Supply as Laos Powers Up', 11 March 2014.

VLGA Observer Mission, 2007. 'Australian Observers: "Timor Leste Parliamentary Elections Declared Free and Fair"', Victorian Local Governance Association, Melbourne, 2 July 2007.

VNS 2015. 'VN to Help Laos Revise Constitution', *Viet Nam News* 10 July 2015.

Vuving, A. 2012. 'Vietnam's Search for Stability', *The Diplomat* 25 October 2012.

Wahyudi Soeriaatmadja 2015. 'Strained Party Relations May Hinder Jokowi', *The Straits Times* 13 April 2015.

Wassana N. 2015. 'Prawit Defends PM's "Close the Country" Gaffe', *Bangkok Post* 30 October 2015.

Wassana, N. and Wassayos, N. 2015. 'Army Hunts Rajabhakti Park Clues', *Bangkok Post* 13 November 2015.

WBG 2015. 'Lao Economic Monitor', World Bank Group, Washington, DC, April 2015.

Weber, M. 1948. 'Politics as a Vocation', trans. and eds H. Gerth and C.W. Mills, *From Max Weber: Essays in Sociology* Routledge and Kegan Paul, London.

Weber, M. 1958. 'The Three Types of Legitimate Rule', trans. Hans Gerth, *Berkeley Publications in Society and Institutions* Vol. 4, No. 1, pp. 1–11.

Weber, M. 1964. *Theory of Social and Economic Organization* The Free Press, New York.

Weber, M. 2004 (1919). 'Politics as Vocation', in M. Weber, *The Vocation Lectures: Science As a Vocation, Politics As a Vocation*, eds D. Owen and T. Strong, trans. R. Livingstone, Hackett Publishing, Indianapolis.

Weaver, M. 2008. 'What Next for Thailand?' *The Guardian* 3 December 2008.

Wikileaks 2011. 'The Contenders: How Elite Cadre Advance, Prospects for 2011', Cable 09HANOI881_a. https://www.wikileaks.org/plusd/cables/09HANOI881_a.html (accessed 19 January 2015).

Wines, M. 2004. 'In South Africa, Democracy May Breed One-Party Rule', *The New York Times* 14 April 2004.

Winters, J. 2011a. *Oligarchy* Cambridge University Press, Cambridge.

Winters, J. 2011b. 'Who Will Tame the Oligarchs?', *Inside Indonesia* No. 104, April–June 2011. www.insideindonesia.org/who-will-tame-the-oligarchs (accessed 26 May 2016).

World Bank 2009. 'Development Research Group', Washington, DC.

World Bank 2011. *World Development Report 2011: Conflict Security and Development* World Bank, Washington, DC.

World Bank 2012a. '2012 Investment Climate Statement – Laos', World Bank, Washington, DC.

World Bank 2012b. 'Timor-Leste: Data', Washington, DC.

World Bank 2014. 'Poverty Has Fallen, Yet Many Cambodians Are Still at Risk of Slipping Back into Poverty, New Report Finds', 20 February 2014. www.worldbank.org/en/news/press-release/2014/02/20/poverty-has-fallen-yet-many-cambodians-are-still-at-risk-of-slipping-back-into-poverty (accessed 6 December 2015).

World Bank 2015a. 'Cambodia: Overview'. www.worldbank.org/en/country/cambodia/overview (accessed 5 December 2015).

World Bank 2015b. 'Data: Laos'. http://data.worldbank.org/country/lao-pdr (accessed 26 August 2015).

World Bank 2015c. 'Data: Thailand'. http://data.worldbank.org/country/thailand (accessed 24 August 2015).

World Bank 2016. 'Growing Challenges: World Bank East Asia and Pacific Economic Update', Washington, DC.

Wurfel, D. 1964. 'The Philippines', in G. Kahin (ed.), *Governments and Politics of Southeast Asia*, 2nd ed., Cornell University Press, Ithaca, NY.

Wurfel, D. 1988. *Filipino Politics: Development and Decay* Cornell University Press, Ithaca, NY.

Xinhua 2010. 'New Steel Plant Expedites State Infrastructure Building in Myanmar: State Media', Xinhua English News, 23 March 2010. http://news.xinhuanet.com/english2010/business/2010-03/23/c_13221494.htm (accessed 11 July 2013).

Zakaria, F. 1994. 'A Conversation with Lee Kwan Yew', *Foreign Affairs* March/April 1994.

Zaw, H. and Slodkowski, A. 2015. 'Burma Gags Media Linked to Shwe Mann, Adding to Concerns About Reforms', *The Irrawaddy* 14 August 2015.

Zin Linn 2012. 'Burma and the International Development Aid and FDI', *Asian Tribune* 2 June 2012.

Index